Approved
publication
OCR
RECOGNISING ACHIEVEMENT

MEI

HIGHER
MEI GCSE
MATHEMATICS

SERIES EDITOR: ROGER PORKESS

AUTHORS:

CATHERINE BERRY   VAL HANRAHAN

PAT BRYDEN   ROGER PORKESS

DIANA COWEY   PAUL SANDERS

DAVE FAULKNER   JULIAN THOMAS

NIGEL GREEN   CHRISTINE WOOD

Hodder Murray

A MEMBER OF THE HODDER HEADLINE GROUP

Acknowledgements

The Publishers would like to thank the following for permission to reproduce copyright material:

Photo credits: p.107 © www.purestockX.com; p.116 © iStockphoto.com/Duncan Walker; p.177 © Antarctic Meteorological Research Center Space Science and Engineering Center, University of Wisconsin-Madison; p.190 © Science Photo Library; p.285 (left) © iStockphoto.com/Olga Petrova; (middle) © iStockphoto.com/AtWaG; (right) © iStockphoto.com/Stephan Hoerold; p.288 © iStockphoto.com/Creativa image; p.318 © Diane Healey/Botanica/photolibrary.com.

London Examinations, a division of Edexcel Foundation, NatWest Bank, AQA (NEAB)/AQA/AQA (SEG) examination questions are reproduced by permission of the Assessment and Qualifications Alliance, MEG, MEI, Royal Bank of Scotland, OCR, SEG, SMP.

Edexcel Foundation, London Examinations accepts no responsibility whatsoever for the accuracy or method of working in the answers given at the back of this book. The answers at the back of this book are the sole responsibility of the publishers and have not been provided or approved by SEG. Every effort has been made to trace all copyright holders, but if any have been inadvertently overlooked the Publishers will be pleased to make the necessary arrangements at the first opportunity.

Although every effort has been made to ensure that website addresses are correct at time of going to press, Hodder Murray cannot be held responsible for the content of any website mentioned in this book. It is sometimes possible to find a relocated web page by typing in the address of the home page for a website in the URL window of your browser.

Hodder Headline's policy is to use papers that are natural, renewable and recyclable products and made from wood grown in sustainable forests. The logging and manufacturing processes are expected to conform to the environmental regulations of the country of origin.

Orders: please contact Bookpoint Ltd, 130 Milton Park, Abingdon, Oxon OX14 4SB. Telephone: (44) 01235 827720. Fax: (44) 01235 400454. Lines are open 9.00 – 5.00, Monday to Saturday, with a 24-hour message answering service. Visit our website at www.hoddereducation.co.uk

First published in 1999 by

Hodder Murray, an imprint of Hodder Education,
a member of the Hodder Headline Group,
An Hachette Livre UK Company
338 Euston Road
London NW1 3BH

Second edition published 2001

This third edition first published 2007

Impression number   10 9 8 7 6 5 4 3 2 1
Year   2011 2010 2009 2008 2007

Cover photo © Michael Abbey/Science Photo Library
Illustrations by Tom Cross, Jeff Edwards, Phil Ford, Joseph McEwan, Tony Wilkins and Barking Dog Art.
Typeset in 10.5/12pt New Baskerville by Pantek Arts Ltd, Maidstone, Kent.
Printed in Dubai

A catalogue record for this title is available from the British Library

ISBN: 978 0340 94054 9

Contents

Contents

How to use this book

This symbol next to a question means you need to use your calculator.
If a question has neither this icon nor the non-calculator icon below, you have the option of whether to use a calculator or not. On the one hand, it is good to practise for the non-calculator examination questions, but on the other hand you also need to work quickly enough to get through plenty of examples.

This symbol next to a question means you are not allowed to use your calculator.

This symbol means you will need to think carefully about a point and may want to discuss it.

Caution. You will need to think carefully about this point. There may well be a mistake which is easily made.

Many of the exercises end with a starred question. These are designed to be more thought provoking, in many cases introducing you to ideas that you may follow up later if you go on to A Level.

The quadratic equation

The roots of $ax^2 + bx + c = 0$, where $a \neq 0$, are given by $x = \dfrac{-b \pm \sqrt{(b^2 - 4ac)}}{2a}$

Area

Area of a triangle

$= \dfrac{1}{2} \times \text{base} \times \text{height}$

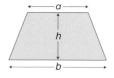

Area of parallelogram

$= \text{base} \times \text{vertical height}$

Area of trapezium $= \dfrac{1}{2}(a + b)\, h$

Lines and angles

A straight **line** goes on forever in both directions.

A **line segment** is a finite part of a straight line.

Parallel lines run in the same direction.

Vertically opposite angles are equal.
Corresponding angles are equal.
Alternate angles are equal.

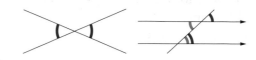

Circles

Circumference of circle $\quad = \pi \times$ diameter
$\qquad\qquad\qquad\qquad\quad\; = 2 \times \pi \times$ radius

Area of circle $= \pi \times (\text{radius})^2$

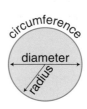

Solid figures

Cuboid	Volume = length × width × height
Prism	Volume = area of cross-section × length
Cylinder	Volume = $\pi r^2 \times$ length
	Curved surface area = $2\pi r \times$ length
Cone	Volume = $\frac{1}{3}\pi r^2 \times$ height
	Curved surface area = $\pi r \times$ slant length
Sphere	Volume = $\frac{4}{3}\pi r^3$
	Surface area = $4\pi r^2$

Trigonometry

$$\sin\theta = \frac{\text{opposite}}{\text{hypotenuse}} = \frac{y}{h}$$

$$\cos\theta = \frac{\text{adjacent}}{\text{hypotenuse}} = \frac{x}{h}$$

$$\tan\theta = \frac{\text{opposite}}{\text{adjacent}} = \frac{y}{x}$$

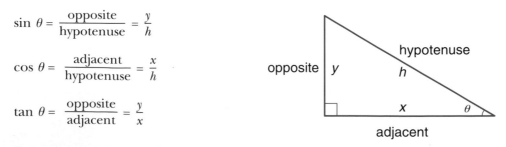

Pythagoras' theorem: $x^2 + y^2 = h^2$

Units

Metric system

Length

k   1 kilometre $= 10^3$ metres $= 1000$ metres

d   1 decimetre $= 10^{-1}$ metres $= \dfrac{1}{10}$ metre

h   1 hectometre $= 10^2$ metres $= 100$ metres

c   1 centimetre $= 10^{-2}$ metres $= \dfrac{1}{100}$ metre

da   1 decametre $= 10^1$ metres $= 10$ metres

m   1 millimetre $= 10^{-3}$ metres $= \dfrac{1}{1000}$ metre

The units for mass and capacity follow the same pattern as length. Thus:

1 kilogram = 1000 grams   1 litre = 1000 millilitres.

Notice also that: 1 tonne = 1000 kg.

Imperial

12 inches = 1 foot   16 ounces = 1 pound

3 feet = 1 yard   14 pounds = 1 stone

1760 yards = 1 mile   8 stones = 1 hundredweight (cwt)

20 cwt = 1 ton

Chapter 1

Basic arithmetic

Before you start this chapter you should be able to:

★ work with units, including changing between Imperial and metric
★ recall integer squares, the corresponding square roots, and cubes
★ add, subtract, multiply and divide directed numbers
★ carry out operations in the correct order
★ work with fractions, decimals and percentages.

Use the questions in the next exercise to check that you still remember these topics.

Review exercise 1.1

1 Chris is cycling in France and passes this sign. The distances are in kilometres. How many miles is it to

a) Lyon? **b)** Paris?

LYON 40km
PARIS 440km

2 Jo's petrol tank has a capacity of 50 litres. It is half full. Approximately how many gallons does it contain?

3 Write down the values of
a) $5^2 = 25$ **b)** $11^2 = 121$ **c)** $15^2 = \cancel{176}\ 225$ **d)** $4^3 = 64$
e) $5^3 = 125$ **f)** $\sqrt{64} = 8$ **g)** $\sqrt{144} = 12$ **h)** $\sqrt{196} = 13$

4 Work out
a) $-3 + 8 = 5$ **b)** $2 - 5 = -3$ **c)** $-4 + 1 = -3$ **d)** $9 - 4 = 5$
e) $-6 - 5 = -11$ **f)** $3 - 2 + 1 = 2$ **g)** $4 - 5 - 2 = -3$ **h)** $-2 + 3 - 6 = -5$

5 Work out
a) $(-4) \times (+6) = -24$ **b)** $(-7) \times (-3)$ **c)** $(+8) \times (-5)$ **d)** $(-10) \div (+2)$
e) $\frac{(+12)}{(-3)} = -4$ **f)** $\frac{(-3) \times (+10)}{(-6)}$ **g)** $(-2)^3$ **h)** $\frac{(-20)}{(-5)} + \frac{(+12)}{(-3)}$

6 Work out
a) $(2 + 3) \times 4$ **b)** $2 + (3 \times 4)$ **c)** $2 + 3 \times 4$ **d)** $(10 - 6) \div 2$
e) $10 - (6 \div 2)$ **f)** $10 - 6 \div 2$ **g)** $11 - 3 + 4$ **h)** $3 + [4 \times (5 - 2)]$

7 Work out
a) $\frac{1}{4} + \frac{3}{8} = \frac{5}{8}$ **b)** $\frac{3}{4} - \frac{5}{16} = \frac{7}{16}$ **c)** $\frac{1}{2} - \frac{2}{5} = \frac{1}{10}$ **d)** $\frac{3}{4} + \frac{2}{3} = \frac{17}{12} = 1\frac{5}{12}$
e) $\frac{3}{4} \times \frac{5}{6} = \frac{35}{24}$ **f)** $\frac{3}{10} \times \frac{4}{9} = \frac{12}{90}$ **g)** $\frac{1}{2} \div 4 = \frac{1}{8}$ **h)** $\frac{3}{4} \div \frac{5}{8} = \frac{24}{20}$

Review exercise 1.1 *continued*

8 Change these mixed numbers to improper fractions.

a) $1\frac{1}{4} = \frac{5}{4}$ b) $3\frac{2}{3} = \frac{11}{3}$ c) $4\frac{3}{5} = \frac{23}{5}$ d) $3\frac{7}{16} = \frac{55}{16}$

9 Change these improper fractions to mixed numbers.

a) $\frac{3}{2} = 1\frac{1}{2}$ b) $\frac{11}{4} = 2\frac{3}{4}$ c) $\frac{23}{6} = 3\frac{5}{6}$ d) $\frac{53}{8} = 6\frac{5}{8}$

10 £20 000 is shared between Anna, Harry, Kashmir and Paul. Anna gets a quarter.

$\frac{1}{4} \times 20000 = £5000$

Harry gets $\frac{2}{5}$ of the remainder. $\frac{2}{5} \times 15000 = 6000$

Kashmir gets $\frac{2}{3}$ of what remains.

Paul gets the rest. $= 3000$ $\frac{2}{3} \times 9000 = £6000$

a) How much does each person get?

b) What fraction of the £20 000 does Paul get? (Give your answer in its simplest form.)

11 Work out

a) $2.6 + 4.73$ b) $7 - 0.4 = 6.6$ c) $2.7 - 0.803$ d) $1 + 0.2 - 0.03$

12 Arrange in order of size, smallest first.

a) $\frac{7}{10}, 0.67, \frac{3}{4}, \frac{2}{3}, 0.72$ b) $0.33, \frac{7}{20}, 0.3, \frac{1}{3}, 0.04$

$2/3 \quad 0.67 \quad \frac{7}{10} \quad 0.72$

13

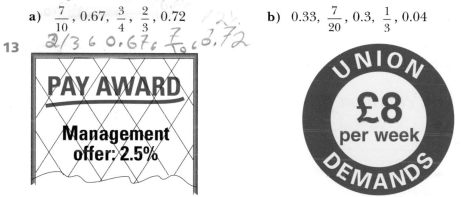

a) Nick earns £300 a week. Which award gives him more?

b) Emily earns £400 a week. Which award gives her more?

c) Karen works out that it makes no difference to her. How much does she earn?

14 Tickets for Greenhill Gardens are £1.50 for one person and £5 for a family. On an average day 400 one-person tickets and 150 family tickets are sold.

$400 \times 1.50 = 600 \quad 5 \times 150 = 750 \quad 600 + 750 = \boxed{1350}$

a) Calculate how much is taken on an average day.

The ticket prices are increased for one person by 30% and for a family by 20%. Following this increase, the number of one-person tickets sold decreases by 8% and the number of family tickets sold decreases by 10%.

£1.95

£6   368 $\times$ 5.52   135

b) Calculate how much more money is taken on an average day.

$717.6 + 810 = 1527.6$

15 Repeat questions 5, 6 and 7 using your calculator. Check that you get the same answers.

Prime factorisation

 Which of these are prime numbers?

15, 17, 19, 21

If a number is not itself prime then it can be written as the product of primes.

e.g. $20 = 2 \times 2 \times 5$ ◄ Each of these is a prime

and $84 = 2 \times 2 \times 3 \times 7$ ◄ Each of these is a prime

This is called **prime factorisation** (or **prime factor decomposition**).

Ian and Lin are both finding the prime factorisation of 20.

Ian writes this.   Lin writes this.

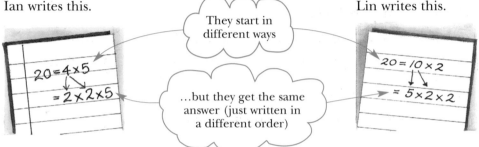

They start in different ways

…but they get the same answer (just written in a different order)

Remember that you must go on factorising until all the numbers are primes. Sometimes it may take several lines of working.

 What is the prime factorisation of 360?

$2 \times 2 \times 2 \times 3 \times 3 \times 5 = 360$

Highest common factor (HCF)

You can find the HCF of 12 and 20 like this:

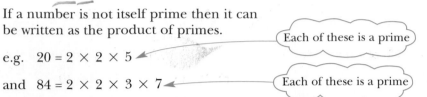

The factors of 12 are   1 2 3 ④ 6 12
The factors of 20 are   1 2 ④ 5 10 20
The HCF of 12 and 20 is 4

The common factors are 1, 2, 4

4 is the highest factor in the list

The HCF of 12 and 20 is 4.

 Another method is to write $12 = 2^2 \times 3$, $20 = 2^2 \times 5$. How does this help you find the HCF?

Lowest common multiple (LCM)

You can find the LCM of 9 and 6 like this:

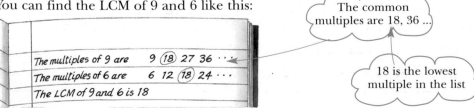

The multiples of 9 are   9 ⑱ 27 36 ···
The multiples of 6 are   6 12 ⑱ 24 ···
The LCM of 9 and 6 is 18

The common multiples are 18, 36 …

18 is the lowest multiple in the list

 Another method is to write $9 = 3^2$, $6 = 2 \times 3$. How does this help you find the LCM?

1: Basic arithmetic

Exercise 1.2

1 Find the prime factorisation of each of these numbers.

   a) 14 2×7 **b)** 15 3×5 **c)** 28 $2 \times 2 \times 7$ **d)** 36 $= 2 \times 2 \times 3 \times 3$

   e) 30 $= 2 \times 3 \times 5$ **f)** 27 $= 3^3$ **g)** 90 $= 2 \times 32 \times 5$ **h)** 126

   i) 150   **j)** 210   **k)** 539   **l)** 1540

2 Find the HCF of each of these.

   a) 10, 25 $= 5$ **b)** 3, 8 $= 1$ **c)** 18, 45 $= 3$ **d)** 14, 10 $= 2$

   e) 21, 49 $= 7$ **f)** 22, 33 $= 11$ **g)** 63, 36 $= 9$ **h)** 56, 126 $= 2$

   i) 12, 24, 54 $= 2$ **j)** 56, 24, 32 $= 2$

3 Find the LCM of each of these.

   a) 6, 10 $= 30$ **b)** 3, 7 $= 21$ **c)** 27, 18 $= 54$ **d)** 16, 8 $= 32$

   e) 14, 35 $= 70$ **f)** 8, 20 $= 40$ **g)** 9, 12, 8 $= 72$ **h)** 6, 10, 15 $= 30$

4 **a)** Write down the LCM of 5 and 7. $= 35$

   b) Write $\frac{2}{5}$ as a fraction with denominator 35. $\frac{2 \times 7}{5 \times 7} = \frac{14}{35}$

   c) Write $\frac{3}{7}$ as a fraction with denominator 35. $\frac{15}{35}$

   d) Which is larger, $\frac{2}{5}$ or $\boxed{\frac{3}{7}}$? $\frac{14}{35} = 0.4 < \frac{3}{7} = 0.42$

5 Look at these gear wheels.

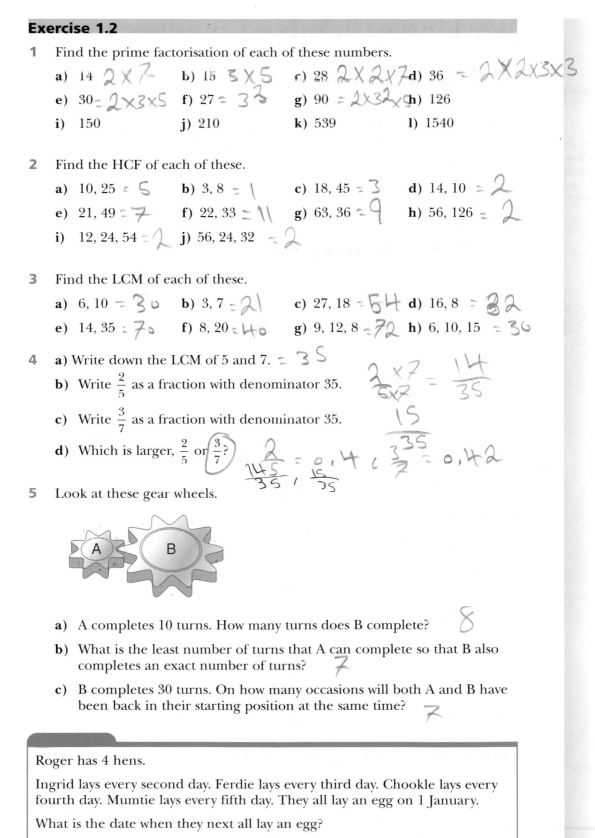

   a) A completes 10 turns. How many turns does B complete? 8

   b) What is the least number of turns that A can complete so that B also completes an exact number of turns? 7

   c) B completes 30 turns. On how many occasions will both A and B have been back in their starting position at the same time? 7

Roger has 4 hens.

Ingrid lays every second day. Ferdie lays every third day. Chookle lays every fourth day. Mumtie lays every fifth day. They all lay an egg on 1 January.

What is the date when they next all lay an egg?

On how many days in the year do they all lay an egg?

7

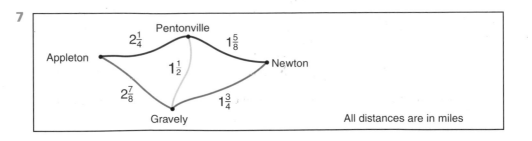

a) How far is it from Appleton to Newton via Pentonville?

b) How far is it from Appleton to Newton via Gravely?

c) How much further is it from Appleton to Gravely via Pentonville than from Appleton to Gravely direct?

d) What is the shortest route from Appleton to Newton which calls at both Pentonville and Graveley and how far is it?

8 Scott works in a service station.

For a normal 38 hour week, he is paid £6.00 an hour. The first 6 hours overtime are paid at 'time and a quarter' and any further overtime is paid at 'time and a half'.

a) How much is Scott paid in a week when he works 45 hours?

b) Last week, Scott earned £258. How many hours did he work?

9 A box is 24" long, 21" wide and $13\frac{1}{2}$" deep. How many packets 4" by $1\frac{3}{4}$" by $1\frac{1}{2}$" fit into the box?

10 Look at the sequence $1, 1\frac{1}{2}, 1\frac{1}{3}, 1\frac{1}{4}, 1\frac{1}{5}, \ldots$

Define P_n as the product of the first n terms of the sequence.

So, for example, $P_3 = 1 \times 1\frac{1}{2} \times 1\frac{1}{3}$.

a) Work out the value of (i) P_2 (ii) P_3 (iii) P_4

b) Work out the value of (i) P_{10} (ii) P_{100} (iii) P_n

c) For what values of n is P_n a whole number?

d) What is the value of $\dfrac{P_n + P_{n+2}}{P_{n+1}}$?

Decimals

Multiplication and division

When you multiply or divide decimals, be careful to get the decimal point in the right place in your answer.

You are doing a multiple choice test. Without using a calculator and without writing anything down, decide which of the following answers is correct. Explain your choice.

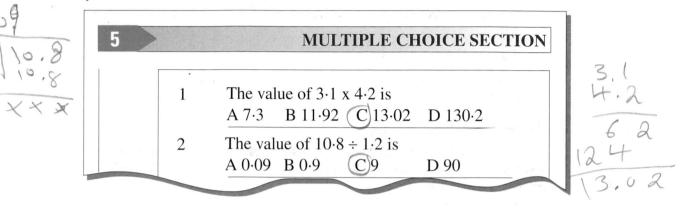

5	**MULTIPLE CHOICE SECTION**
1	The value of 3·1 × 4·2 is A 7·3 B 11·92 C 13·02 D 130·2
2	The value of 10·8 ÷ 1·2 is A 0·09 B 0·9 C 9 D 90

A rough check tells you whether an answer is sensible or not.

The following examples look at different ways to multiply and divide decimals. Carry out a rough check on the answers.

Example

Work out 2.1 × 0.35.

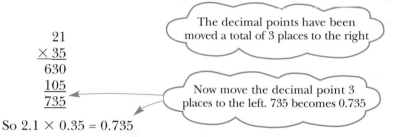

Solution

Make the decimals into whole numbers, so 2.1 becomes 21 and 0.35 becomes 35. Then multiply the whole numbers and finally replace the decimal point.

$$
\begin{array}{r}
21 \\
\times 35 \\
\hline
630 \\
105 \\
\hline
735
\end{array}
$$

> The decimal points have been moved a total of 3 places to the right

> Now move the decimal point 3 places to the left. 735 becomes 0.735

So 2.1 × 0.35 = 0.735

Why must the answer be 0.735 and not 7.35 or 0.0735?

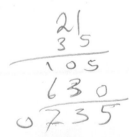

Example

One paving slab costs £2.69. How much do 10 cost?

Solution

£26.9

The cost of 10 slabs is £2.69 × 10 = £26.90.

> Multiplying by 10 moves the decimal point 1 place to the right. 2.69 becomes 26.9 and £26.9 is written as £26.90

What is £0.30 × 100? *30*

Example

Work out 4.3 ÷ 0.08.

43
8
0.344

Solution

Multiply top and bottom by a power of 10 to make the denominator a whole number and then divide out.

$$4.3 \div 0.08 = \frac{4.3}{0.08}$$

> Multiply top and bottom by 100

$$= \frac{430}{8}$$

> $8\overline{)430.00}$ 53.75

$$= 53.75$$

53.75
8)430

Why must the answer be 53.75 and not 537.5 or 5.375?

because we ee don't need decimal in everywhere. and

Example

Work out 2.8 ÷ 10. *= 0.28*

Solution

$$2.8 \div 10 = 0.28$$

> Dividing by 10 moves the decimal point 1 place to the left. 2.8 becomes 0.28

What is 56 ÷ 1000?

0.056

Investigation

Some fractions, such as $\frac{1}{8}$ = 0.125, have a decimal form that terminates.

Others, such as $\frac{1}{12}$ = 0.08333..., have a decimal form that recurs.

Investigate which fractions have terminating decimal forms and which have recurring decimal forms.

$\frac{1}{7}$ = 0.1428571428571... has a recurring pattern of length 6.

What is the longest recurring pattern that you can find?

1: Basic arithmetic

Exercise 1.4

1 Work out

a) 2.4×0.3 b) 8.1×0.02 c) 0.7×32 d) 0.45×1.7

e) 0.4×0.2 f) 10.3×0.15 g) 2.34×0.65 h) 0.03^2

2 Work out

a) $7.2 \div 0.4$ b) $30 \div 1.2$ c) $6 \div 0.03$ d) $11.4 \div 0.25$

e) $0.42 \div 1.2$ f) $0.8 \div 0.2$ g) $18.15 \div 2.4$ h) $2.7 \div 0.015$

3 Work out

a) 4.2×100 b) $3.9 \div 10$ c) $0.2 \div 100$ d) 14.7×1000

e) 300×5.7 f) 80×0.06 g) $4.7 \div 40$ h) $6000 \div 0.0002$

4

1 kg is about 2.2 lbs.

a) What is Amy's weight to the nearest lb?

b) What is Ben's weight to the nearest kg?

c) What is Claire's weight to the nearest kg?

5 a) What is the mass of 3.5 cm^3 of aluminium?

b) What is the mass of 2.4 cm^3 of copper?

c) What is the volume of 14.8 g of silver?

d) What is the volume of 25.3 g of gold?

Metal	Density (g/cm^3)
Aluminium	2.70
Copper	8.93
Silver	10.50
Gold	18.88

Remember:

$$\text{Density} = \frac{\text{Mass}}{\text{Volume}}$$

6 One inch is about 25.4 mm.

a) How many mm are there in 3 inches?

b) How many mm are there in 7.2 inches?

c) What is 600 mm to the nearest inch?

d) What is 1500 mm in feet and inches to the nearest inch?

Investigation

Two numbers, x and y are multiplied together to give z. So $z = xy$.

What can you say about y in each of these cases?

a) $z = 1$ b) $z = x$ c) $z > x$ d) $z < x$?

Percentages

Fractions and percentages

 Which school has the higher proportion of pupils going to university?

Fractions and percentages are common ways of writing proportions but you need to be able to compare them.

 What is $\frac{5}{8}$ as a percentage?

$\frac{5}{8} \times 100 = 62.5$ so $\frac{5}{8}$ is 62.5%   or $62\frac{1}{2}$%

$$\frac{5}{8} \times 100 = 62.5$$

 What is $\frac{3}{8}$ as a percentage?

$$\frac{3}{8} \times 100 = 37.5$$

Making comparisons

Martine works for a travel company. She analyses the surveys which are carried out on return flights. The question 'Would you recommend this holiday to a friend?' was answered as follows.

 Which destination is more strongly recommended?

Martine compares the figures by writing each as a percentage.

$$\frac{149}{188} \times 100 = 79.25\%$$

 Work out the corresponding figures for Greece.
Which destination is more strongly recommended?

You can check these calculations like this:

For Spain: work out 77.5% of 240 and check you get 186.

$$77.5\% \text{ of } 240 = \frac{77.5}{100} \times 240 = 186$$

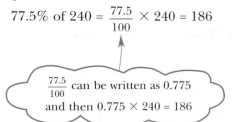

$\frac{77.5}{100}$ can be written as 0.775
and then $0.775 \times 240 = 186$

Percentage calculations

Calculations involving a percentage increase or decrease (such as adding on VAT) are common. Adding on VAT gives you the price including VAT (inc VAT). Taking it back off gives you the price excluding VAT (ex VAT).

VAT stands for Value Added Tax

£1200 ex 17.5% VAT

What is the total cost of this computer?

The VAT is 17.5% of £1200.

$$17.5\% \text{ of } 1200 = \frac{17.5}{100} \times 1200 = 210$$

The total cost of the computer is £1410.

What do you multiply £1200 by to get the price inc VAT?

$$\frac{117.5}{100} \times 1200 = 1410$$

You can check your answer for the total cost by starting with the price of £1410 inc VAT and working back to the price ex VAT:

Price ex VAT + VAT = Price inc VAT

100%   17.5%   117.5%

The price inc VAT is £1410 so

117.5% is 1410

1% is $\frac{1410}{117.5}$

100% is $\frac{1410}{117.5} \times 100 = 1200$

So the cost of the computer ex VAT is £1200 (the right answer).

What do you divide £1410 by to get the price ex VAT?

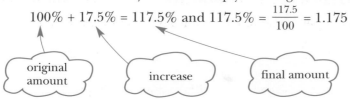
For a 17.5% increase, you can multiply the original amount by 1.175.

$$100\% + 17.5\% = 117.5\% \text{ and } 117.5\% = \frac{117.5}{100} = 1.175$$

> original amount
> increase
> final amount

This method is used in the following example.

Repeated percentage change

Example

Sophie earns £15 000 a year. She gets a 5% pay rise on 1 March and a 3% pay rise on 1 October.

How much does she earn after 1 October?

1.03 × 15 000 = 15 450

Solution

A 5% pay rise means her salary after 1 March will be

$$1.05 \times £15\ 000 = £15\ 750$$

The 3% increase is worked out on her new salary of £15 750.

A 3% pay rise means her salary after 1 October will be

$$1.03 \times £15\ 750 = £16\ 222.50$$

 What difference does it make if Sophie gets the 3% pay rise on 1 March and the 5% pay rise on 1 October?

No difference but in 1 March she will get less money.

Percentage change

Here are Bethany's latest sales figures.

B. MORRIS	SALES REPORT
MONTH	SALES (£000)
APRIL	50
MAY	60
JUNE	75

She works out her sales increase between April and May as a percentage.

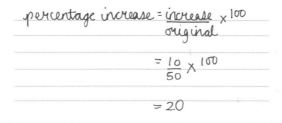

percentage increase = $\frac{\text{increase}}{\text{original}} \times 100$

= $\frac{10}{50} \times 100$

= 20

 Work out the percentage change in sales between May and June.

Work out the percentage change in sales between April and June.

Explain why the percentage change between April and June is not 20% + 25% = 45%.

Exercise 1.5

1 Write these fractions as percentages. (Give your answers to 1 decimal place.)

a) $\frac{2}{9}$ ×100

b) $\frac{3}{7}$×100 = 42.8 c) $\frac{13}{16}$ 350

d) $\frac{7}{15}$ 46-6

2 Gina sees the same office desk for sale in three different shops.

17.5×429 =
100

17.5 × 369
100

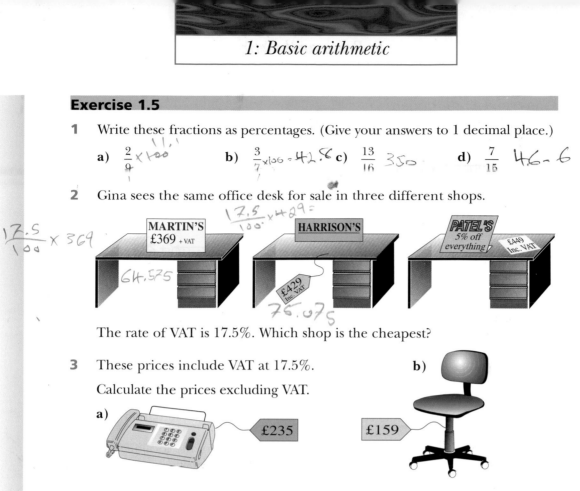

64.575

£429
Inc. VAT

75.075

The rate of VAT is 17.5%. Which shop is the cheapest?

3 These prices include VAT at 17.5%.

Calculate the prices excluding VAT.

a) £235

b) £159

4 22% of a sports club's income is from subscriptions, 36% is from social events and the remainder, amounting to £3150, is from fundraising. Work out the income from

a) subscriptions.

b) social events.

c) Richard shows the club's income on a pie chart. Work out, to the nearest degree, the angles for each of these three areas.

5 Liz, Ben and Josie each receive a pay rise of 2% + £400 a year.

a) Ben earns £18 000. What is his new salary?

b) What percentage increase has Ben received?

c) Liz's new salary is £26 300. How much does she earn before the rise?

d) The pay award gives Josie a 4% rise. How much does she earn before the rise?

6 Abigail's car cost her £12 000. Each year it decreases in value by 25% of its value at the start of that year.

a) What is the value of Abigail's car

(i) after 1 year?

(ii) after 3 years?

b) Work out a formula for the value of Abigail's car after n years.

c) When does the value of the car first fall below £3000?

More applications of percentages

Percentages are used in countless ways. Here are four of the commonest.

Profit and loss

Candice owns a clothes shop.
She buys these jackets at £40 and
trousers at £20.

Her profit on a jacket is £70 – £40 = £30

selling price   cost price

How much profit does she make on the trousers?

Are they more profitable than the jackets for Candice?

Profit figures alone do not tell the whole story. Profit must be related to the
cost price. You do this by working out profit as a percentage of the cost price.

$$\textbf{Percentage profit} = \frac{\textbf{Profit}}{\textbf{Cost price}} \times \textbf{100}$$

For the jackets,

$$\text{Percentage profit} = \frac{£30}{£40} \times 100 = 75$$

What is the percentage profit on the trousers?

Income and tax

Shola's **gross income** is £40 000. She has a **tax-free allowance** of £4500. She
pays no tax on this part of her income. She pays tax on the remainder, which is
£35 500. This is called her **taxable income**.

Shola pays tax at 23p in the pound on the first £27 000 of taxable income and
at 40p in the pound on the remainder.

She calculates her tax like this:

$$23\% \text{ of } £27\,000 = \frac{23}{100} \times £27\,000 = £6210$$

$$40\% \text{ of } £8500 = \frac{40}{100} \times £8500 = £3400$$

$$\text{tax to pay} = £6210 + £3400 = £9610$$

Shola's **net income** is the amount she actually receives.

How much is Shola's net income?

What percentage of her gross income does Shola pay in tax?

Simple interest

Andrew invests £4000 for three years in Oldtown Building Society.

Amount invested	Rate of interest
£1 – £999	4% p.a.
£1000–£4999	5% p.a.
£5000 and over	5.5% p.a.

What rate of interest does he get?

The interest he gets in one year is 5% of £4000.

$$5\% \text{ of } £4000 = \frac{5}{100} \times £4000 = £200$$

If the interest is paid straight to Andrew (not into his account), the account has the same amount in it during the second year, so the interest is again £200.

How much interest does Andrew get in total after three years?

This is the formula for calculating the interest, I.

$$I = \frac{PRT}{100}$$

where P is the money invested (sometimes called the **principal**)

   R is the rate in % p.a.

   T is the time in years.

This situation, where the amount in the account stays the same, is called **simple interest**.

Compound interest

When the interest is paid into the account at the end of each year the interest for the following year is calculated on a slightly increased amount. This is called **compound interest**.

Andrew decides to have the interest paid into his account at the end of each year. He does these calculations.

Year 1: Interest = 5% of £4000 = $\frac{5}{100} \times £4000 = £200$

Amount at end of year 1 = £4000 + £200 = £4200

Year 2: Interest = 5% of £4200 = $\frac{5}{100} \times £4200 = £210$

Amount at end of year 2 = £4200 + £210 = £4410

The amount after year 2 could also be calculated as £4000 × $(1.05)^2$. Explain why this gives the same answer.

How much does Andrew have in his account at the end of year 3?

What other uses of percentages have you met?

Exercise 1.6

1 Becky owns an antiques shop.

handwritten: $100\% + 60\% \Rightarrow \frac{160}{100} \times 45 = 72$

  a) Find the selling price of

   (i) a chair bought for £45 and sold at a 60% profit   *handwritten: 27*

   (ii) a lampstand bought for £32 and sold at a 40% profit.   *handwritten: 44.8*

  b) Becky bought a bookcase for £80 and eventually sold it for £70.
  What percentage loss did she make?   *handwritten: $\frac{80}{70} \times 90 =$*

  c) Becky makes a 45% profit when she sells a picture frame for £58.
  How much did it cost Becky?

2 Chloe buys 30 of these coats at £60 each and 20 of these skirts at £25 each.

She attaches these price tags to them and puts them out in her shop.

  a) What percentage profit does she make on

   (i) a coat?   (ii) a skirt?

  b) Two of the coats are damaged and sold at half price.
  All the other items are sold at full price.

   (i) Calculate how much she takes altogether.

   (ii) Calculate the total profit and write it as a percentage of the total cost.

3 Gareth has a clothes stall on the market. He buys 40 shirts at £16 each and
prices them at a 40% profit. He also buys 50 ties at £8 each and prices
them at a 30% profit.

He sells 36 shirts and 40 ties at these prices. He sells the remainder in a
'20% off marked prices' sale.

  a) Work out Gareth's total takings.

  b) How much profit does he make?

  c) What is this profit as a percentage of how much Gareth paid?
  (Give your answer to the nearest whole number.)

4 Ravi has a gross annual income of £38 000. He has a tax-free allowance of
£5200. He pays tax at 22p in the pound on the first £27 500 of taxable
income and at 40p in the pound on the remainder.

  a) What is Ravi's net income?

  b) What percentage of his gross income is paid in tax?

5 Martha's gross income is £26 500. She has a tax-free allowance of £4800. She pays tax at 10p in the pound on the first £3500 of taxable income and at 24p in the pound on the rest.

a) How much tax does she pay?

b) What is her net income?

c) The rates are changed so that the first £4000 of taxable income is taxed at 9p in the pound and the rest at 25p in the pound. How will this affect Martha's net income? (Her gross income and allowances are unchanged.)

6 Karen, Mark and Tiffany want to invest money in a building society and obtain the highest rate of interest. They have this information.

What is the maximum amount of simple interest that can be obtained by

a) Karen investing £800 for 2 years?

b) Mark investing £4500 for 3 years?

c) Tiffany investing £1500 for 2 years?

d) Karen and Tiffany decide to put their money together in a joint account to get the best interest rate. They agree to share the interest in proportion to the amounts they invest. How much extra interest does each get by investing in a joint account?

7 Jack invested £4000 in an account that pays 3.7% per year compound interest.

He makes no withdrawals.

a) Copy and complete the statement.

After 1 year the total amount in the account is £4000 × ....

b) How much will be in the account after 5 years?   *MEI*

8 Calculate the compound interest when

a) Bryony invests £2000 for 3 years at 5% p.a.

b) Erin invests £600 for 4 years at 5.8% p.a.

c) Nikki invests £7500 for 3 years at 6.75% p.a.

Exercise 1.6 *continued*

9   James invests £10 000 in an account offering compound interest at 6% p.a.

   a) Work out a formula giving the amount in his account at the end of
       n years.

   b) When will James become a millionaire?

Investigation

Francis Rayleigh presents a document to the government in 2002. It says that his ancestor Sir Jasper Rayleigh lent the government £7 in 1572 at 5% compound interest. Can the government afford to repay him?

Finishing off

Now that you have finished this chapter you should be able to:

★ add, subtract, multiply and divide mixed numbers

★ multiply and divide decimals

★ change fractions to percentages

★ make comparisons

★ work out percentage problems where the original amount is unknown

★ work out percentage changes

★ work with percentages to solve problems on profit and loss, tax, simple interest and compound interest.

Use the questions in the next exercise to check that you understand everything.

Mixed exercise 1.7

1 Work out

a) $4\frac{7}{16} - 1\frac{3}{4}$　　b) $2\frac{5}{6} + 5\frac{3}{4}$　　c) $3\frac{1}{4} \times 1\frac{3}{5}$　　d) $8\frac{3}{4} \div 2\frac{1}{3}$

e) $(3\frac{1}{2} - 1\frac{5}{8}) \times 1\frac{1}{3}$　f) $13 \div (1\frac{1}{2} + \frac{2}{3})$　g) $5\frac{1}{4} + 3\frac{2}{3} + 1\frac{5}{6}$

h) $(2\frac{3}{7} - \frac{1}{3}) \div 3\frac{2}{3}$　　i) $3\frac{1}{3} \times 2\frac{1}{4} \times \frac{3}{5}$　　j) $(2\frac{1}{2})^2 + \sqrt{2\frac{1}{4}}$

2 A water tank is five eighths full. 3500 litres of water are used. The tank is now two thirds empty. How much water does it now contain?

3 One pint is about 0.57 litres.

a) How many litres are there in a 4-pint container of milk?

b) How many pints are there in a 1.5-litre bottle of lemonade? Give your answer to the nearest tenth of a pint.

4 Andrew is doing a survey to compare households on two estates, Riverside and Southwood. He gets 224 replies from Riverside and 172 from Southwood. Here are some of his results.

Estate	Riverside	Southwood
Have computer	131	105
Have car	193	117

Mixed exercise 1.7 *continued*

    a) Which estate has the higher proportion of households with a computer and what percentage is this?

    b) Which estate has the higher proportion of households with a car and what percentage is this?

    c) In Southwood 50% of households have both a computer and a car. What percentage of households have neither?

5 Mike owns a clothing shop. The marked prices give him a 45% profit on shirts and a 40% profit on ties.

£15·95   £7·98

$\frac{145}{100} \times £9.45 \quad £11.455$

    a) How much did he pay for a shirt?

    b) How much did he pay for a tie?

  Mike bought 20 shirts and 24 ties. He sold all the shirts and half the ties before selling the remaining ties in a sale offering a third off marked prices.

    c) How much profit does Mike make on the whole deal?

    d) Work out this profit as a percentage of Mike's initial outlay.

6 Anna has a gross income of £24 300. She has a tax-free allowance of £5600. She pays tax at 10p in the pound on the first £4000 of taxable income and at 22p in the pound on the remainder.

    a) What is Anna's net income?

    b) What percentage of her gross income is paid in tax?

    c) Next year, the 10p tax band is extended to the first £5000 of taxable income. The remainder is still taxed at 22p in the pound. Anna's gross income and her tax-free allowance stay the same.

      How much less tax will she pay?

7 Abigail invests £2000 for 3 years at a fixed rate of interest. She is paid interest at the end of each year. At the end of the first year there is £2090 in her account.

    a) What annual rate of interest does she get?

    b) How much does Abigail have in her account at the end of 3 years?

8

Daily News

House prices are rising by 7% each year

A national survey has just reported

The price of a house is £100 000. Assuming house prices continue to rise at the same rate, predict the price of this house in 3 years' time.

MEI

Mixed exercise 1.7 *continued*

9   Hannah invests £600 in a building society account for 2 years.

The account pays 5% per annum compound interest.

Calculate the interest she will receive.   *MEI*

10 Jack invested £1400 at 5.5% per annum compound interest.

How much was his investment worth after 5 years?   *MEI*

Investigation

The Fibonacci numbers 1, 1, 2, 3, 5, 8, 13, 21, ... are defined by $F_1 = 1$, $F_2 = 1$ and $F_{n+2} = F_n + F_{n+1}$.

a) Explain whether F_{125} is odd or even.

b) Explain what happens to the ratio $\dfrac{F_{n+1}}{F_n}$ as n increases.

c) Explain why the highest common factor of any two successive Fibonacci numbers is 1.

Investigation

A credit card company advertises the following arrangements for repayment of loans:

- **2% interest is charged on the first day of the month on the sum owing on that day;**
- **on the last day of each month the borrower must repay 5% of the amount borrowed or £5, whichever is the greater amount.**

On 1 June Mark owes the credit card company £200 **before** the interest is added.

a)   How much will the interest be?

b)   How much will he owe on 29 June?

c)   How much will he have to pay on the last day of June?

d)   How much will he then owe?

e)   How much must he pay on the last day of July?

Use a spreadsheet to investigate how long it takes Mark to pay off his debt.

Chapter 2

Shapes and angles

Before you start this chapter you should:

★ be able to classify triangles

★ recognise different types of quadrilateral

★ be able to find pairs of equal angles where two lines cross or where a line intersects parallel lines

★ know that angles round a point add up to 360° and angles on a straight line add up to 180°

★ know that the angle sum of a triangle is 180°.

Reminder

- Where two lines intersect, **opposite angles** are equal.

- Where a line intersects with two parallel lines, **corresponding angles** are equal.

- Where a line intersects with two parallel lines, **alternate angles** are equal.

Look for the letter Z

Look for the letter F

- The angles in a triangle add up to 180°. These are the **interior angles**.

- The angles in a quadrilateral add up to 360°.

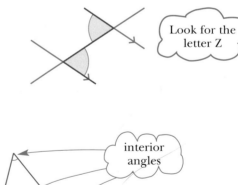

interior angles

You can show this by dividing the quadrilaterial into two triangles.

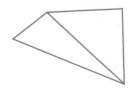

- A line with fixed end points is called a **line segment**.

A ————————— B

Angles and triangles

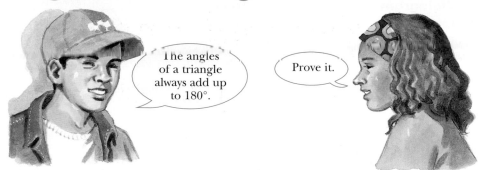

The angles of a triangle always add up to 180°.

Prove it.

Look at this triangle. One side has been extended.

These angles are **interior** angles

This is an **exterior** angle

 What do the words interior and exterior mean?

Notice the arrows on two of the lines in the diagram below.

 What do they tell you?

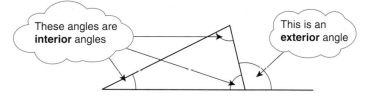

 Why are the angles marked x the same size?
because they are parcallel line

Why are the angles marked y the same size?
because they are alternate

The exterior angle of the triangle is $x + y$.

> **The exterior angle of the triangle is equal to the sum of the interior opposite angles.**

Look at the straight line which forms the exterior angle.

 What do you know about $x + y + z$?
add up to 180

> **The angles of a triangle always add up to 180°**

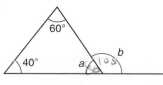

 What are the sizes of a and b in this diagram?

60+40=100
180-100=80
a=80

a=b=a

180-80=100

Area of a parallelogram

A **parallelogram** is a shape with two pairs of parallel sides.

The rule for working out the area of a parallelogram is

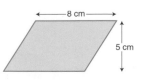

Area of a parallelogram = base × vertical height

For this parallelogram,

Area (in cm^2) = 8 × 5 = 40

 Explain why the rule works. This diagram may help.

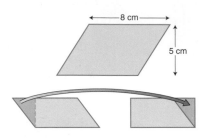

Area of a triangle

The rule for area of a triangle is

Area of a triangle = $\frac{1}{2}$ × base × vertical height

 Explain why this rule works.

Hint: Can you put two identical triangles together so that they make a parallelogram?

Area of a trapezium

A **trapezium** is a shape with one pair of parallel sides.

The rule for working out the area of a trapezium is

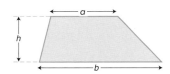

Area of a trapezium = $\frac{1}{2}$ $(a + b)\, h$

For this trapezium,

Area (in cm^2) = $\frac{1}{2}$ × (4 + 6) × 3

= $\frac{1}{2}$ × 10 × 3

= $\frac{1}{2}$ × 30

= 15

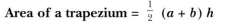

 Explain why the rule works. This diagram may help. It shows two trapezia fitted together to make a parallelogram.

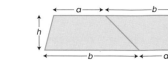

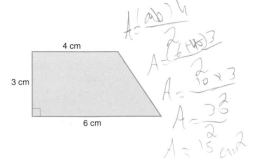

Special quadrilaterals

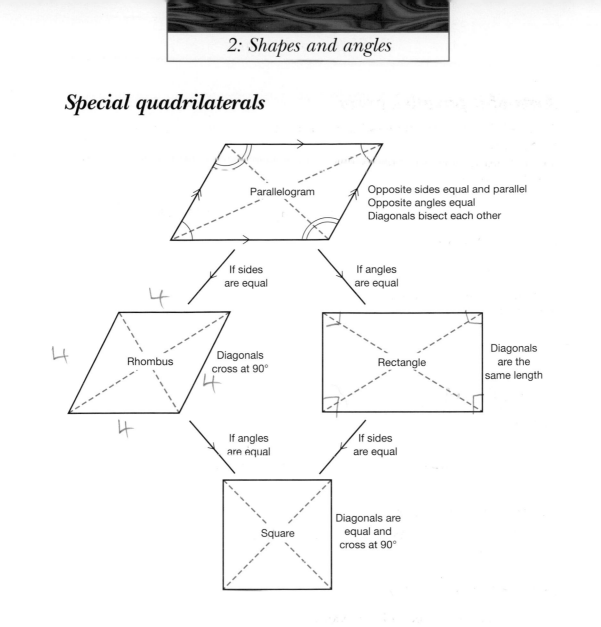

Parallelogram
Opposite sides equal and parallel
Opposite angles equal
Diagonals bisect each other

If sides are equal

If angles are equal

Rhombus
Diagonals cross at 90°

Rectangle
Diagonals are the same length

If angles are equal

If sides are equal

Square
Diagonals are equal and cross at 90°

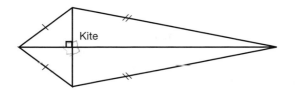

Kite
Two pairs of adjacent sides equal
Diagonals are perpendicular

Review exercise 2.1

1 Find the angles marked with letters in these diagrams.

The diagrams are not drawn accurately.

a)

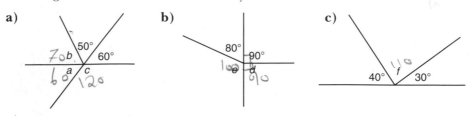

70 b
50°
60°
60
a
c
120

b)

80°
90°
100
e
d
90

c)

110
f
40°
30°

2 Find the angles marked with letters in these diagrams.

a)

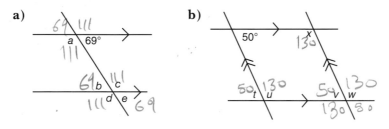

69 ///
a 69°
///
69 b ///c
d e
/// 69

b)

50°
x
130
50 130
t u
50 130
v w
130 80

3 Find the angles marked with letters.

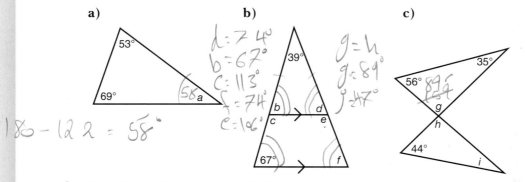

a)

53°
69°
58 a
$180 - 122 = 58°$

b)

d = 7 40
b = 67°
c = 113°
f = 74°
e = 106°

39°
b
c
67°
f

g = h
g = 89°
j = 47°

c)

35°
56° 89
g
h
44°
i

4 Find the angles marked with letters.

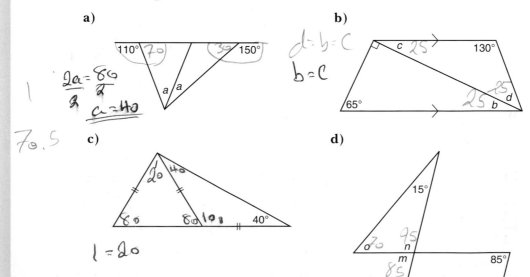

a)

110° 70
35 150°
a a
$\frac{2a = 80}{2}$
$a = 40$
70.5

b)

d = b = c
b = c

c 25
130°
65°
25
25 b
d

c)

20 40
80
80 100
40
$1 = 20$

d)

15°
95
20
n
m
85
85°

Revision exercise 2.1 *continued*

5 Find the areas of these shapes.

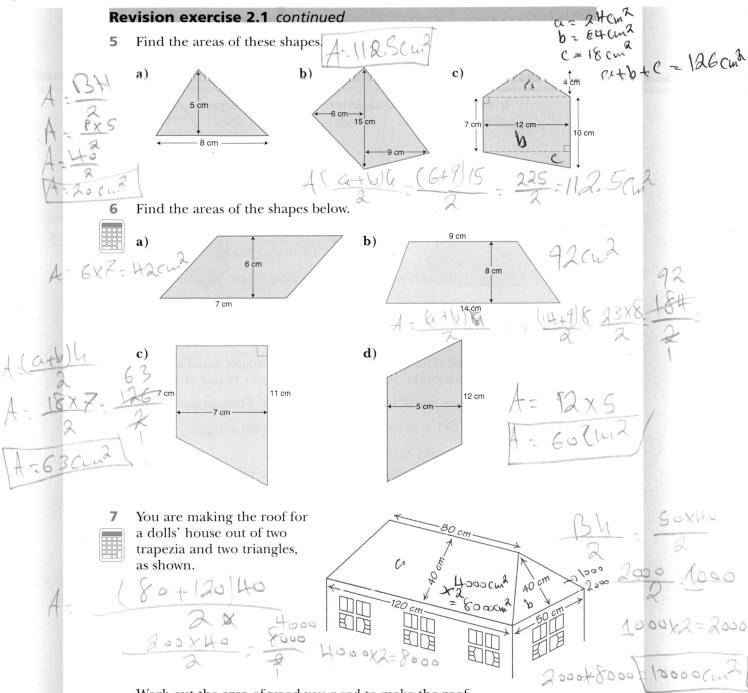

a)

5 cm
8 cm

b)

6 cm
15 cm
9 cm

c)

4 cm
7 cm   12 cm   10 cm

Handwritten annotations:
$A = \dfrac{BH}{2}$
$A = \dfrac{8 \times 5}{2}$
$A = \dfrac{40}{2}$
$A = 20\,cm^2$

$A = 112.5\,cm^2$

$a = 24\,cm^2$
$b = 84\,cm^2$
$c = 18\,cm^2$
$a+b+c = 126\,cm^2$

$A\left(\dfrac{a+b}{2}\right)h = \dfrac{(6+9)15}{2} = \dfrac{225}{2} = 112.5\,cm^2$

6 Find the areas of the shapes below.

a)

6 cm
7 cm

$A = 6 \times 7 = 42\,cm^2$

b)

9 cm
8 cm
14 cm

$92\,cm^2$

$A = \dfrac{(a+b)h}{2} \Rightarrow \dfrac{(14+9)8}{2} = \dfrac{23 \times 8}{2} = \dfrac{184}{2} = 92$

c)

7 cm   11 cm
7 cm

$A = \dfrac{(a+b)h}{2}$
$A = \dfrac{18 \times 7}{2} = \dfrac{126}{2} = 63$
$A = 63\,cm^2$

d)

5 cm   12 cm

$A = 12 \times 5$
$A = 60\,cm^2$

7 You are making the roof for a dolls' house out of two trapezia and two triangles, as shown.

80 cm
40 cm
120 cm
40 cm
50 cm

$A = \dfrac{(80+120)40}{2} = \dfrac{200 \times 40}{2} = \dfrac{8000}{2} = 4000$

$4000\,cm^2 \times 2 = 8000\,cm^2$

$\dfrac{BH}{2} = \dfrac{50 \times 40}{2} = \dfrac{2000}{2} = 1000$

$1000 \times 2 = 2000$

$2000 + 8000 = 10000\,cm^2$

Work out the area of wood you need to make the roof.

8 Copy and complete the following table.

Quadrilateral	Number of lines of symmetry	Order of rotational symmetry
Parallelogram	0	2
Rhombus	2	2
Rectangle	2	2
Square	4	4

Exercise 2.2

1 a) Write down the name of each polygon below and say whether it is regular or irregular.

b) Find the sum of the interior angles of each polygon.

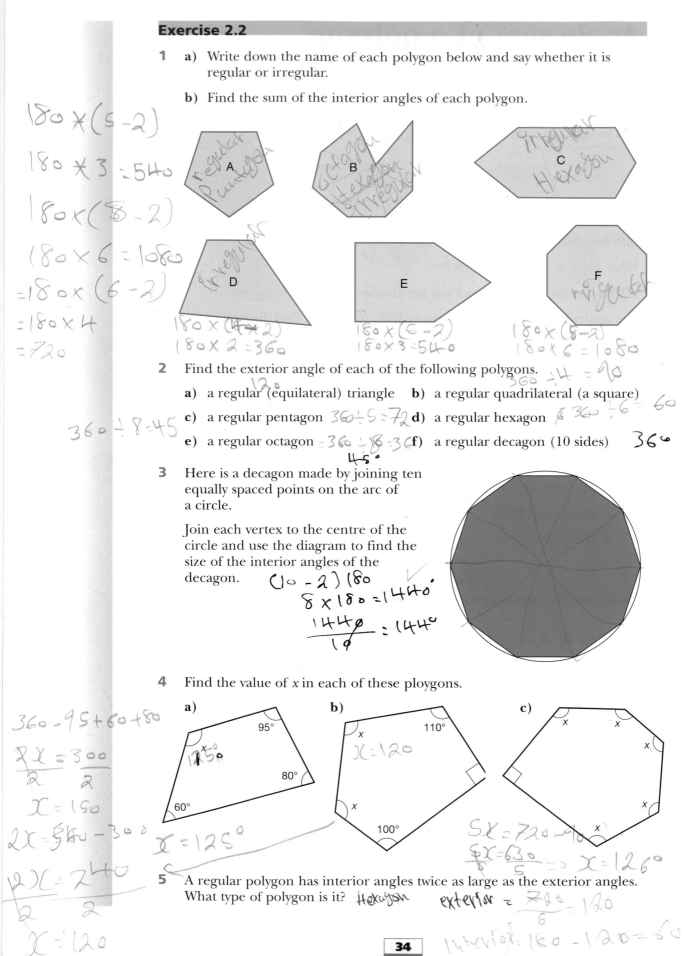

Handwritten working (left margin):

$180 \times (5-2)$
$180 \times 3 = 540$
$180 \times (8-2)$
$180 \times 6 = 1080$
$= 180 \times (6-2)$
$= 180 \times 4$
$= 720$

A — regular Pentagon
B — octagon hexagon irregular
C — irregular Hexagon
D — irregular
E
F — regular

$180 \times (4-2)$
$180 \times 2 = 360$

$180 \times (5-2)$
$180 \times 3 = 540$

$180 \times (8-2)$
$180 \times 6 = 1080$

2 Find the exterior angle of each of the following polygons. $360 \div 4 = 90$

a) a regular (equilateral) triangle $120°$ **b)** a regular quadrilateral (a square)

c) a regular pentagon $360 \div 5 = 72$ **d)** a regular hexagon $360 \div 6 = 60$

e) a regular octagon $= 360 \div 8 = 45°$ **f)** a regular decagon (10 sides) $36°$

$360 \div 8 = 45$

3 Here is a decagon made by joining ten equally spaced points on the arc of a circle.

Join each vertex to the centre of the circle and use the diagram to find the size of the interior angles of the decagon.

$(10-2)180$
$8 \times 180 = 1440°$
$\dfrac{1440}{10} = 144°$

4 Find the value of x in each of these ploygons.

a) 95°, $x°$, 60°, 125°

$360 - 95 + 60 + 80$
$\dfrac{2x = 300}{2} = \dfrac{300}{2}$
$x = 150$
$2x = 540 - 300$
$2x = 240$
$\dfrac{2x}{2} = \dfrac{240}{2}$
$x = 120$
$x = 125°$

b) x, 110°, 80°, x, 100° $x = 120$

c) x, x, x, x, x

$5x = 720 - ...$
$5x = 630 \Rightarrow x = 126°$

5 A regular polygon has interior angles twice as large as the exterior angles. What type of polygon is it? Hexagon

exterior $= \dfrac{720}{6} = 120$

interior: $180 - 120 = 60$

Finishing off

Now that you have finished this chapter you should be able to:

★ prove that the exterior angle of a triangle equals the sum of the interior opposite angles

★ prove that the angle sum of a triangle is 180°

★ calculate areas of parallelograms and trapezia

★ recognise special quadrilaterals

★ find the sum of the interior angles of any polygon

★ find the interior and exterior angles of any regular polygon.

Mixed Exercise 2.3

1 Find the area of each of thse shapes.

a)

6 cm

8 cm

$A = 8 \times 6$
$A = 48 \, cm^2$

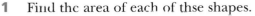

$\frac{(a+b)h}{2}$

$\frac{(8+7)3}{2}$

$\frac{10 \times 3}{2} = \frac{30}{2} = 15 \, cm^2$

b)

3 cm 3 cm

a

7 cm 5 cm

b

c)

A   B

D   C

base AC = 6 cm
height BD = 8 cm

$6 \times 8 = \boxed{48 \, cm^2}$

2 Find the sizes of the angles marked with letters.

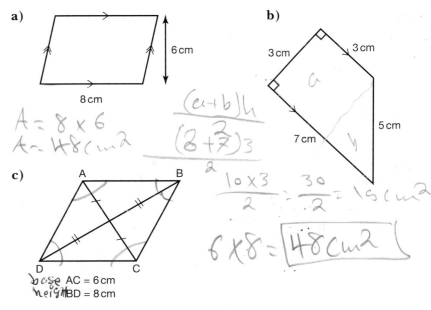

a)

135°
a

47°   133°

$2a = 366 - 94$
$2a = 266$
$\frac{2a}{2} = \frac{266}{2}$ $a = 133$

b)

c

118° b $b = 118$

40° $118 + 118 + 40$
276

360 − 276
$c = 84$

c)

58°

100°
d

e

$d = 80$

$e = 22$
$c = 58$

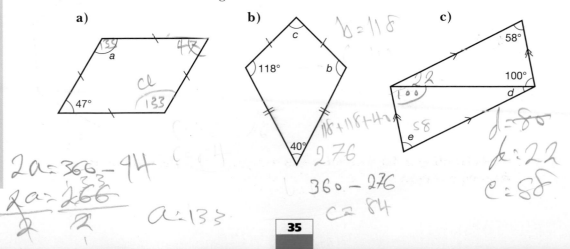

3 Copy and complete the following table.

Shape	Number of lines of symmetry	Order of rotational symmetry
Equilateral triangle	3	3
Square	4	4
Regular pentagon	5	5
Regular hexagon	6	6
Regular octogon	8	8

What do you notice? *I notice that Regular Polygon has same symmetry line and rotational*

4 Four of the exterior angles of a pentagon are 42°, 53°, 71° and 92°.

Calculate the size of the remaining exterior angle.   ***MEI***

102°

5 Hexagons like those drawn below have three lines of symmetry.

a) Derive an expression for the value of *a* in terms of *b*.

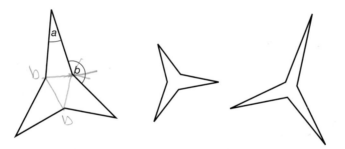

b) Explain why it is not possible for *b* to equal 110°.   ***MEI***

Chapter 3

Equations and inequalities

> **Before you start this chapter you should:**
>
> ★ understand the symbols <, >, ≤ and ≥
>
> ★ be able to simplify expressions by collecting like terms
>
> ★ be able to expand brackets
>
> ★ be able to solve simple equations.

Reminder

$3 \times a$ is written $3a$ $a \times b$ is written ab

$a \times a$ is written a^2 $a \div b$ is written $\dfrac{a}{b}$

Inequality symbols

< means *is less than*   ≤ means *is less than or equal to*

> means *is greater than*   ≥ means *is greater than or equal to*

Expanding brackets

Each term in the bracket is multiplied by the term outside the bracket.
For example,

$$3(a + 2b) = 3a + 6b$$

$$x(x - 3y) = x^2 - 3xy$$

$$2q(p - 2q + 4r) = 2pq - 4q^2 + 8qr$$

Solving simple linear equations

Always remember to apply the same mathematical operation to both sides of the equation, so that the two sides stay equal.

If you are not sure what order to do things in, think about what has been done to the unknown. You must reverse the order when you solve the equation. The examples that follow show how to do this.

Example

Solve these equations.

a) $3x + 2 = 11$ $x = 3$

b) $\dfrac{x}{4} - 1 = 5$ $x = 16$

c) $\dfrac{2x - 1}{5} = 3$ $x = 8$ ⟹ $2x - 1 = 15$

$2x = 16$

Solution

a) In this equation, x has been multiplied by 3 and then 2 has been added. You must undo these operations in reverse order.

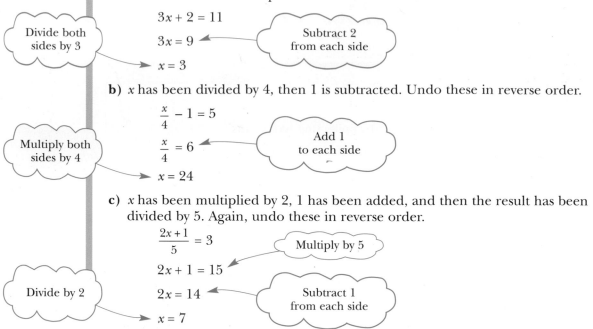

$$3x + 2 = 11$$

Divide both sides by 3

Subtract 2 from each side

$$3x = 9$$

$$x = 3$$

b) x has been divided by 4, then 1 is subtracted. Undo these in reverse order.

$$\frac{x}{4} - 1 = 5$$

Multiply both sides by 4

Add 1 to each side

$$\frac{x}{4} = 6$$

$$x = 24$$

c) x has been multiplied by 2, 1 has been added, and then the result has been divided by 5. Again, undo these in reverse order.

$$\frac{2x + 1}{5} = 3$$

Multiply by 5

$$2x + 1 = 15$$

Divide by 2

Subtract 1 from each side

$$2x = 14$$

$$x = 7$$

Use the questions in the next exercise to check that you still remember these topics.

Review exercise 3.1

1 Simplify these expressions by collecting like terms.
   a) $3x + 2 + x - 4 - 2x + 1$ ⟹ $2x - 1$
   b) $5a + 2b - 3a + 3 - 6b$ = $2a - 4b + 3$
   c) $4p + 3q + 7p - 3pq - q - 2p + 5pq - 2q$ ⟹ $9p + 2pq$

2 Write these statements using inequality signs.
   a) x is greater than 3 $x > 3$
   b) x is less than or equal to -2 $x \le -2$
   c) x is greater than or equal to -1 and less than 5 $-1 \le x < 5$

3 Simplify these expressions.
   a) $2a \times 3b$ = $6ab$
   b) $3x \times 5x$ = $15x^2$
   c) $3p \times 4q \times p$ ⟹ $12p^2q$
   d) $a \times 2a \times 3a$ = $6a^3$
   e) $(-2c) \times 6d$ ⟹ $-12cd$
   f) $3x \times (-y) \times (-2y)$ = $+6xy^2$
   g) $(2s)^2$ = $4s^2$
   h) $(-3z)^2 \times 2z$ ⟹ $9z^2 \times 2z = 18z^3$

4 Remove the brackets from the following expressions.
   a) $3(a + 2)$ $3a + 6$
   b) $4(x - y)$ ⟹ $4x - 4y$
   c) $3(2p - 3q)$ ⟹ $6p - 9q$
   d) $2(a - 4b + 2c)$ = $2a - 8b + 4c$
   e) $5(2x - 3)$ $10x - 15$
   f) $m(m + 2n)$ ⟹ $m^2 + 2mn$
   g) $3d(3d - 2e)$ $9d^2 - 6de$
   h) $xy(x + y)$ ⟹ $x^2y + xy^2$ ⟹ x^3y^3
   i) $4a(ab - bc)$ $4a^2b - 4abc$
   j) $2pq(3p - 4r)$ $6p^2q - 8r$

Review exercise 3.1 *continued*

5 Expand the brackets and simplify each of these expressions.

a) $2(3x + 1) + 5(x - 3)$ *6x + 2 + 5x - 15 ⇒ 11x - 13*

b) $3(a - 3b) - 2(2a - b)$ *3a - 9b - 4a + 2b ⇒ -a - 7b*

c) $5(2p + 3q - 1) + 3(2p + 4) - 4(1 - 2q)$ *10p + 15q - 5 + 6p + 12 - 4 + 8q ⇒ 16p + 23q + 3*

d) $m(2n + 3) + n(m - 4)$ *2mn + 3m + mn - 4n ⇒ 3mn + 3m - 4n*

e) $a(2a - 1) - 4a(2 - 3a) + 5(2a - 1)$ *2a² - a - 8a + 12a² + 10a - 5 ⇒ 14a² + a - 5*

f) $2x(x - 3y) - 3y(2x + y)$ *2x² - 6xy - 6xy + 3y² ⇒ 2x² - 12xy + 3y²*

6 Solve the following equations.

a) $a + 4 = 7$ *a = 3*

b) $5b = 30$

c) $2x + 3 = 15$

d) $4y - 2 = 18$

e) $3p + 4 = -5$

f) $6t - 5 = 16$

g) $\dfrac{d}{3} - 2 = 1$

h) $\dfrac{x - 3}{2} = 4$

i) $\dfrac{3y + 5}{2} = 1$

j) $\dfrac{x - 3}{2} + 8 = 2$

k) $\dfrac{x}{3} - \dfrac{x}{4} = 2$ *x = 24*

l) $\dfrac{x}{2} - \dfrac{x}{4} = 3$ *x = 12*

m) $\dfrac{3}{4}x - \dfrac{x}{6} = 49$ *x = 84*

n) $\dfrac{2}{3}x = 5 + \dfrac{1}{6}x$ *x = 10*

o) $\dfrac{2}{3}x = 11 - \dfrac{1}{3}x$

7 Solve these equations. (Start each time by multiplying out the brackets and simplifying.)

a) $4(2a + 3) + a = 30$ *8a + 12 + a = 30 ⇒ 9a = 18 ⇒ a = 2*

b) $2(3x + 1) + 3(x - 4) = 17$

c) $5(3y - 2) - 4(2 - y) = 1$

d) $2(3 - z) + 6(2 + 3z) = 2$

8 Janice hires a car for a day. Her bill comes to £82.40.

Let m stand for the number of miles she drove.

Write down an equation involving m, and use it to find how many miles she drove.

-50 + 0.4m = 82.4 - 50
0.4m = 32.4 ⇒
0.4m = 32.4
──── ───
0.4   0.4
m = 81

CAR HIRE
£50 per day
+
40p per mile

9 A coach party of 50 people are going to a zoo. The total entrance cost for the whole party is £256.

Let n stand for the number of children in the group.

a) Write down an expression for the number of adults in the group.

b) Write down an equation involving n.

c) Solve your equation to find the number of children and the number of adults in the group.

ZOO ENTRANCE

Adults.........£6
Children.....£4

Exercise 3.2

1 Solve these equations.

a) $5 - 2x = 4$ $x = \frac{1}{2}$

b) $9 - 4x = 16$ $x = -\frac{7}{4}$

c) $8 = 11 - 5x$ $x = \frac{5}{3}$

d) $14 = 8 - 2x$ $x = -3$

e) $1 - \frac{x}{2} = 4$ $x = -3$

f) $6 = 10 - \frac{2x}{3}$

g) $\frac{1-x}{3} = 4$ $x = -11$

h) $\frac{2-5x}{4} = 6$

2 Solve these equations.

a) $6x - 3 = 2x + 4$

b) $3x + 1 = 4 - x$

c) $2x - 5 = 4x + 1$

d) $1 - 3x = 4 - 5x$

e) $3 - 7x = 3x + 4$

f) $3(2x - 1) = 4x + 3$

g) $\frac{2x+3}{5} = x - 3$

h) $\frac{1-x}{2} = \frac{2x+5}{3}$

3 Solve these equations.

a) $\frac{3}{x} = 4$

b) $\frac{7}{2x} = 5$

c) $\frac{3}{x+3} = 2$ $x = 6$

d) $\frac{4}{3x-2} = 1$

e) $\frac{2}{x} = \frac{1}{x+3}$

f) $\frac{3}{2x-1} = \frac{5}{x-4}$ $x = -1$

g) $\frac{4}{1-2x} + 3 = 1$ $x = 1.5$

h) $\frac{6}{4x-1} - 3 = 2$ $x = \frac{11}{20}$

4 A group of children are sharing out some sweets. There are 5 each and 2 sweets are left over. Then three more children join them, and they share out the sweets again. This time there are 3 each and 5 sweets are left over.

a) Let n be the number of children to start with. Write down an equation in n and solve it to find the number of children.

b) How many sweets were there?

5 Andrew's grandmother is 5 times as old as he is. Andrew works out that in 4 years she will be 4 times as old as he is.

a) Work out Andrew's age and his grandmother's age.

b) When will Andrew's grandmother be

(i) three times as old as he is?   (ii) twice as old as he is?

6 Solve these equations.

a) $\frac{2x+1}{3} - \frac{x+5}{4} = 1$ $x = -2\frac{1}{5}$

b) $\frac{x+1}{x+3} = \frac{x-2}{x+5}$ (Hint: use brackets and multiply out.)

c) $\frac{1}{x} + \frac{1}{x+1} = \frac{2}{x-2}$ (Hint: multiply each term by $x(x+1)(x-2)$.)

Simultaneous equations

A book club is running a special offer.

Philip wants to know how much each type of book costs in the special offer. Using p to represent the cost of one paperback, in pence, and h for the cost of one hardback, in pence, he writes down two equations:

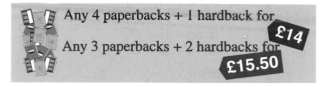

Any 4 paperbacks + 1 hardback for £14

Any 3 paperbacks + 2 hardbacks for £15.50

$$4p + h = 1400 \quad \leftarrow \textcircled{1}$$
$$3p + 2h = 1550 \quad \leftarrow \textcircled{2}$$

This pair of equations is an example of **simultaneous equations**.

There are two unknowns, p and h, and so two equations are needed to solve them.

To solve the equations, the first step is to find an equation which involves just one of the unknowns. This is how you can do it:

> First multiply equation ① by 2 so that both equations involve the term $2h$

① × 2	$8p + 2h = 2800$
②	$3p + 2h = 1550$
Subtract:	$5p = 1250$
	$p = 250$
Substitute into ①	$4 \times 250 + h = 1400$
	$1000 + h = 1400$
	$h = 400$

> Then subtract equation ② from equation ① to get rid of the terms in h

> Now you can find h by substituting the value for p into either of the original equations

So a paperback costs £2.50 and a hardback costs £4.00.

Check that these answers fit the statement in the advertisement.

Example

Solve the simultaneous equations

> ① $3x + 2y = 10$
> ② $2x + 5y = 3$

Solution

In this example you cannot multiply just one equation by a number to get the same term in both equations. However, you could multiply equation ① by 2 and equation ② by 3, so that both equations involve the term $6x$.

① × 2	$6x + 4y = 20$
② × 3	$6x + 15y = 9$
Subtract:	$-11y = 11$
	$y = -1$
Substitute into ②:	$2x + -5 = 3$
	$2x = 8$
	$x = 4$

Substitute these values for x and y into equation ① to check.

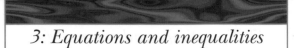
Finishing off

Now that you have finished this chapter you should be able to:

★ solve a variety of linear equations

★ solve simultaneous linear equations algebraically and graphically

★ solve linear inequalities algebraically.

Use the questions in the next exercise to check that you understand everything.

 Mixed exercise 3.5

1 Solve these equations.

a) $7 - 2x = 8$ $x = -\frac{1}{2}$ b) $10 = 1 - 3x$ $x = -3$ c) $5 - \frac{x}{3} = 3$ $x = 6$

d) $\frac{1-3x}{4} = 4$ $x = -5$ e) $5x - 3 = 2x + 9$ f) $1 - 4x = 3x + 8$

g) $2 - 3x = 7 - x$ h) $2(3x - 4) = x + 5$ i) $3(x - 1) = 4(2x + 7)$ $x = -6.2$

j) $\frac{1-5x}{4} = 7 - 2x$ k) $\frac{3x+1}{2} = \frac{2x-4}{3}$ $x = 22$ l) $\frac{6}{x} = 5$ $x = 1.2$

m) $\frac{3}{x+1} = 2$ n) $\frac{7}{3x+2} = \frac{4}{2x-3}$

2 Solve each of these pairs of simultaneous equations.

a) $3x + y = 10$
   $2x + 3y = 9$

b) $5a - 2b = 12$
   $2a + b = 3$

c) $3p - 2q = -10$
   $4p + 3q = -2$

d) $2s + 5t = 20$
   $s = 3t - 1$

e) $5c - 3d = 7$
   $3c - 4d = 13$

f) $y = 4x + 2$
   $y = 3x - 1$

g) $3p - 4q = 27$
   $q = 7 - 2p$

h) $4f - 3g = 16$
   $6f + 7g = 1$

i) $c = 4 - 5d$ $c = -1$
   $d = 2c + 3$ $d = 1$

$g = 2$ $f = 2.5$

3 Solve these inequalities.

a) $4x - 1 > 8$ $x > 2.25$

b) $3x + 2 \leq x - 4$

c) $4 - 5x > 2x - 3$

d) $2(2x - 1) \leq 5x + 1$

e) $2(1 - 3x) < 3(2 - x)$

f) $\frac{2x+3}{4} \geq 6$

g) $\frac{2x-1}{4} \leq \frac{3-x}{3}$

h) $\frac{3-2x}{4} > \frac{3x+1}{5}$

4 In this triangle, angle A is twice the size of angle B, and angle C is 40° greater than angle A.

Write down an equation and solve it to find the sizes of the three angles.

$C = 40$

$40 > A > 2b$

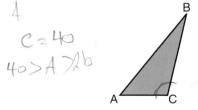

Mixed exercise 3.5 *continued*

5 230 tickets are sold for this double bill. The total amount taken in ticket sales is £920.50.

How many adult tickets and how many children's tickets are sold?

6 Tim cycles to work, a distance of 4 km. He cycles at a speed of 12 km/h. One day, his bicycle gets a puncture part of the way there, and he has to walk the rest of the way to work. He walks at a speed of 5 km/h. The whole journey takes him half an hour. How far from home did the bicycle get a puncture?

7 Two lines have equations

$$y = 2x - 1$$
$$3y + 4x = 6$$

Find the co-ordinates of the point where the lines cross.

8 Three tins of dog food and five tins of cat food costs £3.93.

Two tins of dog food and three tins of cat food costs £2.47.

Find the cost of one tin of dog food and the cost of one tin of cat food.

d = £0.36

C = £0.45

9 Jim is buying some cakes for the people at work. He wants to buy 15 cakes. Doughnuts cost 36p and iced buns 30p. He has a maximum of £5 to spend. Let n be the number of doughnuts he buys.

Write down an inequality and solve it to find the maximum number of doughnuts he could buy.

10 Set up and solve an equation to answer this algebra question from the 1930s.

> If a certain number is added to both the numerator and the denominator of the fraction $\frac{3}{13}$ the result is equivalent to $\frac{4}{9}$.
>
> Find the number.

Mixed exercise 3.5 *continued*

11 Here is a sketch of three straight lines.

The lines intersect at the points A, B and C.

Find the coordinates of B and C.

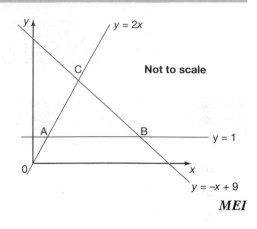

y = 2x

C

Not to scale

A   B

y = 1

x

0

y = −x + 9

MEI

12 This is the graph of *y = 2x*.

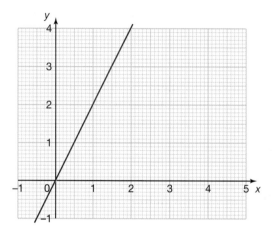

Solve, graphically, the following simultaneous equations.

$$y = 2x$$
$$3x + 4y = 12$$

MEI

Investigation

a) Try to solve the simultaneous equations

$$4x - 2y = 5$$
$$y = 2x - 1$$

What goes wrong? *x is going to cause*

Draw graphs of these two equations and use them to explain why the equations cannot be solved.

b) Try to solve the simultaneous equations

$$6x + 3y = 9$$
$$y = 3 - 2x$$

Explain what happens. Again, you may find it helpful to draw graphs of the two equations.

c) One of parts a) and b) has no solutions, the other has infinitely many solutions. Which is which? Why?

Chapter 4

Statistics review

Before you start this chapter you should be able to:

★ summarise data in a tally chart and frequency table

★ understand the terms categorical, numerical, discrete and continuous

★ draw and interpret a bar chart, pictogram, pie chart and vertical line chart

★ calculate the mean, median, mode and range of a set of data

★ draw a scatter diagram and recognise correlation.

Using statistics

Statistics is used extensively to help people investigate a wide variety of situations in real life, and to make the best decisions about them.

There are several stages in this process:

1. Decide what questions you want to answer.

2. Collect relevant data.

3. Analyse your data. (Suitable displays may help.)

4. Use your findings to answer the questions.

Much of the work in this review chapter fits into the second and third stages.

Data display reminder

A tally chart

Goals	Tally
0	卌 卌 卌 卌 l
1	卌 卌 卌 卌 卌 llll
2	卌 卌 卌
3	ll
4	卌 l
5	l
6	

A frequency table

Number of goals	0	1	2	3	4	5	6
Frequency	21	29	15	2	6	1	0

These two displays refer to the same data, the numbers of goals scored by teams in the English football league (Premier League, Divisions 1, 2 and 3) one Saturday.

These displays illustrate six sets of data. Are the data categorical or numerical?

A bar chart

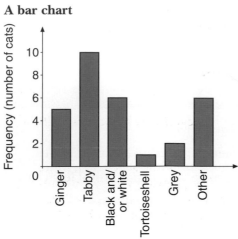

This bar chart refers to pet cats on a small housing estate.

A pictogram

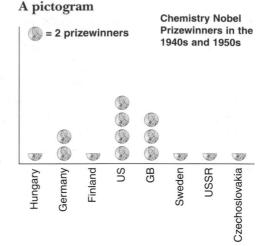

This pictogram shows the nationalities of winners of the Nobel Prize for Chemistry in the 1940s and 1950s.

A pie chart

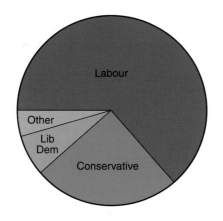

This pie chart shows the representation of the political parties at Westminster after the 1997 General Election.

A vertical line chart

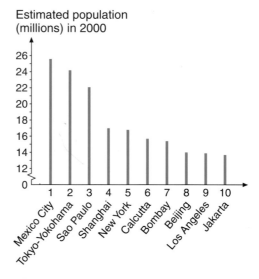

This vertical line chart illustrates the population of the world's ten largest cities, ranked by size.

Stem and leaf diagram

```
2 | 8
3 | 0 6
4 | 0 0 3 4 4 5 5 6
5 | 0 0 3
6 | 4 6
7 | 1 7
8 | 0 7
```

This club obtained 45 points

This stem and leaf diagram shows the number of points won by football teams in the English Premier league during the 2001/2 season.

Key: 2|8 refers to a club that won 28 points.

Sometimes data displays are drawn so as to give a false impression.

- In pictograms, the icons should always be the same size.

  £ = 1 million pounds   £££ = 3 million pounds ✓

  £ = 1 million pounds   £ = 3 million pounds ✗

- In bar charts and vertical line charts, the vertical scale should normally be continuous, starting at the origin.

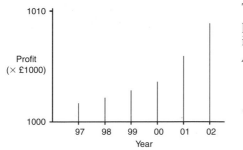

This makes it look as though the profit is growing very fast whereas it is actually changing very little. A false impression may be intended.

✗

- Sometimes you may genuinely want to break the vertical scale to show a particular point and in that case you should use the broken line symbol ⌇ to show it.

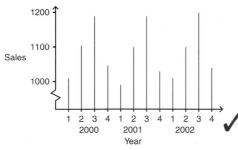

This vertical line chart shows the quarterly sales of a magazine. It has been drawn to bring out the seasonal sales pattern. No deception is intended.

✓

Review exercise 4.1

1   Use the data displays above and on the previous pages to answer the following questions.

   a) How many teams scored less than 3 goals in the English League on the Saturday shown?

   b) How many cats are referred to in the bar chart?

   c) How many people received the Nobel Prize for Chemistry in the 1940s and 1950s?

   d) Which party came second in the 1997 General Election?

   e) What is the population of Shanghai?

Review exercise 4.1 *continued*

2   A newspaper editor wishes to know whether the reporters on her paper are writing simply enough. She takes a sample of 50 words from each reporter's work and writes down their lengths. Here are the figures from Nigel's sample.

11	6	6	3	5		4	7	3	6	2
4	7	6	7	4		10	8	6	3	7
4	4	11	2	8		2	1	5	2	2
5	3	7	4	6		6	6	11	2	3
6	7	7	4	2		8	10	3	7	6

a)   Construct a tally chart for these data.

b)   Construct a frequency table.

c)   Display the data on a vertical line chart.

The diagrams below illustrate the sample data from two other reporters.

d)   Compare the samples from the three reporters.

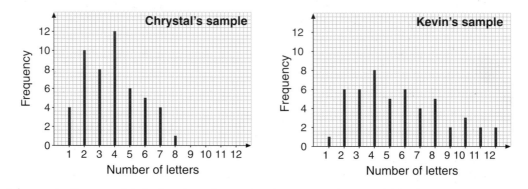

e)   Do you think the data from the three samples would be better illustrated on pie charts? Give your reasons.

3   A school is preparing a booklet for new students. They want to include information about how students travel to school. The bar chart illustrates data for the present first-year students.

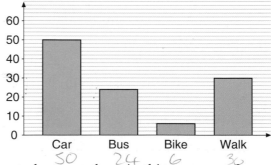

a)   How many students are there in this year group?

b)   Which is the most popular method of travelling to school?

c)   Use the same data to draw a pictogram and then a pie chart.

d)   Which of the three diagrams would you choose for the booklet? Give a brief explanation for your choice.

4   A local politician wishes to present the case that the residents in his area are quite poor. He collects data on the ages of cars in a small car park in the area. (He uses the cars' registration letters to find their ages.) He is going to give an illustrated talk, and considers these three displays.

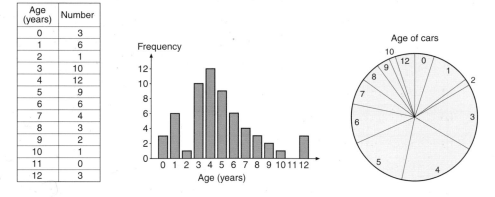

Age (years)	Number
0	3
1	6
2	1
3	10
4	12
5	9
6	6
7	4
8	3
9	2
10	1
11	0
12	3

a) Which display do you think is best? Explain your choice briefly.

b) The politician says, 'Only 5% of people in my area have a new car.'

Explain

   (i) how he obtained the figure of 5%

   (ii) whether you agree with his statement.

5   The following headlines and data displays could have occurred in a newspaper. Comment on them in terms of:

(i) whether they are designed to give a misleading impression

(ii) if so, how they should have been drawn.

a)

STEEP FALL IN SUPPORT FOR GOVERNMENT

Support for the government has plummeted to an all time low.

b)

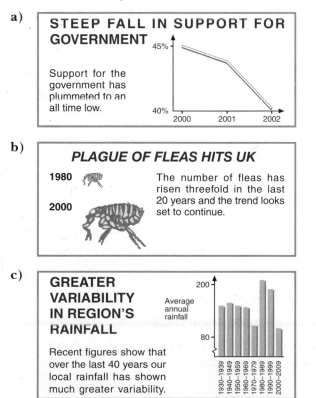

PLAGUE OF FLEAS HITS UK

1980

2000

The number of fleas has risen threefold in the last 20 years and the trend looks set to continue.

c)

GREATER VARIABILITY IN REGION'S RAINFALL

Recent figures show that over the last 40 years our local rainfall has shown much greater variability.

Review exercise 4.1 *continued*

6 Andrew throws two dice and records their total many times over. The results are shown on the tally.

Total of two dice	Tally
2	||
3	~~||||~~ |||
4	~~||||~~ ~~||||~~ |
5	~~||||~~ ~~||||~~ |||
6	~~||||~~ ~~||||~~ ~~||||~~ ||
7	~~||||~~ ~~||||~~ ~~||||~~ ~~||||~~ |
8	~~||||~~ ~~||||~~ ||||
9	~~||||~~ ~~||||~~ |||
10	~~||||~~ ||||
11	~~||||~~ |||
12	||||

a) How many times did he throw the dice?

b) What score was

(i) the mode

(ii) the median

(iii) the mean?

7 Sheila found the mode, median and mean of sets of five numbers. Her results are shown in the table.

Numbers	Mode	Median	Mean
1, 1, 2, 3, 4	1	2	2.2
1, 2, 3, 4, 4	4	3	2.8
1, 3, 4, 5, 5	5	4	3.6
1, 2, 2, 3, 4	2	2	2.4
2, 2, 4, 6, 7	2	4	4.2

Sheila said: 'The mean can never be between the mode and the median.'

Investigate whether she is correct by considering other sets of five numbers.

MEI

Collecting data

Questionnaires

What data do you need to collect? The answer depends on what you want to know, and why, but even then it is probably not entirely obvious. It is often helpful to start with a brainstorming session for those involved. Imagine this situation.

A superstore is considering setting up a play area for small children so that their parents can shop without being distracted. They want to judge whether the extra sales will make the cost of the play area worthwhile.

What data would help the superstore?

They decide to ask their customers to fill in a questionnaire.

What questions should it contain?

You need to be very careful about how you ask the questions. Here is a check-list to apply to each one.

- Is it absolutely clear what the question is asking?

- Are you sure it is what you want to ask?

- Is the wording misleading? Does it encourage a particular answer?

It is usual to ask people to respond to most of the questions by ticking a box. This makes their answers easier to process.

- Do the boxes allow for all possible answers?

- Is it possible to tick more than one box?

It is common to include a few questions on other subjects in a questionnaire. It does not have to be restricted to its main purpose.

The superstore asks two employees to devise a questionnaire about the children's play area. Which of their questions are suitable and which are not?

ALEX

1. How often do you shop here? ....

2. Do you have children under 10? ....

3. Are they naughty when they come shopping?
   ☐ yes   ☐ no

4. Free range eggs are good for your children. Would you be prepared to pay a little more for them?
   ☐ yes   ☐ no

5. What is your typical bill here?
   ☐   ☐   ☐   ☐
   Up to £10   £10-£30   £20-£50   Over £40

VAL

1. How many times have you come to this shop in the last 7 days?
   ☐ 1   ☐ 2   ☐ 3   ☐ 4   ☐ 5 or more

2. How many children under 10 do you have?
   ☐ 0   ☐ 1   ☐ 2   ☐ 3   ☐ 4 or more

3. If we provide a play area, do you think your children would use it?
   ☐ Hardly ever   ☐ Sometimes   ☐ Often   ☐ Almost always

4. How much extra would you be prepared to pay for 12 eggs if they were free range?
   ☐ Nothing   ☐ 5p   ☐ 10p   ☐ 15p

5. Please pin today's receipt to this questionnaire. Is this bill
   ☐ Less than usual   ☐ typical   ☐ More than usual

Before you use a questionnaire you should always try it out on a few people first. Once you have given it out for real, it is too late to find out that some of the questions don't work.

Exercise 4.3

1 Say whether you think there will be positive correlation, negative correlation or no correlation in the following bivariate data.

    a) average hours per week watching television and average books read per week

    b) time to run 100 metres and time to run 200 metres

    c) population of a town and number of doctors practising in the town

    d) size of shoe worn and IQ

2 Ten students took tests in Mathematics and Music. The marks obtained by each student are shown in this table.

Student	A	B	C	D	E	F	G	H	I	J
Maths	34	91	59	24	29	11	83	20	97	42
Music	28	70	71	42	26	22	49	11	82	33

    a) Plot a scatter diagram.

    b) Does the scatter diagram suggest that students who are good at Mathematics are also likely to be good at Music?

3 A number of people were selected at random to carry out a fitness test. The following table shows their age (in months) and the time taken (in seconds) to complete the test.

Person	A	B	C	D	E	F	G	H	I	J
Age (months)	240	252	260	265	280	300	310	328	360	375
Time (secs)	35	40	43	46	45	52	48	56	55	60

    a) Plot a scatter diagram of these data.

    b) Calculate the mean values of the ages and of the times.

    c) Draw a line of best fit on your graph.

    d) Use your line of best fit to predict the time taken by someone who is 340 months old.

4 Seven runners took part in both a 5000 m and a 10 000 m race. The table below shows their time for each in minutes.

5000 m (minutes)	14.2	14.7	15.1	15.6	16.0	17.5	19.8
10 000 m (minutes)	31.3	30.7	34.5	33.1	33.9	40.2	42.7

    a) Plot a scatter diagram of these data.

    b) Draw a line of best fit on the scatter diagram and hence predict the 10 000 m time of a runner who took 16.5 minutes to run 5000 m.

MEI

Exercise 4.3 *continued*

5   A market gardener believes that the number of tomatoes per plant might be increased by the use of a special fertiliser. He tests this by a controlled experiment in which some plants are fed with specific quantities of fertiliser and the number of tomatoes per plant is recorded.

The scatter diagram of results is shown here.

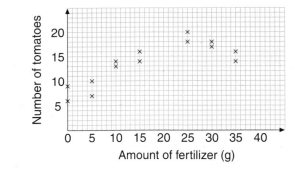

a) Predict the number of tomatoes found if 20 g of fertiliser are used.

b) Suggest why it is not appropriate to predict the number of tomatoes if 10 g of fertiliser are used.

6   The following data concern the percentage of arable land and the percentage of land over 500 m high in seven districts.

District	Percentage of land over 500 m	Percentage of arable land
Barnston	24	62
James-le-wick	73	24
York Ridge	69	31
Deangate	62	36
Raisley	56	47
Ormton Episcopi	38	56
Hartlebury Magna	33	58

a) Plot the data on a scatter diagram.

b) Calculate the means for the percentage of land over 500 m and the percentage of arable land. Plot the mean point on your diagram.

c) Draw a line of best fit.

d) Comment on the correlation between the percentage of land over 500 m and the percentage of arable land.

e) The district of Barker's Down has 45% of its land at a height over 500 m. Use your graph to predict the percentage of arable land in Barker's Down.

f) Joyce Meadows is by the sea and only has 0.5% of its land over 500 m. Can you predict the percentage of arable land?

Exercise 4.3 *continued*

7 The scatter graph shows the number of hours spent watching TV last week and the homework marks for 10 students in Mathematics.

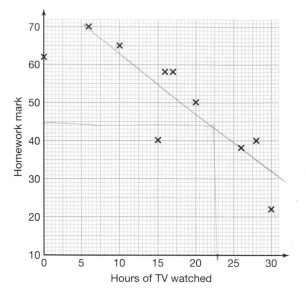

Another student watched 23 hours of TV last week.

Estimate the homework mark for that student.

Show your method.

MEI

Statistical measures

Statistics usually involves large or very large data sets. The example which follows is based on a small set (size 7) to make it easy to see how certain measures are calculated. When you read it, remember that most real statistics involves much larger sets.

The number of callers to a Local Health Emergency Hotline on each day in one week is recorded.

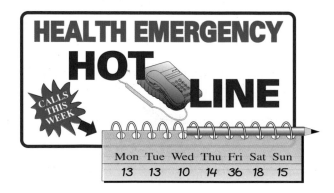

Mean

To find the mean, the numbers are added up and divided by how many there are:

$$\frac{13 + 13 + 10 + 14 + 36 + 18 + 15}{7} = 17$$

So 17 is the mean number of calls.

 How can you use the statistics functions on your calculator to find the mean of a data set?

Median

This is the middle number when they are placed in order:

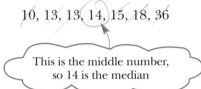

10, 13, 13, 14, 15, 18, 36

This is the middle number, so 14 is the median

If there is an even number of items of data, there is no single middle number. In this case, the median is half-way between the two numbers nearest to the middle:

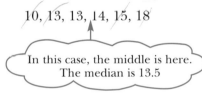

10, 13, 13, 14, 15, 18

In this case, the middle is here. The median is 13.5

Mode

This is the most common number.

There are two 13s in 13, 13, 10, 14, 36, 18, 15 so 13 is the mode.

Which average?

Which average is best? The answer will depend on what it is to be used for.

- The mean takes account of all callers in the seven days.

  If there are not many data items, the mean can be unduly affected by extreme values. In this case the 36 callers on Friday have raised the mean.

 What reasons can you think of to explain the large number of calls on Friday? Do you think the mean gives a good 'typical value' in this case?

- The median is just the middle number, so it is not affected by an extreme value, such as the 36 calls on Friday.

 Suppose you have a large data set. Is the median easy to find?

- The mode is often the easiest to pick out. Like the median, it is not affected by extreme values. There may not be a mode, or there may be more than one mode.

Example

2, 5, 7, 8, 9   has no mode

3, 3, 5, 6, 6   has two modes, 3 and 6: it is **bimodal**.

The mode may not always be representative. A cricketer's scores in ten matches are

26, 0, 102, 44, 0, 68, 163, 18, 35, 95

The mode of these scores is 0, but the cricketer is actually a high scorer.

Think of another situation where the mode is unrepresentative.

Range

The mean, median and mode provide information about where a set of data is centred. They are often called measures of central tendency.

The **range** provides information about the spread of the data. It is the difference between the largest data value and the smallest.

So for the Health Emergency Hotline data,

Range = 36 – 10 = 26

What would the range be without Friday's figure? An extreme value like that is called an outlier. What is the effect of outliers on the range?

There are other ways of measuring the spread. One way, the interquartile range, is covered on page 155.

How do you enter statistical data into your calculator?

What statistical measures will it work out for you?

What statistical diagrams does a graphical calculator draw? What about a spreadsheet?

Exercise 4.4

1 **a)** Work out the mean, median, mode, and range of the number of runs scored by the following cricketers. (The players were out each time.)

Alun   8, 9, 12, 6, 23, 14, 0, 12, 20
David   28, 16, 30, 0, 0, 42, 1, 55, 0, 1, 4
Martin   23, 22, 25, 26, 20, 28, 27, 24

   b) (i) Which average do you think best represents the performance of each cricketer? Which cricketer would you want in your team, and why?

   c) Jane's mean score is 24.5 runs, and her range is 30 runs. Compare Martin's mean score and range with those of Jane. Do they tell you who is better at batting?

Exercise 4.4 *continued*

2   A survey is being carried out into the amount of pocket money 15 year olds are given per week. For a class of 30 students, the survey produces the following averages for one week.

>   Mean £4.65   Median £3.50   Mode £5

a) Next week all the students receive the same pocket money except one who gets £5 instead of £8. What are the new mean, median and mode?

b) In a third week, a new boy joins the class. Everyone else's pocket money is the same as in week 2. He gets £6 a week pocket money. What can you say about the new mean, median and mode?

3   Paula asked twelve friends about the number of bus journeys they had made in the last four weeks. They gave the following figures.

>   0   0   0   2   2   3   4   4   5   5   7   40

a) Find the mode, median and mean of these numbers.

b) Which of these averages best represents the figures and why?

c) Paula found that eight of the people she asked had taken bus journeys for social activities, while John travelled by bus to and from work each day. She decided to leave out John's figure. Find the new mean and median.

4   The figures below give the weekly pay of a random sample of ten adults on a housing estate.

>   £0   £250   £200   £0   £2500   £300   £220   £0   £180   £200

a) Find the mean, mode and median of these figures.

b) Which average do you think is the most representative?

c) Which figure would you use if you were

>   (i)   a local politician campaigning against unemployment?

>   (ii) a local shopkeeper trying to decide how much money people have to spend?

5   The table shows the number of occupants in a sample of the cars travelling along a commuter road in the rush hour one morning.

1	2	3	4	5	6 or more
22	8	13	9	2	0

a) Find the mode, median and mean of these data.

b) Which of these measures would you quote if you were

>   (i)   campaigning to reduce the number of cars on the road?
>   (ii) estimating the number of people being transported along the road?

Review exercise 5.1 *continued*

3 Katie is trying out this puzzle on her friends.

She says, 'Think of a number. Add 1, then multiply by 2, then subtract 5, then multiply by 3, then add 4.'

a) Write down and simplify an expression for the answer that each person will get.

b) Michelle thinks of the number 3. What is her result?

c) Jayne thinks of the number –2. What is her result?

d) How could Katie work out the numbers from the results?

4 Work these out.

a) –1 + 2   **b)** 4 + –6   **c)** –2 + –5

d) 4 – 9   **e)** –3 – 8   **f)** –2 – –6

g) –2 × 5   **h)** –7 × –3   **i)** $(-4)^2$

j) 12 ÷ –3   **k)** –15 ÷ 3   **l)** –63 ÷ –7

5 Work these out.

a) –2 + (3 × –5)   **b)** 5 – (–2 × –6)

c) $\dfrac{-2+8}{-3}$ **d)** $\dfrac{5-(-3\times4)}{2}$

e) $(-4)^2 - (-3)^2$ **f)** $\dfrac{(-2)^2-10}{5}$

g) $\dfrac{(-3-5)^2}{-4}$ **h)** $\dfrac{12}{-2} - \dfrac{-16}{8}$

i) $\dfrac{-18}{-2} - \dfrac{(-4)^2}{-1}$ **j)** $\dfrac{(-5)^2-(-3)^2}{-4\times2\times-1}$

6 The formula

$v = u + at$

gives the final speed, v, of an object moving with constant acceleration in terms of the initial speed, u, the acceleration, a, and the time taken, t.

Find v when

a) $u = 3$, $a = 2$, $t = 5$

b) $u = 10$, $a = -1$, $t = 4$

c) $u = -5$, $a = -3$, $t = 8$

7 $y = \dfrac{a^2 - b}{c}$

Work out y when

a) $a = 5$, $b = 3$, $c = 2$

b) $a = -2$, $b = 1$, $c = -5$

c) $a = -4$, $b = -3$, $c = 2$

8 $p = \dfrac{q^2 + r^2}{2q - r}$

Work out p when

a) $q = 2$, $r = -1$

b) $q = -1$, $r = 3$

c) $q = -3$, $r = -4$

Manipulating formulae and expressions

Expanding two brackets

The nth term of the quadratic sequence

$$12, 20, 30, 42....$$

is given by the formula

$$n\text{th term} = (n + 2)(n + 3)$$

In this expression, $n + 2$ is being multiplied by $n + 3$. This is like finding the area of a rectangle with length $n + 2$ and width $n + 3$.

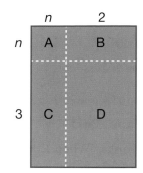

Write down an expression for the area of each section A, B, C and D. Then write down an expression for the total area of the rectangle.

Look at the expression you have found. Notice how each of the four terms is obtained by multiplying one term from the first bracket and one from the second bracket.

Some people find it helpful to draw lines or arrows connecting each pair of terms which are multiplied together.

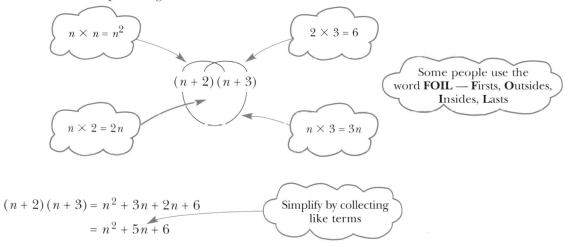

$n \times n = n^2$

$2 \times 3 = 6$

$(n + 2)(n + 3)$

Some people use the word **FOIL** — **F**irsts, **O**utsides, **I**nsides, **L**asts

$n \times 2 = 2n$

$n \times 3 = 3n$

$$(n + 2)(n + 3) = n^2 + 3n + 2n + 6$$

Simplify by collecting like terms

$$= n^2 + 5n + 6$$

Check that this is the same as the expression you found for the area of the rectangle.

Example

Multiply out   **a)** $(x + 1)(x - 3)$

                b) $(2a - 1)(3b + 2)$

Solution

a) $(x + 1)(x - 3) = x^2 - 3x + x - 3$

Simplify by collecting like terms

$$= x^2 - 2x - 3$$

b) $(2a - 1)(3b + 2) = 6ab + 4a - 3b - 2$

$-6ab$

Exercise 5.2 *continued*

3 **a)** Multiply out the following.

(i) $(x + 2)(x - 2)$ (ii) $(2y + 3)(2y - 3)$ (iii) $(3p + 1)(3p - 1)$

b) What do you notice? Explain why this happens.

4 **a)** Multiply out the following.

(i) $(a + 3)^2$ (Hint: write it as $(a + 3)(a + 3)$.)

(ii) $(z - 4)^2$

(iii) $(2n + 1)^2$

b) What do you notice?

c) Use your answer to part b) to multiply out the following.

(i) $(b + 2)^2$ (ii) $(3q - 1)^2$ (iii) $(1 - x)^2$

5 Expand the brackets and simplify.

a) $(x + 3)(x - 1) + (x + 2)(2x - 5)$

b) $(x + 2)^2 - (x - 1)^2$

c) $(2x + 3)(3x - 2) - (x + 5)(3x - 1)$

6 Solve these equations.

a) $(x + 2)(x - 1) = x(x + 3)$ **b)** $(x - 3)(x - 2) = (x + 1)(x + 4)$

c) $(x + 2)^2 = (x - 2)(x + 1)$ **d)** $(2x - 3)(x + 1) = 2x(x - 1)$

e) $(x - 1)(4x - 3) = (2x - 5)(2x + 1)$ **f)** $(2x - 1)(x + 5) = (x - 1)^2 + (x + 3)^2$

7 Simplify these fractions.

a) $\dfrac{6x}{3y}$ **b)** $\dfrac{x^2}{5x}$ **c)** $\dfrac{3y^2}{2y}$ **d)** $\dfrac{xy}{y}$

e) $\dfrac{x^2 - x}{2x}$ **f)** $\dfrac{(x + 4)^2}{3(x + 4)}$ **g)** $\dfrac{x^3 + x^2}{4x^2}$

8 Copy and complete this algebraic multiplication grid.

Do no leave any brackets in your answers.

$\times$	$x + 1$	$x + 2$	....
$x - 1$	....	$x^2 + x - 2$	$2x^2 - 3x + 1$
$x + 2$	$x^2 + 3x + 2$	....	$2x^2 + 3x - 2$

MEI

9 Expand these brackets.

a) $(2a + b + 1)(a - 3b - 2)$ **b)** $(x + 2)(2x - 1)(x + 3)$

c) $(x^2 + 2x - 3)^2$ **d)** $(s + 2)^3$

Rearranging formulae

Kelly is doing an experiment. She is finding the acceleration, a, of a block sliding down a ramp. She has a table of results for the initial speed, u, of the block, the final speed, v, of the block and the time taken, t. She is going to use this formula to work out a each time:

$$v = u + at$$

If Kelly substitutes each set of results into the formula, she will have to solve an equation to find a each time. It will be quicker if she rearranges the formula first, to make a the subject of the formula. This means that a will appear on its own on the left-hand side of the formula, and nowhere else.

Rearranging a formula is just like solving an equation, except that you are using letters instead of numbers.

Rearranging Kelly's formula is like solving the equation

$$9 = 3 + 2a$$

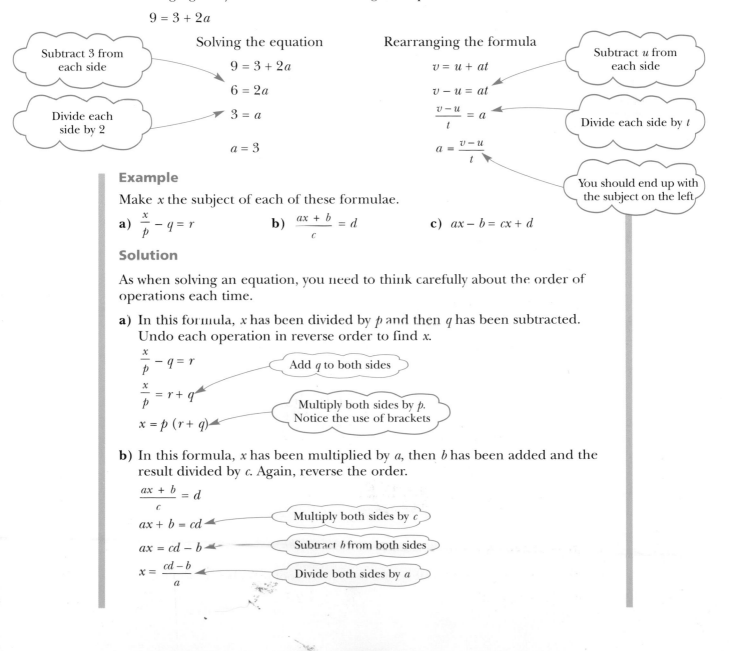

Solving the equation	Rearranging the formula

Subtract 3 from each side

$$9 = 3 + 2a$$ $$v = u + at$$ Subtract u from each side

$$6 = 2a$$ $$v - u = at$$

Divide each side by 2

$$3 = a$$ $$\frac{v-u}{t} = a$$ Divide each side by t

$$a = 3$$ $$a = \frac{v-u}{t}$$

You should end up with the subject on the left

Example

Make x the subject of each of these formulae.

a) $\dfrac{x}{p} - q = r$ 　　　b) $\dfrac{ax + b}{c} = d$ 　　　c) $ax - b = cx + d$

Solution

As when solving an equation, you need to think carefully about the order of operations each time.

a) In this formula, x has been divided by p and then q has been subtracted. Undo each operation in reverse order to find x.

$$\frac{x}{p} - q = r$$

Add q to both sides

$$\frac{x}{p} = r + q$$

Multiply both sides by p. Notice the use of brackets

$$x = p\,(r + q)$$

b) In this formula, x has been multiplied by a, then b has been added and the result divided by c. Again, reverse the order.

$$\frac{ax + b}{c} = d$$

Multiply both sides by c

$$ax + b = cd$$

Subtract b from both sides

$$ax = cd - b$$

Divide both sides by a

$$x = \frac{cd - b}{a}$$

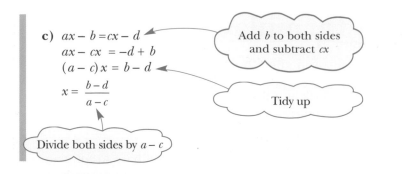

c) $ax - b = cx - d$ Add b to both sides and subtract cx

$ax - cx = -d + b$

$(a - c)x = b - d$ Tidy up

$x = \dfrac{b - d}{a - c}$

Divide both sides by $a - c$

Formulae with fractions

This is the formula for the density, D, of an object with mass M and volume V.

$$D = \frac{M}{V}$$

Suppose you want to make V the subject of this formula. It is similar to solving the equation

$$2 = \frac{6}{V}$$

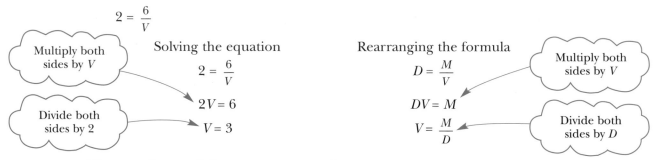

Solving the equation

Multiply both sides by V

$$2 = \frac{6}{V}$$

$$2V = 6$$

Divide both sides by 2

$$V = 3$$

Rearranging the formula

$$D = \frac{M}{V}$$

Multiply both sides by V

$$DV = M$$

$$V = \frac{M}{D}$$

Divide both sides by D

Formulae with squares and square roots

So far, you have used inverse operations such as adding to undo a subtraction, or dividing to undo a multiplication. In the same way, you can undo a square by using the square root, and vice versa.

This formula connects the initial speed, u, the final speed, v, the acceleration, a, and the distance travelled, s, of an object moving with constant acceleration:

$$v^2 = u^2 + 2as$$

Paul and Peter are trying to make u the subject of the formula.

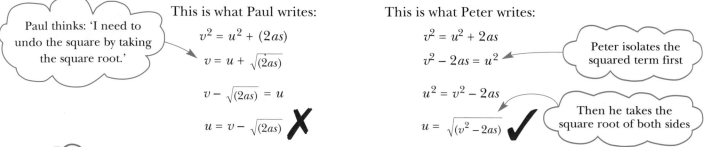

Paul thinks: 'I need to undo the square by taking the square root.'

This is what Paul writes:

$$v^2 = u^2 + (2as)$$

$$v = u + \sqrt{(2as)}$$

$$v - \sqrt{(2as)} = u$$

$$u = v - \sqrt{(2as)} \quad \textbf{X}$$

This is what Peter writes:

$$v^2 = u^2 + 2as$$

$$v^2 - 2as = u^2$$

$$u^2 = v^2 - 2as$$

$$u = \sqrt{(v^2 - 2as)} \quad \checkmark$$

Peter isolates the squared term first

Then he takes the square root of both sides

Explain why Paul's work is wrong and Peter's is right.

To get rid of a square root, you isolate the square root term before squaring.

5: Formulae and expressions

Example

Make x the subject of the formula

$$z - \sqrt{(x+y)} = w$$

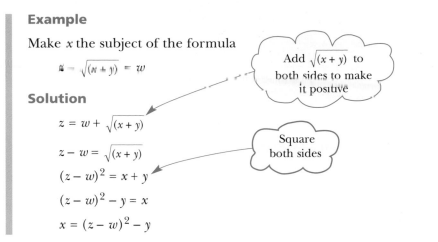

Solution

$$z = w + \sqrt{(x+y)}$$

$$z - w = \sqrt{(x+y)}$$

$$(z-w)^2 = x + y$$

$$(z-w)^2 - y = x$$

$$x = (z-w)^2 - y$$

Add $\sqrt{(x+y)}$ to both sides to make it positive

Square both sides

Exercise 5.3

1 Make x the subject of each of these formulae.

a) $x + a = b$

b) $xy = z$

c) $px - q = r$

d) $\dfrac{x}{m} = n$

e) $\dfrac{x+a}{b} = c$

f) $\dfrac{rx}{s} - t = v$

g) $g - x = h$

h) $c - dx = e$

i) $\dfrac{y-x}{w} = z$

j) $p - \dfrac{x}{q} = r$

k) $\dfrac{ax}{b} = \dfrac{c}{d}$

l) $\dfrac{mx+n}{m} = n$

m) $px - q = rx + s$

n) $px - 5 = 2x + s$

o) $ax + b = cx - d$

p) $ax - b = d - cx$

2 Make p the subject of each of these formulae.

a) $p^2 - q = r$

b) $(p+a)^2 = b$

c) $\sqrt{p} + m = n$

d) $\sqrt{(p+r)} = s$

e) $\dfrac{p^2 + x}{y} = z$

f) $\sqrt{(bp+c)} = d$

g) $\sqrt{\dfrac{p}{w}} - x = y$

h) $r - p^2 = s$

i) $\left(\dfrac{p}{a} + b\right)^2 = c$

j) $\sqrt{\dfrac{q-p}{r}} = s$

k) $\dfrac{f - p^2}{h} = g$

l) $\dfrac{q - \sqrt{p}}{q} = r$

3 Make a the subject of each of these formulae.

a) $\dfrac{p}{a} = q$

b) $\dfrac{b}{a} - c = d$

c) $\dfrac{x}{a+y} = z$

d) $r - \dfrac{s}{a} = t$

e) $\dfrac{f}{g-a} = h$

f) $\dfrac{p}{a^2 - q} = r$

g) $\sqrt{\dfrac{b}{a}} + c = d$

h) $\dfrac{m}{n - \sqrt{a}} = p$

i) $\dfrac{w}{(x-a)^2} = y$

4   Make r the subject of each of these formulae.

   a) $C = 2\pi r$ **b)** $A = \pi r^2$

   c) $V = \dfrac{1}{3}\pi r^2 h$ **d)** $V = \dfrac{4}{3}\pi r^3$

5   The area of a trapezium is given by the formula $A = \dfrac{1}{2}(a + b)h$.

   a) Make h the subject of the formula.

   b) Make a the subject of the formula.

6   The formula $T = 2\pi\sqrt{\dfrac{l}{g}}$ gives the period, T, of a pendulum.

   a) Make l the subject of the formula.

   b) Make g the subject of the formula.

7   The formula $\dfrac{1}{u} + \dfrac{1}{v} = \dfrac{1}{f}$ is used to find the frequency, f, of a wave

   formed from two other waves.

   a) Make f the subject of the formula.

   b) Make u the subject of the formula.

Finishing off

Now that you have finished this chapter you should be able to:

★ multiply out two brackets

★ factorise an expression

★ cancel algebraic fractions

★ rearrange a formula.

Use the questions in the next exercise to check that you understand everything.

Mixed exercise 5.4

1 Find a formula for the nth term of each of these sequences.

   a) 3, 7, 11, 15....

   b) –5, –3, –1, 1....

   c) 3, 6, 11, 18....

   d) 7, 4, 1, –2....

   e) 6, 12, 20, 30....

2 Expand the brackets and simplify if possible.

   a) $(a + 2)(b + 3)$

   b) $(x + 5)(x - 2)$

   c) $(2p + 1)(p + 3)$

   d) $(2s - 1)(t - 4)$

   e) $(3z - 2)(2z + 5)$

   f) $(1 - d)(2d + 1)$

   g) $(x + 4)^2$

   h) $(4q - 3)(2q - 5)$

   i) $(2y - 3)(2y + 3)$

   j) $(3a - 2)^2$

   k) $(2p + 1)(3q - 2) - (p - 3)(2q + 3)$

   l) $(2x + 3)(2x - 1) + (x - 1)^2$

3 Factorise these expressions.

   a) $pq + 2pr$

   b) $2a - 6b$

   c) $12x - 8y + 16z$

   d) $m^2n - mn$

   e) $3x^2 + 9xy$

   f) $5fg - 10f^2 - 15fh$

   g) $6c^2d - 8cd^2$

   h) $4st + 8s^2t - 4st^2$

   i) $p^2q^3 + p^3q^2$

   j) $2x^2yz^2 - 10xy^2z$

   k) $6a^2b^2 - 3ab$

   l) $18r^2s - 24rs^2 + 12s$

4 Expand the brackets in each of these expressions, simplify them and then factorise the simplified expression as far as possible.

   a) $p(2p + q) + 3q(p + 2p^2)$

   b) $3c(2c + 3d) - 2(d + 3c^2)$

   c) $(x + 1)(x + 2) - (x - 4)(x + 3)$

   d) $(2y + 1)(y + 4) + (y + 2)(3y - 2)$

   e) $(a + 3b)(a + 4b) - (a - 2b)(a + b)$

   f) $(3s + 2)^2 - (s - 2)^2$

Mixed Exercise 5.4 *continued*

5 Simplify these fractions.

a) $\dfrac{6a}{2b}$ **b)** $\dfrac{p^2}{4p}$ **c)** $\dfrac{uv}{vt}$

d) $\dfrac{(x+2)^2}{3(x+2)}$ **e)** $\dfrac{x^2+5x}{x}$ **f)** $\dfrac{x^2+5x}{x+5}$

g) $\dfrac{2x+4}{3x+6}$ **h)** $\dfrac{(x+y)}{3(x+y)}$ **i)** $\dfrac{(a-b)^3}{a-4b}$

6 Make x the subject of each of these formulae.

a) $px - q = r$ **b)** $\dfrac{xy}{z} = \dfrac{z}{y}$ **c)** $\dfrac{fx}{g} + h = g$

d) $s - \dfrac{x}{t} = r$ **e)** $\dfrac{a-x}{b} = c$ **f)** $\dfrac{x^2}{p} + q = r$

g) $\dfrac{\sqrt{x-y}}{w} = z$ **h)** $\dfrac{(f-x)^2}{g} = h$ **i)** $\dfrac{r}{x} = \dfrac{s}{r}$

j) $\dfrac{a}{x-b} = c$ **k)** $p - \dfrac{q}{x^2} = r$ **l)** $\sqrt{\dfrac{c}{d-x}} = e$

7 The surface area of a cone is given by the formula

$$S = \pi r l + \pi r^2$$

a) Make l the subject of the formula.

b) Factorise the original formula as far as possible.

c) Make l the subject of this factorised formula.

d) Show that your answers to parts a) and c) are the same.

8 Simplify   **a)** $\dfrac{(x+9)^2}{3(x+9)}$ **b)** $(2x^4)^3$ *MEI*

9 **a)** Simplify $\dfrac{8p^2q}{4p^2q^4}$

b) Given that $0 < q < 1$, what can you say about the value of the expression in part a)?

     Explain your reasoning.   *MEI*

10 **a)** $A = \dfrac{h}{2}(a+b)$.

     Rearrange this formula to make b the subject.

b) Make t the subject of $s = \dfrac{1}{2}at^2$.

c) Make u the subject of this formula.

$$v^2 = u^2 + 2as$$ *MEI*

11 Expand

a) $(1-x)(1+x)$ **b)** $(1-x)(1+x+x^2)$

c) $(1-x)(1+x+x^2+x^3)$

How can these results be generalised?

Chapter 6

Ratio, proportion and variation

Before you start this chapter you should be able to:

★ relate a ratio to fractions, decimals and percentages

★ write a ratio in its simplest form

★ share an amount in a given ratio.

Use the questions in the next exercise to check that you still remember these topics.

Review exercise 6.1

1 Abi makes orange paint by mixing two parts red with three parts yellow.

   a) How many litres of yellow paint are needed to make ten litres of orange?

   b) What fraction of the mixture is red?

   c) What percentage of the mixture is yellow?

   d) Abi has twelve litres of red paint and unlimited yellow. How much orange paint can she make?

2 Write each ratio in its simplest form.

   a) 9:12 _3:4_   **b)** 20:25 _4:5_   **c)** 100:40 _5:2_   **d)** 15:45

   e) 21:35 _3:5_   **f)** 75:30 _15:6_   **g)** 48:72 _12:18 2:3_   **h)** 60:84 _20:24_

   i) 4:8:16 _2:4:8 1:2:4_   **j)** 20:25:50 _4:5:10_   **k)** 18:24:39   **l)** 28:42:84

3 Write each ratio in a common unit and then express it in its simplest form.

   a) 2 hours : 24 minutes _120:24 30:6 5:1_   **b)** 50 mm : 2 cm

   c) 2 kg : 750 g _2,000:1750_   **d)** 250 ml : 1.5 l

   e) £7 : 280p   **f)** 5 km : 1500 m

   g) 2 cm : 1 km   **h)** 1.2 kg : 400 g

   i) 12 pints : 2 gallons   **j)** 8 cm : 0.2 mm

   k) $2\frac{1}{2}$ minutes : 90 seconds _250_   **l)** 625 mm : 0.5 m

4 In each of these pairs of similar triangles, find the length of the side marked with a question mark. (Note: the triangles are not drawn to scale.)

a)

b)

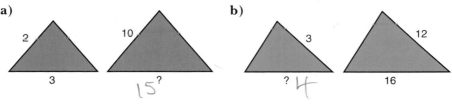

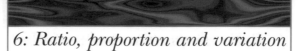

Direct proportion

In the example on page 103, it took Thomas 45 minutes to drive 72 km and you worked out that in 30 minutes he drives 48 km. This calculation assumes that in two thirds of the time he drives two thirds of the distance; in one quarter of the time he drives one quarter of the distance; in one and a half times the time he drives one and a half times the distance; and so on. This is **direct proportion**.

 How far does Thomas drive in 90 minutes?

If you double the time then you double the distance.

You can plot these data to obtain this straight line graph.

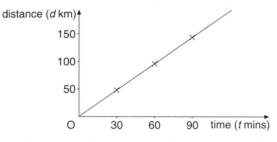

We say that d is **directly proportional** to t or that d **varies directly** as t and write

$d \propto t$ ← $\propto$ means is proportional to

You can work out the gradient of the straight line and this value, k, connects d and t by

$d = k \times t$ ← k is called the **constant of proportionality**

 What is the value of k here?

What does k represent?

Example

y is directly proportional to x.

$y = 24$ when $x = 6$

Find y when $x = 8$

Solution

Since $y \propto x$ then $y = kx$ for some constant k

Substitute $y = 24$ and $x = 6$ to get $24 = k \times 6$

so $k = 4$

The relationship is $y = 4x$

Now substitute $x = 8$ $y = 4 \times 8$

                                       $= 32$

You can see that when x increases by one third (from 6 to 8) then y also increases by one third (from 24 to 32).

Mike is designing a wildlife park. He is including a fenced enclosure for a rare breed of deer. Each deer must be allocated a certain area, so the larger the enclosure the more deer it will accommodate.

Mike plans a square enclosure, with side x metres.

 As x is increased, what happens to

- the total cost of fencing the enclosure?
- the number of deer that the enclosure can accommodate?

You can work out the total cost of the fencing, £F, like this:

$$£F = \text{cost per metre} \times \text{number of metres}$$

$$= \text{cost per metre} \times 4x$$

$$= (4 \times \text{cost per metre}) \times x$$

You can write this as $F = k \times x$ where k is called the **constant of proportionality**.

In this case, k is the cost of 4 m of fencing.

For example, if fencing costs £5 per metre,

$$k = 4 \times 5 = 20$$

When $F = kx$ you can say that

F varies directly with x

or **F is directly proportional to x.**

You can also write this using symbols:

$F \propto x$ Read this as 'is proportional to'

 Does the number of deer, N, vary directly with x?

Doubling the area of the enclosure means there is room for twice as many deer, three times the area means three times as many deer and so on.

The number of deer, N, is directly proportional to the *area* of the enclosure, x^2 square metres, so

$N \propto x^2$

or $N = cx^2$

Notice that c is used here instead of k to avoid confusion with k used earlier

 What does the constant of proportionality, c, represent in this case?

 When x is doubled, what happens to the value of N?

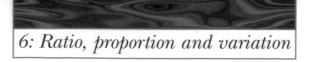

Exercise 6.4 *continued*

5 The wavelength of radio waves is inversely proportional to their frequency.

    a) Copy and complete the following table giving your answers to the nearest whole number.

Station	Wavelength (m)	Frequency (kHz)
Talk Radio	1089	
Radio 4	1515	198
Radio 5		433
Virgin	1215	

    b) Draw a graph of frequency against wavelength.

       Mark each of the radio stations on your graph.

6 The gravitational force, F, between two objects is inversely proportional to the square of the distance, d, between them. When $d = 20$, $F = 0.00625$.

    a) Find a formula connecting F and d.

    b) Find F when $d = 5$.

    c) Find d when $F = 0.00025$.

7 The value of y varies inversely as the square root of x.

    When $x = 225$, $y = 60$.

    a) Find the value of y when $x = 144$.

    b) Find the value of x when $y = 300$.

    c) What change in x leads to the y value doubling?

    d) State the range of values of x for which y exceeds 100.

Investigation

The table below gives the values of z for different values of x and y.

For example when $x = 2$ and $y = 3$ then $z = 60$.

y \ x	1	2	3	4	5
1	5	20	45	80	125
2	10	40	90	160	250
3	15	60	135	240	375
4	20	80	180	320	500

Find the formula giving z in terms of x and y.

a) How would you describe the relationship between x and y in words?

b) How would you represent the information in the table on a graph?

Finishing off

> **Now that you have finished this chapter you should:**
>
> ★ be able to work with ratio
>
> ★ be able to use the unitary method
>
> ★ understand and use direct proportion
>
> ★ understand and use inverse proportion.

Use the questions in the next exercise to check that you understand everything.

Mixed exercise 6.5

1   Andrea and Mark run a business. They share profits in the ratio 5:3.

   a)   In the first year, the profit is £10 000. How much does each get?

   b)   In the second year, Andrea gets £4500 more than Mark. How much is the profit in the second year?

2   Uncle Norman gives £60 000 to his nephews Bob and Ken to be shared in the ratio 3:2. Bob gives 20% of his share to each of his two children, Jack and Alice. Ken gives 30% of his share to his daughter Emily.

   a)   How much does Jack get?

   b)   How much does Emily get?

   c)   Aunt Maureen also has a sum of money which she wishes to be shared in exactly the same way. Explain why Jack gets the same as Emily regardless of how much money is shared.

3

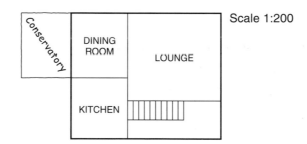

This is a scale drawing of the ground floor of Martin's house with a sketch showing where he plans to build his conservatory.

   a)   What are the real dimensions of the dining room?

   b)   What is the area of the lounge?

   c)   The conservatory will extend the dining room by 2.2 metres. How long will this be on the drawing when it is done accurately?

   d)   What is the actual floor area of the conservatory?

Mixed exercise 6.5 *continued*

4   Helen is an astronaut. She orbits the Earth every 90 minutes. How many orbits does she complete in a day?

5   Miles goes on holiday to Japan. He changes £450 into yen. He gets 182 yen for a pound.

   a) How many yen does he get?

   b) He returns home with 3500 yen and changes them back into pounds. The exchange rate is now 180 yen to the pound and there is a 2% commission charge which the bank deducts. How much, to the nearest penny, does he get?

6   y is directly proportional to x^3 and $y = 50$ when $x = 5$.

   a) What is the relationship between y and x?

   b) Work out the value of y when $x = 4$.

   c) Work out the value of x when $y = 400$.

7   A stone dropped into a well takes t seconds to hit the surface of the water which is s metres below the top. Given that s varies directly as t^2 and that $s = 20$ when $t = 2$, find

   a) the value of s when $t = 1.2$

   b) the value of t when $s = 3.2$.

8   The extension of an elastic spring, x mm, is directly proportional to the mass, m grams, suspended from it. A mass of 300 grams results in an extension of 15 mm.

   a) What mass will produce an extension of 2 cm?

   b) What extension will be produced by a mass of half a kilogram?

9   The £2 coin is made from two alloys.

   The inner circle is cupro-nickel which is copper and nickel in the ratio $3:1$. The outer part is made from nickel-brass which is copper, nickel and zinc in the ration $19:1:5$.

   Which alloy contains the higher proportion of copper? Show your working.   *MEI*

10   The volume, V, of a gas is inversely proportional to its pressure P. When $V = 520$, $P = 630$.

   a) Find the formula connecting V and P.

   b) (i) Find V when $P = 1950$.

         (ii) Find P when $V = 504$.   *MEI*

11   The number, N, of square tiles needed to tile a floor varies inversely as the square of the length, L, of the side of the tile.

   When $L = 0.4$ m, $N = 2000$.

   a) Find a formula connecting N and L.

   b) Calculate the number of tiles needed when $L = 0.6$ m.   *SEG*

Mixed exercise 6.5 *continued*

12

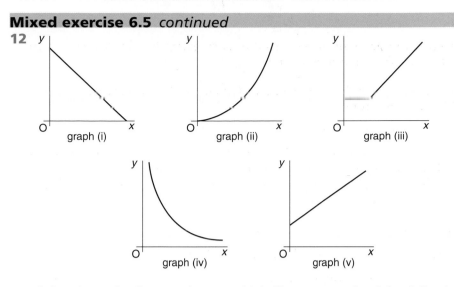

graph (i)   graph (ii)   graph (iii)

graph (iv)   graph (v)

Select from the five graphs one which illustrates each of the following statements.

a) The time (y) taken for a journey is inversely proportional to the average speed (x).

b) The surface area (y) of a sphere is proportional to the square of the radius (x).

c) The cost (y) of an electricity bill consists of a fixed charge plus an amount proportional to the number of units used (x).

MEG

13 The number of coins, N, with diameter d cm and with a fixed thickness, that can be made from a given volume of metal can be found by using the formula $N = \dfrac{k}{d^2}$ where k is a constant.

a) Given that 5000 coins of diameter 2.5 cm can be made from the volume of metal, find the value of k.

b) Calculate how many coins of diameter 2 cm can be made from an equal volume of metal.

c) Rearrange the formula $N = \dfrac{h}{d^2}$ to make d the subject.

d) 2000 coins are to be made using an equal volume of metal. Calculate the diameter of these coins.

MEG

14 Martha has obtained these results from her experiment.

a) Explain why Martha shouldn't assume that $Q \propto P$.

b) Martha thinks that either $Q \propto P^2$ or $Q \propto P^3$. Which of these fits Martha's data better? Why?

c) Suggest a formula connecting Q and P.

d) Do you think Martha has used a sensible scale for her graph?

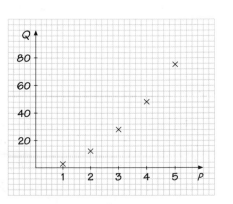

Chapter 7

Trigonometry

★ The early part of this chapter covers work on Pythagoras' theorem and trigonometry which you may have met before.

★ This work will then be extended to cover work in three dimensions.

Pythagoras' theorem

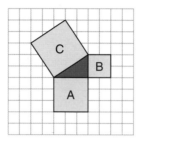

 Find the areas of squares A, B and C in each of the diagrams above.

You will probably find that the easiest way of finding the area of square C is to make it into a larger square and then subtract the areas of the four red triangles.

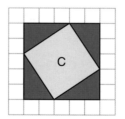

 Draw some more right-angled triangles on squared paper. Draw squares on each side and find their areas. What do you notice?

The rule that you have found is Pythagoras' theorem. It is usually written like this:

$$a^2 + b^2 = c^2$$

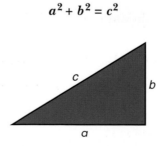

Notice that the side *c* must be the longest side, called the **hypotenuse**.

Example

Find the lengths of the sides marked x in each of the triangles below.

a)

b)

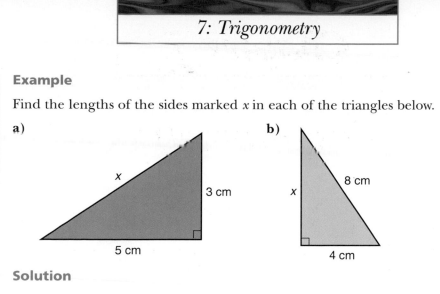

Solution

a) In this triangle the side marked x is the hypotenuse.

$$a^2 + b^2 = c^2$$
$$5^2 + 3^2 = x^2$$
$$25 + 9 = x^2$$
$$34 = x^2$$
$$x = \sqrt{34} = 5.83 \text{ (3 s.f.)}$$

> Sometimes you may wish to leave an answer like this in its exact form, $\sqrt{34}$. The answer 5.83 has been rounded and so is not exact

b) In this triangle the side marked x is one of the shorter sides.

$$a^2 + b^2 = c^2$$
$$x^2 + 4^2 = 8^2$$
$$x^2 + 16 = 64$$
$$x^2 = 64 - 16 = 48$$
$$x = \sqrt{48} = 6.93 \text{ (3 s.f.)}$$

Notice that finding the hypotenuse involves adding the squares of the other two sides, while finding one of the two shorter sides involves subtraction.

To prove Pythagoras' theorem, it is not enough to show that it is true for a few triangles, as you did on the previous page. However, you can prove it by generalising the method you used.

You can use this diagram to prove Pythagoras' theorem.

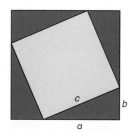

Write down an expression for the area of the large square in terms of a and b.

Write down an expression for the area of each red triangle.

Use your answers to find an expression for the area of the yellow square.

Use this to prove Pythagoras' theorem.

Exercise 7.1

1 Find the lengths of the sides marked with letters in these triangles.

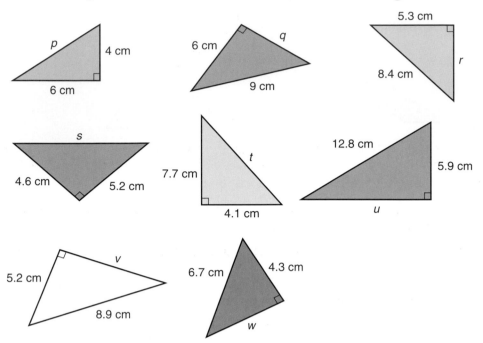

2 The diagram shows two points A (2, 3) and B (5, –2).

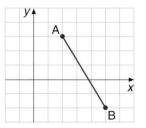

    a) What is the horizontal distance between A and B?

    b) What is the vertical distance between A and B?

    c) Use Pythagoras' theorem to work out the distance AB.

3 Use the method from question 2 to find the distance between each of the following pairs of points.

    a) (4, 1) and (1, 2)   **b)** (–2, 4) and (2, 0)

    c) (3, –1) and (–1, 5)   **d)** (–3,–2) and (4, 3)

Exercise 7.1 *continued*

4   Find the area of this triangle.

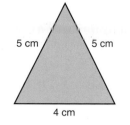

5   A ladder 8 m long is placed leaning against a wall. The foot of the ladder must not be less than 1.5 m from the wall. How far up the wall can the ladder reach?

6   **a)** A ship starts from Dover and sails 5 km south. It then sails 3 km west. How far is the ship from Dover?

   b) Another ship sails 6 km south-east from Dover. How far south and how far east is it from Dover?

7   One way of proving Pythagoras' theorem is to use similar triangles.

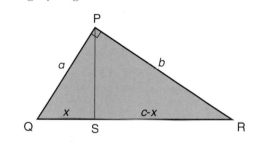

   a) Explain why triangle PQS is similar to triangle PQR.

   b) Find an equation connecting the side lengths of these two triangles.

   c) Explain why triangle PRS is similar to triangle PQR.

   d) Find an equation connecting the side lengths of these two triangles.

   e) Use your answers to prove Pythagoras' theorem.

8   Find the area of this triangle.

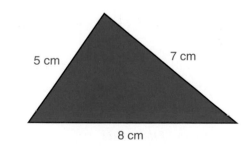

Pythagoras' theorem in three dimensions

Look at this cuboid. It is drawn using three axes, labelled *x*, *y* and *z*. You need three axes because it is a three-dimensional figure, and to specify a point you need three co-ordinates.

Point O is the origin and has co-ordinates (0, 0, 0). The co-ordinates of B are (3, 4, 0) and those of G are (0, 4, 2).

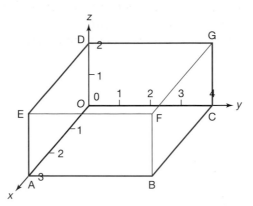

 What are the co-ordinates of the other vertices of the cuboid, A, C, D, E and F?

 The mid-point of the line BG has co-ordinates $(1\frac{1}{2}, 4, 1)$.

How can you use the co-ordinates of B and G to work this out? What are the co-ordinates of the mid-points of OB and OF?

Is the mid-point of AG the same point as the mid-point of OF?

Now look at this diagram. It shows part of a framework of scaffolding. A strut is to be put along the diagonal AG to provide extra stability.

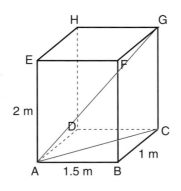

 How could you work out the length of the strut?

AG is the hypotenuse of the right-angled triangle ACG marked in red, so you can use Pythagoras' theorem. However, you do not know the length of the line AC.

AC is the hypotenuse of another right-angled triangle, ABC.

$$AC^2 = AB^2 + BC^2$$
$$= 1.5^2 + 1^2$$
$$= 2.25 + 1$$
$$= 3.25$$

Why is it best just to work out AC^2 and not find the actual length of AC?

Now you can use this value for AC^2 to work out the length of AG.

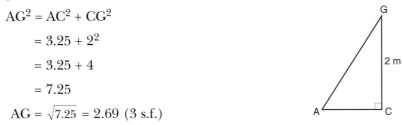

$$AG^2 = AC^2 + CG^2$$
$$= 3.25 + 2^2$$
$$= 3.25 + 4$$
$$= 7.25$$
$$AG = \sqrt{7.25} = 2.69 \text{ (3 s.f.)}$$

The length of the strut is 2.69 metres.

Pythagoras' theorem can be extended to three dimensions to solve problems like this one more quickly.

$$AG^2 = AB^2 + BC^2 + CG^2$$
$$= 1.5^2 + 1^2 + 2^2$$
$$= 2.25 + 1 + 4$$
$$= 7.25$$
$$AG = \sqrt{7.25} = 2.69 \text{ (3 s.f.)}$$

This is Pythagoras' theorem in three dimensions. There are three lengths instead of two to be squared

Explain why these two methods give the same result.

Exercise 7.2

1 Find the length of the diagonal of each of these cuboids.

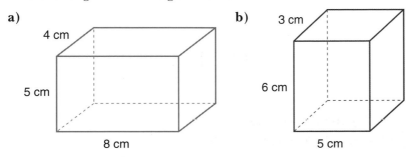

a) 4 cm, 5 cm, 8 cm

b) 3 cm, 6 cm, 5 cm

2 Find the distance between each of the following pairs of points in three-dimensional space.

    a) (1, 3, 2) and (5, 0, 3)   **b)** (4, –1, 3) and (1, 2, –2)

    c) (3, 4, –2) and (0, 4, 1)   **d)** (–3, 5, 2) and (–5, –1, 4)

Exercise 7.2 *continued*

3 Find the height of this pyramid.

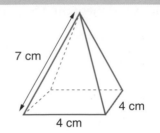

7 cm

4 cm

4 cm

4 An air traffic controller is observing the progress of an aeroplane which has just taken off. He notes at a particular time that the aeroplane is 12 km north and 8 km west of the control tower, and its altitude is 1500 m. After a short time it is 20 km south and 15 km west of the tower, and its altitude is 4600 m. What distance has the aeroplane travelled?

5 The diagram below shows the roof of a doll's house. It has a rectangular base ABCD and consists of two equal isosceles triangles and two trapezia.

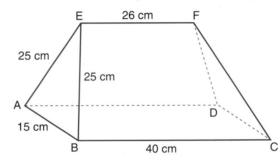

E   26 cm   F

25 cm

25 cm

A

15 cm

B   40 cm   C

D

a) Find the height of the roof.

b) Find the perpendicular distance between E and AB.

c) Find the perpendicular distance between EF and BC.

d) Find the total area of wood needed to make the roof. (Do not include the base.)

Similar figures

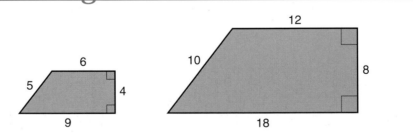

12

6

10

5   4

8

9   18

Look at these two trapezia. They are the same shape but the sides of one are twice as long as those of the other. Figures like these are **similar**. Their sides are in proportion, and their corresponding angles are equal.

To show that two triangles are similar, it is sufficient to show that two angles of one are equal to two angles of the other. The third angles must then be equal and the sides in proportion.

Can you have two quadrilaterals with equal angles that are not similar?

Right-angled triangles

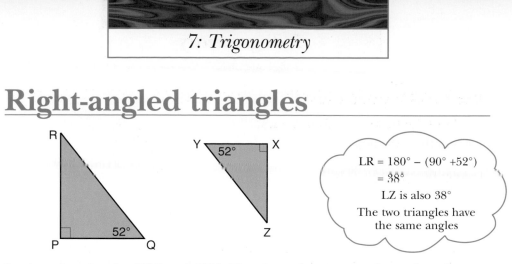

LR = 180° − (90° +52°)
= 38°
LZ is also 38°
The two triangles have
the same angles

Look at the triangles PQR and XYZ. They have the same angles and so they
are similar.

- The side QR corresponds to the side YZ. These sides are the **hypotenuses**.

- The side PR corresponds to the side XZ. These sides are called the **opposite**
  sides, as they are opposite to the angle of 52°.

- The side PQ corresponds to the side XY. These sides are called the **adjacent**
  sides, as they are adjacent to the angle of 52°.

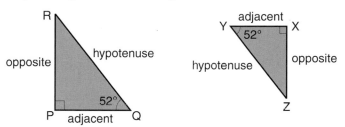

Any other triangle with a right angle and an angle of 52° will also be similar to
these two triangles. For any triangle like this, the ratio $\dfrac{\text{opposite}}{\text{adjacent}}$ is always the same.
It is 1.28 (3 s.f.) This number is called the **tangent** (or **tan**) of 52° and is
written tan 52°.

*Use your calculator to find tan 52°. Check that it is the same as the number
given above (although your calculator will give more decimal places).*

Similarly, the ratio $\dfrac{\text{opposite}}{\text{adjacent}}$ is a fixed number for any right-angled triangle with
a particular angle.

Example

$\tan 34° = \dfrac{x}{7}$

x is the opposite side

7 is the adjacent side

$7 \tan 34° = x$

$x = 4.72 \text{ cm (3 s.f.)}$

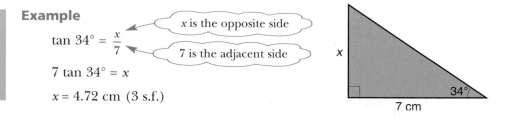

Do this on your calculator and check that you get the same answer.

For a triangle like this one, you cannot use tan to find the opposite side. This is because you do not know the length of the adjacent side, only the hypotenuse. Another ratio, linking the opposite side and the hypotenuse, is needed.

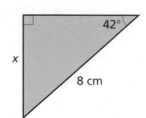

The ratio $\dfrac{\text{opposite}}{\text{hypotenuse}}$ for a particular angle is called the **sine** (or **sin**) of that angle.

In the same way, for some triangles a ratio linking the adjacent side and the hypotenuse is needed.

The ratio $\dfrac{\text{adjacent}}{\text{hypotenuse}}$ for a particular angle is called the **cosine** (or **cos**) of that angle.

You now know the three trigonometry ratios:

$$\sin\theta = \frac{\text{opp}}{\text{hyp}} \qquad \cos\theta = \frac{\text{adj}}{\text{hyp}} \qquad \tan\theta = \frac{\text{opp}}{\text{adj}}$$

Some people use the word SOHCAHTOA to remember these ratios. Can you see how this works?

When you want to find a side length in a triangle using trigonometry, you need to decide which ratio to use. The examples below show how to do this.

Example

In this triangle you are given the hypotenuse and need to find the adjacent side. You need the ratio which links the adjacent and the hypotenuse. This is the cosine.

$\cos 58° = \dfrac{x}{10}$

$10 \cos 58° = x$

$x = 5.30 \text{ cm} \ (3 \text{ s.f.})$

Example

In this triangle you need the ratio which links the opposite side and the hypotenuse. This is the sine.

In this example you have to find the side which is on the bottom of the ratio. This means an extra line of working.

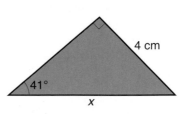

$\sin 41° = \dfrac{4}{x}$

$x \sin 41° = 4$

$x = \dfrac{4}{\sin 41°}$

$x = 6.10 \text{ cm} \ (3 \text{ s.f.})$

Exercise 7.3

1 Use similar triangles to find the sides marked *x* in these triangles. (Lengths are in cm.)

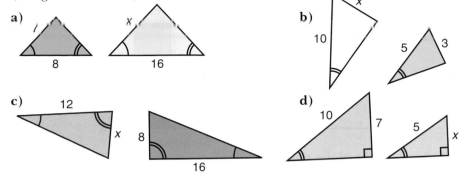

2 Copy these triangles and mark the opposite side (O), adjacent side (A) and hypotenuse (H) in each case.

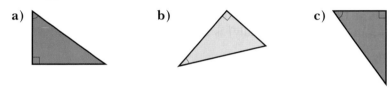

3 Use tan to find the length *x* in these triangles.

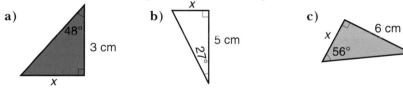

4 Use sin to find the length *x* in these triangles.

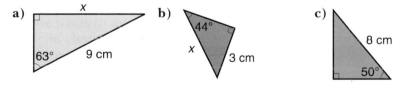

5 Use cos to find the length *x* in these triangles.

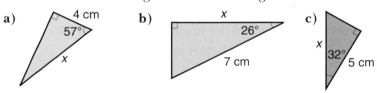

6 Find the sides marked with letters in these triangles.

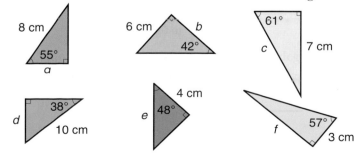

Finding an angle using trigonometry

You can use trigonometry to find an angle in a right-angled triangle if you know two of the sides.

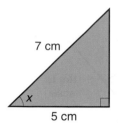

In this triangle you know the adjacent side and the hypotenuse. So the ratio you need is cosine.

$$\cos x = \frac{\text{adj}}{\text{hyp}}$$

$$\cos x = \frac{5}{7}$$

You now need to find out what angle has a cosine of $\frac{5}{7}$.

You need to 'undo' the cosine. To do this you will need to use the inverse cosine on your calculator. It may be labelled $\cos^{-1}$, or arccos, or you may have to press the INV button before pressing cos. Make sure your calculator is in Degree (Deg) mode.

Use your calculator to find the angle x.

(You should get x = 44.4°)

Example

A hiker leaves his camp site and walks 5 km due north and then 3 km due west. What bearing must he walk on to get back to the camp site?

Solution

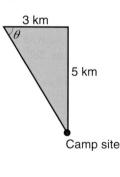

$$\tan \theta = \frac{5}{3}$$

$$\theta = 59°$$

The hiker must walk on a bearing of 149°.

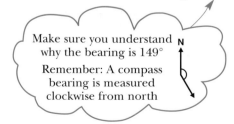

Make sure you understand why the bearing is 149°

Remember: A compass bearing is measured clockwise from north

Exercise 7.4

1 Find the angles marked with letters in these triangles.

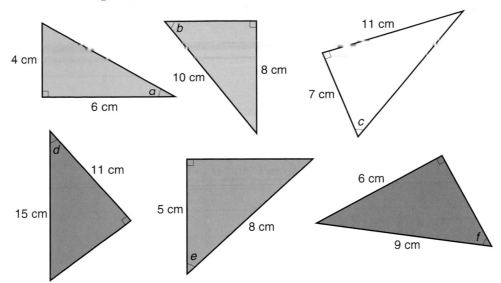

2 A water chute at a swimming pool is 12 m long. The top of the chute is 7.5 m above the ground.

Find the angle that the chute makes with the horizontal.

3 This map shows part of an orienteering course, in which competitors have to use a compass to find their way to each of the points labelled A to F. Each of the squares on the grid represents 100 m.

Calculate the distance and bearing required to go

a) from A to B   **b)** from B to C   **c)** from C to D

d) from D to E   **e)** from E to F.

4 The slope of the road through Hardknott Pass (in the Lake District) is 33% in places. This means that the road rises 0.33 m for each metre measured along the road surface.

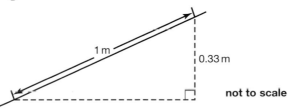

not to scale

Calculate the angle the road makes with the horizontal.   *MEI*

Finishing off

Now that you have finished this chapter you should be able to:

★ use Pythagoras' theorem in two and three dimensions

★ use trigonometry in two and three dimensions

★ find the area of a triangle using the formula $\frac{1}{2}ab\sin C$.

Use the questions in the next exercise to check that you understand everything.

Mixed exercise 7.7

1 Find the lengths of the sides marked x in these triangles.

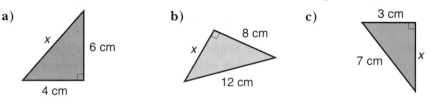

a)

b)

c)

2 Find the lengths of the sides and angles marked with letters in these triangles.

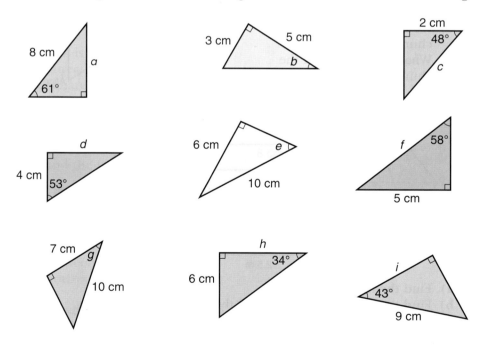

3 Find the distance between each of these pairs of points.

    a) (5, 1) and (−2, 4)   **b)** (−3, 0) and (2, −1)

    c) (2, 3, −1) and (−1, −2, 4)   **d)** (0, 4, −2) and (2, 2, 1)

Mixed exercise 7.7 *continued*

4 John has been bought a kite for his birthday.

    a) The kite is flying on the end of a string 25 m long. The string makes an angle of 64° with the horizontal. How high is the kite?

    b) The diagram shows John's kite.

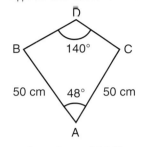

        Explain carefully why

        (i)   BC = 2 × 50 × sin 24°

        (ii) BC = 2 × BD × sin 70°

        and hence calculate BC and BD.

    c) Calculate the area of the kite.

5 **a)** A ship starting from point A sails 15 km on a bearing of 116° to reach point B. How far south and how far east is B from A?

    b) The ship then sails a further 23 km on a bearing of 230° to point C. How far south and how far west is C from B?

    c) What bearing must the ship sail on to return to point A from point C, and what distance will it sail?

6 Joe and Paula are standing in different positions looking at a hot-air balloon in the sky.

    a) Joe is 200 m from a point immediately below the balloon. The angle of elevation of the balloon from where he is standing is 28°.

        Find the height of the balloon.

    b) Paula is 320 m from a point immediately below the balloon.

        What is the angle of elevation of the balloon from where she is standing?

7 In this cuboid ABCDEFGH, P is the mid-point of FG.

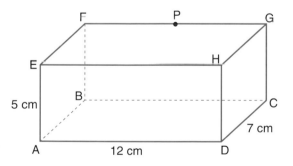

    a) Find the length of the diagonal of the cuboid.

    b) Find the angle between the diagonal of the cuboid and the horizontal.

    c) Find the angle between AP and the horizontal.

    d) Find the angle between AP and DP.

    e) Calculate the area of the triangle ADP.

He groups the data into six classes of equal width, using intervals 21–25, 26–30, and so on and draws a bar chart.

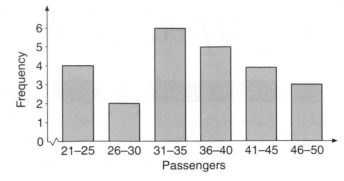

 Do you think the newspaper readers would find the bar chart easy to follow? Do these classes include the numbers at their ends?

Measures of central tendency and spread

What is a typical number of passengers?

The class with the highest frequency is 31 – 35 and this is called the **modal class**.

 What is the mode of the actual data? Which gives the better typical number, the mode or the modal class?

Fergus can work out the exact mean from the actual data like this:

$$\frac{3 \times 21 + 1 \times 25 + 1 \times 27 + \dots + 1 \times 50}{24} = 35.375$$

A newspaper reader has to estimate the mean from the bar chart. The mid-point of the first interval is $\frac{21+25}{2} = 23$; the mid-points of the other intervals are 28, 33, 38, 43 and 48.

$$\text{Estimated mean} = \frac{(4 \times 23 + 2 \times 28 + 6 \times 33 + 5 \times 38 + 4 \times 43 + 3 \times 48)}{24}$$
$$= 35.5$$

 Why do the two calculations of the mean not give quite the same answers? Which is the more accurate?

The median of the 24 numbers lies midway between number 12 and number 13.

 What can you say about the median if
a) you have Fergus's actual data?
b) you only have the bar chart?

It is common to use a cumulative frequency graph to find the median of grouped data and this is covered later in the chapter.

The range of the actual data is $50 - 21 = 29$. What would you be able to say about the range if you only had the bar chart?

The advantage of grouping data is that it is easier to see the overall pattern, or distribution. However, the disadvantage is that the answers to any calculations using grouped data are only approximate.

8: Grouped data

1 A survey was carried out to find out how much time was needed by a group of pupils to complete homework set on a particular Monday evening.

The results are shown in the table.

Calculate an estimate for the mean time spent on homework by the pupils in the group.

Time, t hours, spent on homework	Number of pupils
0	9
$0 < t \leqslant 1$	14
$1 < t \leqslant 2$	17
$2 < t \leqslant 3$	5
$3 < t \leqslant 4$	1

London

2 Bronwen owns a pet shop.

The table gives information about the weights of hamsters in Bronwen's shop.

Calculate an estimate for the mean weight of the hamsters in Bronwen's shop.

Weight w of hamsters in g	Number of hamsters
$28 \leqslant w < 30$	9
$30 \leqslant w < 32$	5
$32 \leqslant w < 34$	4
$34 \leqslant w < 36$	2

London

3 Bumal counted the number of words in the sentences of an article in a newspaper one morning. Here are his results.

Number of words	1–5	6–10	11–15	16–20	21–25	26–30
Frequency	0	5	9	13	17	6

a) Estimate the mean number of words in a sentence.

b) Why is it an estimate?

c) Give the greatest range possible for these data.

4 30 students at a flying school take a theory test. These are their marks.

```
13  65  98  16  57  52  49  88  51  78
40  58  72  63  70  29  66  75   6  11
47  61  43  78  52  61  69  22  67  81
```

The flying school group the data and then draw a bar chart.

The bar chart appears in a report.

a) Group these data into classes of equal width, 0–9, 10–19, and so on.

b) Draw a bar chart.

c) Patrick reads the report and uses the bar chart to estimate the mean mark. What answer does he get?

d) Calculate the true mean mark from the original data.

e) Calculate the error in Patrick's estimate.

8: Grouped data

 Between what limits is it reasonable to expect the weight of a full-term, new-born baby to lie?

Other examples of continuous data include lengths and times.

 Are the readings on the stopwatch really continuous?

To display continuous data they must be grouped.

Frequency charts

This frequency table gives the lengths, t (in minutes), of telephone calls in an office one day.

Length of call, t (minutes)	$0 \leqslant t < 5$	$5 \leqslant t < 10$	$10 \leqslant t < 15$	$15 \leqslant t < 20$	$20 \leqslant t < 25$	$25 \leqslant t < 30$	$30 \leqslant t < 35$
Frequency	10	8	3	0	2	1	1

Notice how the inequality signs are used, ≤ at one end of each class and < at the other. This ensures that if a value falls on the end of one interval, say 5.00, it is clear which class it belongs to.

 Which class would 5.00 belong to?

The data are displayed on a diagram that is often called a frequency chart.

There are several points to notice about this frequency chart.

● It is like a bar chart except that there are no gaps between the blocks. That is because the data are continuous.

● All the classes are of equal width (all 5 minutes).

● The classes are marked at their ends (0, 5, 10, …) and not their middles, as in a bar chart.

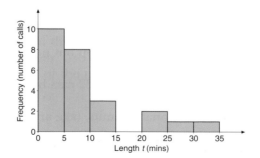

 Why is it essential to group continuous data before you display them?

Histograms

Sometimes continuous data are grouped into classes of unequal width, as in the next example.

The frequency table below gives the weights, w kg, of a sample of 100 pike taken from a large lake.

Weight, w kg	$0 \leqslant w < 0.5$	$0.5 \leqslant w < 1$	$1 \leqslant w < 2$	$2 \leqslant w < 4$	$4 \leqslant w < 12$
Frequency	12	18	24	20	26

Look carefully at these figures. The greatest frequency is the 26 pike for $4 \leqslant w < 12$ but this is a very wide class, 8 kg, and so you might expect a higher frequency there than, say, in $0 \leqslant w < 0.5$, which is only $\frac{1}{2}$ kg wide.

If a display is to give the right impression it must take these differences in class width into account. A histogram does just that.

In a histogram the frequency is represented by the area of each block and not its height.

The height of each block is calculated as $\frac{\text{frequency}}{\text{class width}}$, and called **frequency density**, or (in this case) frequency per kilogram.

This is shown in the table below.

Class	Class width	Frequency	Frequency density = $\frac{\text{Frequency}}{\text{Class width}}$
$0 \leqslant w < 0.5$	0.5	12	24
$0.5 \leqslant w < 1$	0.5	18	36
$1 \leqslant w < 2$	1	24	24
$2 \leqslant w < 4$	2	20	10
$4 \leqslant w < 12$	8	26	3.25

You can now draw the histogram, as shown.

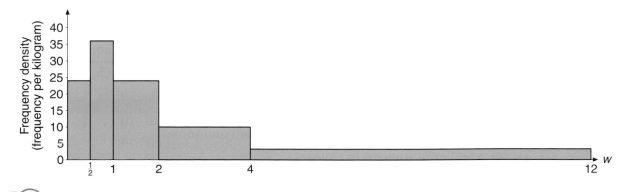

 Does this give a fair impression of the distribution of the pikes' weight? Which is the modal class?

 Under what circumstances do people choose to use unequal class widths?

4   Jack recorded the ages of 120 vehicles.
    The table summarises the data he collected.

Age of vehicle (*a* years)	Frequency
$0 < a \leqslant 2$	36
$2 < a \leqslant 5$	39
$5 < a \leqslant 10$	35
$10 < a \leqslant 20$	10

a) Draw a histogram for the data.

b) What feature of the shape of the histogram is likely to be common to
    all histograms showing the ages of road vehicles?

MEI

5   The table summarises the number of visitors to a museum during its
    first 120 days of operation.

Number of visitors (*n*)	Frequency
$0 < n \leqslant 100$	45
$100 < n \leqslant 150$	40
$150 < n \leqslant 200$	20
$200 < n \leqslant 300$	15

a) Draw a histogram to respresent the data.

b) Estimate the percentage of days that the museum had more than
    130 visitors.

MEI

6   The table shows the distribution of the speeds recorded by a traffic camera
    one afternoon.

Speed (*x* mph)	Frequency
$30 < x \leqslant 50$	96
$50 < x \leqslant 60$	76
$60 < x \leqslant 70$	16
$70 < x \leqslant 100$	12

a) Draw a histogram to illustrate these data.

b) David says that 50 to 60 mph is the modal class.
    Give a reason in support of his choice.

MEI

Exercise 8.2 *continued*

7   Paula decided to investigate the times it took her friends to complete a puzzle. She wrote down their times in minutes and seconds on a rough piece of paper, and then wrote them out neatly giving only the minutes.

6	8	5	3	9	6	2	12	10	13
13	7	20	11	9	6	7	6	13	15
6	11	9	15	9	16	21	18	9	10
8	13	11	19	21	9	6	8	12	10

a)   Shona took 3 minutes 51 seconds. How did Paula record this?

b)   Group the data into classes $0 \leqslant t < 5$, $5 \leqslant t < 10$, …, $20 \leqslant t < 25$.

c)   State the least and greatest possible times, in minutes and seconds, for someone in the class $5 \leqslant t < 10$.

d)   Display the data on a frequency chart.

e)   Calculate the mean of the figures Paula wrote down neatly.

f)   Explain why you would expect the mean of these figures to be less than that of the times they actually took. About how much would you expect the difference to be?

8   Philip records the time it takes him to get to work on a number of days. His data are shown on this histogram.

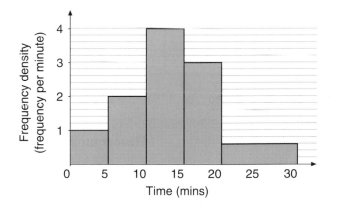

a)   How many values are there in each class?

b)   On the next two days, Philip takes 23 minutes and 27 minutes.

   What will be the new height of the bar representing the 20–30 group on the histogram?

Cumulative frequency graphs

When data come to you already grouped, or when they are very extensive, it can be helpful to draw a cumulative frequency graph, as in the next example.

A leisure centre has collected data on the ages of members of its youth swimming club, and has grouped them as follows.

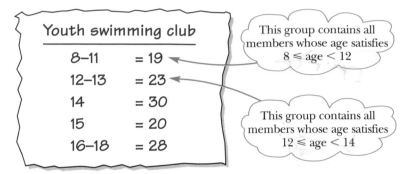

Youth swimming club

8–11	= 19
12–13	= 23
14	= 30
15	= 20
16–18	= 28

This group contains all members whose age satisfies $8 \le age < 12$

This group contains all members whose age satisfies $12 \le age < 14$

These data can be written as a cumulative frequency table, like this:

Age	Frequency
< 12	19
< 14	42
< 15	72
< 16	92
< 19	120

This group includes everyone under 15, that is all the 10, 11, 12, 13 and 14 year olds

These figures are called the **cumulative frequencies**

The last figure, in this case 120, is the total frequency. The swimming club has 120 members

The data are now plotted to give a cumulative frequency graph. This has a characteristic shape, like a sloping letter *S*. Cumulative frequency is plotted on the vertical axis, and the variable, in this case age, on the horizontal axis.

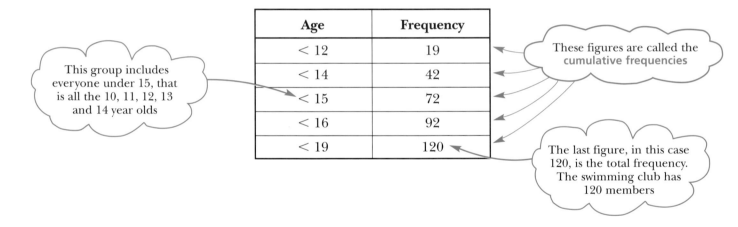

92 swimmers are under 16

Finding the median

There are 120 swimmers. The median is between the 60th and 61st swimmer, that is at $60\frac{1}{2}$. Usually when you are using a cumulative frequency chart, the numbers will be large enough for you to be able to ignore the half and just divide the total frequency by two.

If you ignore the half, in this case the median is the 60th swimmer. You draw a line from 60 on the cumulative frequency axis until it meets the curve. Then you draw another line down to the horizontal axis and read off the age.

It is just over $14\frac{1}{2}$ years, about 14 years and 7 months.

Quartiles and the IQR

Once you have drawn the cumulative frequency curve, you can use it to find the quartiles and the interquartile range, or IQR.

In Chapter 4, you looked at the range of a set of data. (Remember the median tells you where the data is centred and the range measures how spread out the data are.) The **interquartile range** is another measure of spread; it measures the distance between two quartiles.

When the data are ranked, the median and the two quartiles split them into four groups of equal size.

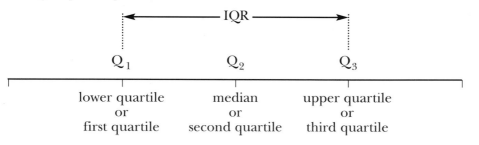

The first quartile (often called Q_1) is a quarter of the way through the data.

The third quartile (often called Q_3) is three quarters of the way through the data.

In the example of the leisure centre swimming club,

$$Q_1 \text{ is the } \frac{120}{4} = 30\text{th swimmer}$$

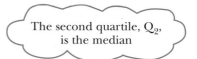

The second quartile, Q_2, is the median

$$Q_3 \text{ is the } 3 \times \frac{120}{4} = 90\text{th swimmer}$$

The interquartile range is the difference between these two quartiles

interquartile range $\longrightarrow$ $\text{IQR} = Q_3 - Q_1$

So the IQR for the swimmers is

$$15 \text{ years } 9\frac{1}{2} \text{ months} - 13 \text{ years } 5\frac{1}{2} \text{ months} = 2 \text{ years } 4 \text{ months}$$

In this example the data set is reasonably large. There are 120 items. It is reasonable to divide the number of items by 4 to find the lower quartile: $120 \div 4 = 30$. You are better not using quartiles with smaller sets of data. If you have to use them, make sure that they divide the data into four equal groups.

What are the quartiles and the median for 5, 6, 7, 7, 11, 12, 12, 14 ?

Box and whisker plots

The ages of the youth swimming club can be represented in **a box and whisker diagram**.

- A number line is drawn to cover the full range of possible ages.

- A line (or whisker) is then drawn from the smallest possible age to the lower quartile.

- A box is drawn from the lower quartile to the upper quartile with a line across at the position of the median.

- Another line (or whisker) is drawn from the upper quartile to the largest possible age.

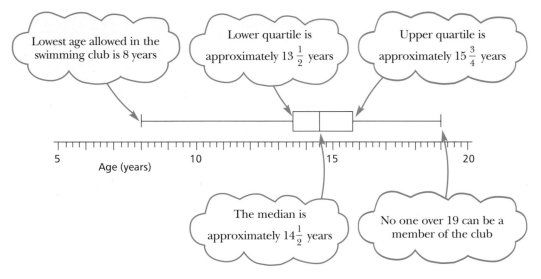

Lowest age allowed in the swimming club is 8 years

Lower quartile is approximately $13\frac{1}{2}$ years

Upper quartile is approximately $15\frac{3}{4}$ years

The median is approximately $14\frac{1}{2}$ years

No one over 19 can be a member of the club

The leisure centre also runs a youth judo club.

The box and whisker diagram for this club is shown below.

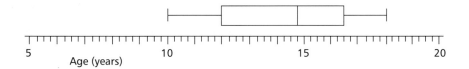

By looking at the box and whisker diagrams, the manager of the leisure centre can see that

- There is not much difference between the average (as measured by the **median**) age of members of the two clubs: the judo club has an average age of about $14\frac{3}{4}$ whilst the swimming club has an average age of about $14\frac{1}{2}$.

- The judo club has a smaller **range** of possible ages than the swimming club: the judo club has children in an 8-year age interval whilst the swimming club has children in an 11-year age interval.

- The spread of ages (as measured by the **interquartile range**) is much greater in the judo club.

 *What information can the manager **not** obtain from the box and whisker diagrams?*

8: Grouped data

Exercise 8.3

1 A group of children were asked to guess the length, l cm, of a piece of string. Their answers are given in the table.

Length l (cm)	$20 \leqslant l < 30$	$30 \leqslant l < 40$	$40 \leqslant l < 50$	$50 \leqslant l < 60$	$60 \leqslant l < 70$
Frequency	8	20	35	24	13

   a) Construct the cumulative frequency table.

   b) Draw the cumulative frequency curve.

   c) The string was actually 44 cm long. Estimate how many children

   (i) underestimated the length

   (ii) overestimated the length.

2 A group of students took an exam. Their marks are given in the table.

Mark	$0 < x \leqslant 10$	$10 < x \leqslant 20$	$20 < x \leqslant 30$	$30 < x \leqslant 40$	$40 < x \leqslant 50$	$50 < x \leqslant 60$
Frequency	4	10	32	22	24	8

   a) Construct the cumulative frequency table.

   b) Draw the cumulative frequency curve.

   c) Estimate the median mark.

   d) Estimate the upper and lower quartiles, and the interquartile range.

   e) The mark for a merit was fixed at 45. Estimate the number of students who were awarded a merit.

   f) 10% failed. Estimate the pass mark.

3 A boy went fishing one day and caught 80 mackerel. Their masses were as shown in this table.

Mass (kg)	0.3 – 0.4	0.4 – 0.5	0.5 – 0.6	0.6 – 0.7	0.7 – 0.8	0.8 – 0.9	0.9 – 1.0	1.0 – 1.1	1.1 – 1.2
Fish	3	5	8	14	20	12	8	6	4

   a) Construct the cumulative frequency table.

   b) Draw the cumulative frequency graph.

   c) Estimate the median and the upper and lower quartiles of the masses of the fish he caught.

   d) Any fish under 0.45 kg were given to Tabby the cat. Estimate how many Tabby got.

   e) The boy sold those fish that were at least 0.85 kg. How many did he sell?

   f) Draw a box and whisker plot to illustrate the masses of the fish that the boy caught.

   g) On the same day, the boy's friend caught 60 fish. A box and whisker plot for these fish is shown below.

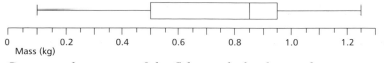

   Compare the masses of the fish caught by the two boys.

Mixed exercise 8.4 *continued*

3 In a long-jump competition the following distances, in metres, were recorded.

4.90   5.10   5.25   5.30   5.40   5.45   5.55   5.55   5.60
5.75   5.80   5.95   6.15   6.25   6.50

Draw a box plot for these data.   *MEI*

4

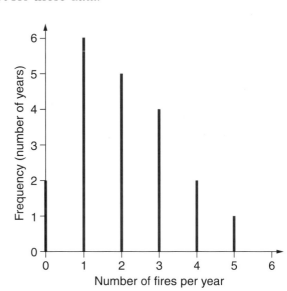

The vertical line chart shows the frequency of fires in a small town over a period of 20 years. Which of the following statements are true and which false?

a) The mode is 6.

b) The upper quartile is 3.

c) The chart shows that fires were more frequent during the first 10 years than during the second 10 years.

d) There is a probability of 0.4 that, in a year chosen at random, the number of fires is less than the median.

SMP (adapted)

5 Angus has been commissioned by an airline to carry out a small survey into the weight of luggage that passengers bring. He looks at internal and trans-Atlantic flights. In both cases he collects data from a random sample of passengers.

His data are shown in the table here.

Weight (kg)	Internal	Trans-Atlantic
$0 \leqslant w < 10$	10	3
$10 \leqslant w < 15$	18	10
$15 \leqslant w < 20$	14	12
$20 \leqslant w < 25$	8	11
$25 \leqslant w < 30$	0	9
$30 \leqslant w < 40$	0	2
$40 \leqslant w < 50$	0	3

8: Grouped data

Mixed exercise 8.4 *continued*

a) Draw a histogram for each set of data.

b) Estimate the mean of each set.

c) Construct a cumulative frequency table for each set of data.

d) Draw the cumulative frequency curve for each set of data on the same graph.

e) Estimate the median and the interquartile range and draw a box and whisker plot for each set of data.

f) Angus has to write a report for the airline. What points should he make?

6   A group of students are going on an adventure weekend. They will need special clothes and have to send their heights to the adventure centre beforehand. Fred sends in this histogram together with his estimate of the mean and a statement of the modal class.

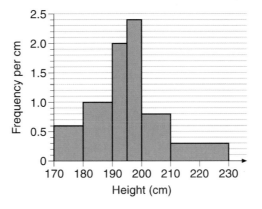

a) Draw up a frequency table for the number of students in each class.

b) What is the modal class?

c) Estimate the mean.

d) Is the information about the modal class and the mean likely to be of any use to the centre?

e) Could Fred have drawn the histogram better?

f) How do you think Fred should have presented the information?

7   A naturalist catches 80 hedgehogs and records the number of fleas on each.

Fleas	Up to 10	11–20	21–30	31–40	41–50	51–60	61–70
Hedgehogs	3	5	16	20	19	10	7

a) Construct a cumulative frequency table.

b) Draw the cumulative frequency graph.

c) Find the median, and the upper and lower quartiles of the number of fleas per hedgehog.

d) What percentage of the hedgehogs have more than 55 fleas?

Mixed exercise 8.4 continued

8 a) Gavin measured the lengths (in cm) of some leaves from a tree in a thick wood.

He then grouped the data as in the table below.

Length of leaf	Frequency
$5.0 \leqslant l < 7.0$	4
$7.0 \leqslant l < 9.0$	11
$9.0 \leqslant l < 11.0$	23
$11.0 \leqslant l < 13.0$	8
$13.0 \leqslant l < 17.0$	4

(i)   Draw a histogram to display these data.

(ii) Estimate the mean length.

(iii) State the maximum and minimum possible values of the range.

b) He also measured the same number of leaves from a tree in his back garden.

His table was as follows.

Length of leaf	Frequency
$5.0 \leqslant l < 7.0$	0
$7.0 \leqslant l < 9.0$	6
$9.0 \leqslant l < 11.0$	26
$11.0 \leqslant l < 13.0$	11
$13.0 \leqslant l < 17.0$	7

(i)   Draw a histogram to display these data.

(ii) Estimate the mean length.

(iii) State the maximum and minimum possible values of the range.

c) Compare the two samples and comment.

9 The lengths of telephone calls, in minutes, received at a switchboard during the first hour of one day were recorded, with the following results:

Length of calls	Frequency
0–5	2
5–8	5
8–11	10
11–14	10
14–18	3

Note: 5–8 means at least 5 and less than 8.

a) On squared paper draw a histogram of these data.

b) Calculate an estimate of the mean length of the calls and explain briefly why this is only an approximation.

MEI (adapted)

Mixed exercise 8.4 *continued*

10 The table below shows the annual incomes, *x*, in thousands of pounds, of the inhabitants of Wyedale.

Income	$0 \leqslant x < 10$	$10 \leqslant x < 15$	$15 \leqslant x < 20$	$20 \leqslant x < 30$	$30 \leqslant x < 50$
Frequency	82	158	185	112	63

a) By drawing a cumulative frequency graph obtain estimates of

  (i) the median income of these people

  (ii) the interquartile range of the incomes.

b) Draw a box-and-whisker diagram to illustrate the data.

The incomes of the inhabitants of Avonford have a median of £18 500 and an interquartile range of £7300.

c) Compare the distribution of incomes in the two towns.

11 A survey was conducted into the length of time, *t*, a small class of pupils spent on their homework on Tuesday and Wednesday last week. The results for Tuesday are presented on the histogram below.

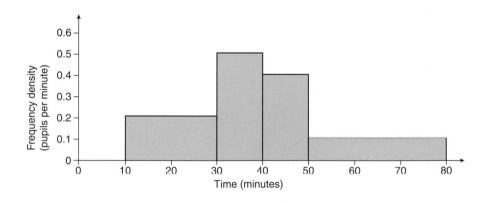

a) Copy and complete the frequency distribution table for this data.

Time (minutes)	$10 \leqslant t < 30$	$30 \leqslant t < 40$	$40 \leqslant t < 50$	$50 \leqslant t < 80$
Frequency	4			

b) Calculate an estimate for the mean of this distribution.

The length of time spent on the homework on Wednesday night had a mean of 48.5 minutes and a range of 25 minutes.

c) Compare the lengths of time spent on homework by these pupils on the two nights.

Mixed exercise 8.4 *continued*

12 The table below shows the length of service, *t*, in years, of teachers at Avonford High School.

Length of service	$0 \leqslant t < 5$	$5 \leqslant t < 10$	$10 \leqslant t < 15$	$15 \leqslant t < 25$	$25 \leqslant t < 40$
Number of teachers	8	12	19	12	5

  a) Obtain the median and the interquartile range of the lengths of service.

  b) Represent the data with a box-and-whisker diagram.

The box-and-whisker plot below shows the length of service, in years, of teachers at Wyedale School.

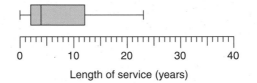

Length of service (years)

  c) Compare the lengths of service of teachers at the two schools.

13 A doctor's patients are divided by age into groups as shown in the table below.

Age (*x*) in years	$0 \leqslant x < 5$	$5 \leqslant x < 15$	$15 \leqslant x < 25$	$25 \leqslant x < 45$	$45 \leqslant x < 75$
Number of patients	14	41	59	70	16

  a) Draw a histogram to represent this distribution. The vertical scale should be 'Patients per year of age'.

  b) The doctor wishes to choose a stratified sample of 40 patients. Explain, with any appropriate calculations, how this can be done.

MEI

Mixed exercise 8.4 *continued*

14 A student is studying the distribution of lengths of worms in a sample of topsoil from a field. The distribution of lengths is shown in this histogram.

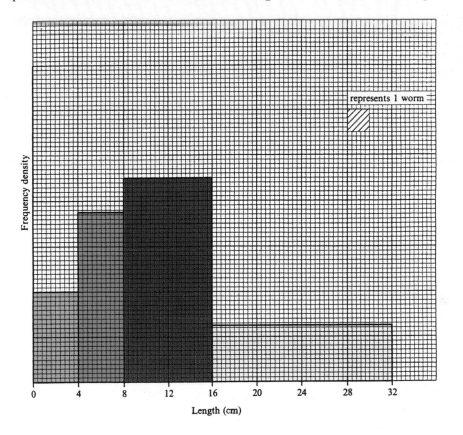

a) Write down the number of worms with lengths less than 4 centimetres.

b) Write down the number of worms with lengths greater than or equal to 8 centimetres and less than 16 centimetres.

c) Calculate the total number of worms in the sample.

d) The area of the part of the field from which the student took her sample of topsoil was 10 m².

The area of the whole field was 160 m².

Estimate the number of worms in the topsoil of the whole field.

London

Chapter 9

More about numbers

Before you start this chapter you should be able to:

★ write a number in index form

★ write a number as the product of its prime factors.

Reminder

Index form: $3 \times 3 \times 3 \times 3 \times 3 = 3^5$

$3^1 = 3$

Prime factors: $360 = 2^3 \times 3^2 \times 5$

> 5 is called the **index** or the **power**.
> 3 is called the **base**

Rules of indices

It is often convenient to write numbers in index form. That means that you need to know the rules for working with them – how to multiply, divide and so on.

Multiplication

What happens when you multiply two numbers given in index form, for example $3^6 \times 3^4$?

$$3^6 \times 3^4 = \underset{1 \quad 2 \quad 3 \quad 4 \quad 5 \quad 6}{(3 \times 3 \times 3 \times 3 \times 3 \times 3)} \times \underset{7 \quad 8 \quad 9 \quad 10}{(3 \times 3 \times 3 \times 3)}$$

$$= 3^{10}$$

You can see that you add the powers: $6 + 4 = 10$

This can be written as a general rule:

$$x^m \times x^n = x^{m+n}$$

When you talk about a general rule, what does the word 'general' mean?

You must be careful when multiplying numbers in index form. They must have the same base.

Look at $2^5 \times 3^4$.

You cannot add the powers in this case because the numbers have different bases, 2 and 3. All you can do is multiply them out as ordinary numbers:

$$2^5 \times 3^4 = 32 \times 81 = 2592$$

Division

You can find the rule for dividing numbers in index form in the same way.

What is $3^6 \div 3^4$?

$$3^6 \div 3^4 = \frac{\cancel{3} \times \cancel{3} \times \cancel{3} \times \cancel{3} \times 3 \times 3}{\cancel{3} \times \cancel{3} \times \cancel{3} \times \cancel{3}}$$

$$= 3^2$$

This time you subtracted: $6 - 4 = 2$

The general rule is:

$$x^m \div x^n = x^{m-n}$$

Example

Simplify $\dfrac{5^5 \times 5^2}{5^4}$

Solution

$5^{5+2-4} = 5^3$ or 125

What keys would you press to do this on your calculator?

A power of a power

Another rule concerns $(x^m)^n$. Carry out this investigation to find this rule for yourself.

Investigation

Work out the values of

a) $(2^2)^6$ **b)** $(2^3)^4$ **c)** $(2^4)^3$ **d)** $(2^6)^2$ **e)** 2^{12}

What does this suggest to you about $(x^m)^n$?

The answer is included in the set of rules at the top of page 188. Look there to check that you got it right.

Power zero

What is the value of $3^5 \div 3^5$?

There are two ways of working this out:

$3^5 \div 3^5 = 3^{5-5} = 3^0$ $3^5 \div 3^5 = \dfrac{\cancel{3} \times \cancel{3} \times \cancel{3} \times \cancel{3} \times \cancel{3}}{\cancel{3} \times \cancel{3} \times \cancel{3} \times \cancel{3} \times \cancel{3}} = 1$

This shows you that $3^0 = 1$.

You can do the same with any number, not just 3, and so the general rule is:

$$x^0 = 1$$

This is an exciting result! It gives meaning to a power of zero.

Any number to the power zero is one.

Negative powers

What about negative powers? Look at $3^2 \div 3^6$. Again you can write this two ways:

$3^2 \div 3^6 = 3^{2-6} = 3^{-4}$ $3^2 \div 3^6 = \dfrac{\cancel{3} \times \cancel{3}}{\cancel{3} \times \cancel{3} \times 3 \times 3 \times 3 \times 3} = \dfrac{1}{3^4}$

So $3^{-4} = \dfrac{1}{3^4}$, and in general:

$$x^{-n} = \dfrac{1}{x^n}$$

Exercise 9.4 *continued*

10 a) The diagram shows an equilateral triangle of side 2 cm.

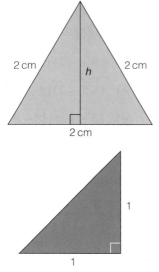

2 cm   2 cm
h
2 cm

  (i)   Use Pythagoras' theorem to prove that $h = \sqrt{3}$.

  (ii) Hence find the *exact* values of $\sin 30°$, $\cos 30°$ and $\tan 30°$.

  (iii) Also find the *exact* values of $\sin 60°$, $\cos 60°$ and $\tan 60°$.

b) The diagram shows a right-angled isosceles triangle.

1

1

  (i)   Find the length of the hypotenuse of this triangle.

  (ii) Hence prove that $\sin 45° = \dfrac{1}{\sqrt{2}} = \dfrac{\sqrt{2}}{2}$.

  (iii) Determine *exact* values for $\cos 45°$ and $\tan 45°$.

Recurring decimals

Some fractions, like $\dfrac{1}{8} = 0.125$ and $\dfrac{3}{50} = 0.06$, have decimal forms that terminate. Others, like $\dfrac{1}{3} = 0.33333\ldots$, give rise to **recurring decimals**.

Those that terminate all have denominators whose only prime factors are 2 and 5. If the denominator of the fraction, in its simplest form, has any prime factor other than 2 or 5 then the decimal form of the fraction will recur.

What is special about the numbers 2 and 5?

How is a recurring decimal converted back into a fraction?

As an example, look at $0.27777\ldots (= 0.2\dot{7})$.
You can work out what fraction it represents like this.

Let $x = 0.27777\ldots$ Then $10x = 2.7777\ldots$

Now subtract $x = 0.27777\ldots$

$9x = 2.5$ ← This is exact. All the other digits are 0

$x = \dfrac{2.5}{9} = \dfrac{25}{90} = \dfrac{5}{18}$.

So $0.2\dot{7} = \dfrac{5}{18}$.

Now use exactly the same method to try to convert $0.\dot{6}\dot{3}$ *into a fraction.*
What happens? How can you adapt the method to make it work?

The power of 10 by which you multiply x depends on the length of the recurring cycle.

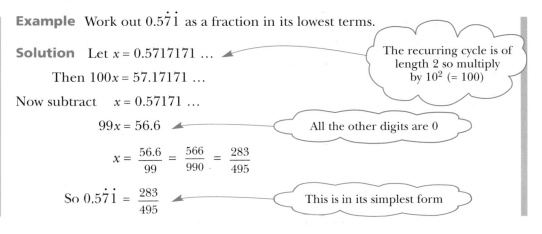

Example Work out $0.5\dot{7}\dot{1}$ as a fraction in its lowest terms.

Solution Let $x = 0.5717171\ldots$

Then $100x = 57.17171\ldots$

Now subtract $x = 0.57171\ldots$

$$99x = 56.6$$

$$x = \frac{56.6}{99} = \frac{566}{990} = \frac{283}{495}$$

So $0.5\dot{7}\dot{1} = \frac{283}{495}$

The recurring cycle is of length 2 so multiply by 10^2 (= 100)

All the other digits are 0

This is in its simplest form

Exercise 9.5

1 Write each of the following numbers as a fraction in its lowest terms.

a) $0.\dot{2}$ b) $0.\dot{5}\dot{4}$ c) $1.\dot{0}\dot{8}$ d) $0.8\dot{5}$

e) $2.4\dot{3}\dot{8}$ f) $0.11\dot{3}$ g) $0.\dot{9}6\dot{3}$ h) $0.\dot{1}4285\dot{7}$

2 Given that $p = 0.\dot{5}\dot{7}$,

a) write p as a fraction, giving your answer in its simplest form

b) find p^2, giving your answer as a fraction in its simplest form.

$0.\dot{9}6\dot{3}$ means 0.963963963 …

3 Given that $q = 0.\dot{1}\dot{5}$, and $r = 0.\dot{1}2\dot{6}$, express $q + r$ both as a recurring decimal and as a fraction in its simplest form.

☆

Finishing off

Now that you have finished this chapter you should be able to:

★ remember and use these rules of indices:

$$x^m \times x^n = x^{m+n} \qquad\qquad x^m \div x^n = x^{m-n}$$

$$x^0 = 1 \qquad\qquad x^{-n} = \frac{1}{x^n}$$

$$x^{\frac{1}{n}} = \sqrt[n]{x} \qquad\qquad (x^m)^n = x^{mn}$$

★ work with fractional indices

★ work with numbers in standard form

★ work with surds

★ write a recurring decimal as a fraction in its simplest form.

Use the questions in the next exercise to check that you understand everything.

Mixed exercise 9.6

1 Write these as ordinary numbers.

   a) 3^5 **b)** 4^3 **c)** $8^{\frac{1}{3}}$

   d) 2^{-4} **e)** $27^{\frac{2}{3}}$ **f)** 8^0

   g) 0^8 **h)** $9^{-\frac{1}{2}}$ **i)** $9^{-1\frac{1}{2}}$

2 Write these numbers in index form.

   a) 625 **b)** $\sqrt{11}$ **c)** $\dfrac{1}{49}$

   d) $\sqrt{343}$ **e)** 4096 **f)** $\dfrac{\sqrt{3}}{27}$

3 State which rule of indices (as given above) is illustrated by each of these statements. State the values of x and, where relevant, m and n.

   a) $25^{\frac{1}{2}} = 5$ **b)** $3^4 \times 3^2 = 3^6$ **c)** $2^{-3} = \dfrac{1}{8}$

   d) $19^0 = 1$ **e)** $5^{17} \div 5^{11} = 5^6$ **f)** $(4^3)^2 = 4^6$

4 Work out the following. Where you can, give your answer in index form; otherwise give it as an ordinary number.

   a) $\dfrac{3^4 \times 3^2}{3^3}$ **b)** $(2^3)^4$ **c)** $2^6 + 2^6$

   d) $3^4 + 3^3$ **e)** 27×3^{-2} **f)** $7 \times \sqrt{7}$

5 Write these figures in standard form.

   a) The radius of the Earth is (approximately) $630\,000\,000$ centimetres.

   b) It takes light $0.000\,000\,000\,003\,3$ seconds to travel one millimetre.

Mixed exercise 9.6 *continued*

6   Carry out these calculations, giving your answers in standard form.

   a) $(3.2 \times 10^{16}) \times (5 \times 10^4)$ b) $(3.2 \times 10^{16}) \div (5 \times 10^4)$

   c) $(6 \times 10^{-10})^2$ d) $(1 \times 10^{-5}) \times (3 \times 10^{-4})$

   e) $\dfrac{(3.3 \times 10^6) \times (1.2 \times 10^4)}{9 \times 10^5}$ f) $\dfrac{(6 \times 10^{-5}) \times (8.8 \times 10^{-7})}{1.1 \times 10^{-12}}$

   g) $(3 \times 10^5) + (4 \times 10^6)$ h) $(5.21 \times 10^4) - (3 \times 10^2)$

   i) $(2.61 \times 10^{-2}) - (4.1 \times 10^{-3})$ j) $\sqrt{(4.9 \times 10^{11})}$

7   State, as powers of 10, the number of

   a) millimetres in 1 metre   b) milligrams in 1 kilogram

   c) litres in 1 millilitre   d) centimetres in 1 kilometre

   e) tonnes in 1 microgram.

8   The speed of sound is 3.3×10^2 metres per second.

   How long does sound take to travel a distance of 1.2×10^4 metres?

   Give your answer to the nearest second.

   MEI

9   $p^{1.5} \times \sqrt{p} \times p^{-5} = p^x$

   Work out the value of *x*.

10 a) Find the value of *n* in the equation $2^n = \sqrt{8}$.

   Triangle ABC has an area of 32 cm².

   b) Calculate the value of *k*.

   London

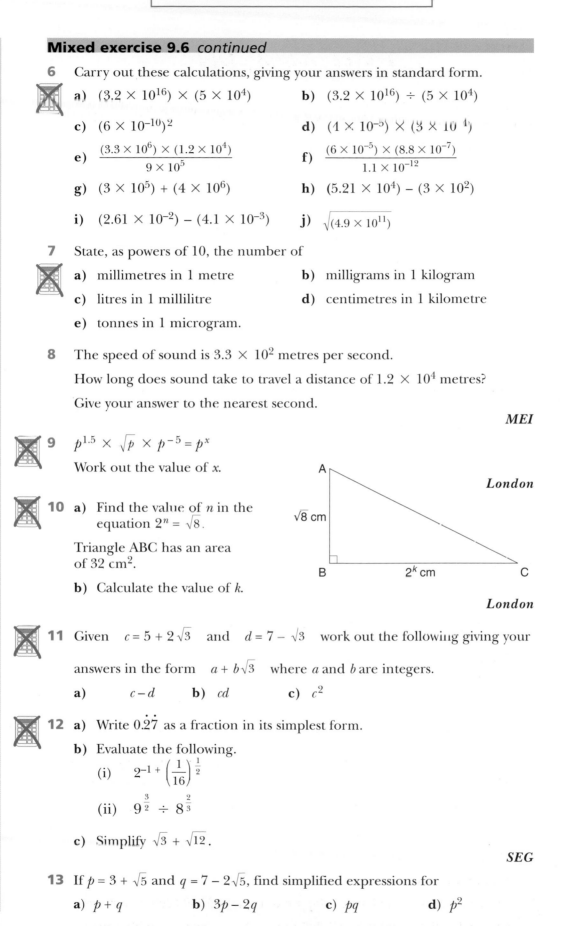

A — London

$\sqrt{8}$ cm

B 2^k cm   C

11 Given $c = 5 + 2\sqrt{3}$ and $d = 7 - \sqrt{3}$ work out the following giving your answers in the form $a + b\sqrt{3}$ where *a* and *b* are integers.

   a) $c - d$ b) cd c) c^2

12 a) Write $0.\dot{2}\dot{7}$ as a fraction in its simplest form.

   b) Evaluate the following.

      (i) $2^{-1} + \left(\dfrac{1}{16}\right)^{\frac{1}{2}}$

      (ii) $9^{\frac{3}{2}} \div 8^{\frac{2}{3}}$

   c) Simplify $\sqrt{3} + \sqrt{12}$.

   SEG

13 If $p = 3 + \sqrt{5}$ and $q = 7 - 2\sqrt{5}$, find simplified expressions for

   a) $p + q$ b) $3p - 2q$ c) pq d) p^2

Mixed exercise 9.6 *continued*

14 Simplify the following expressions.

a) $\dfrac{3}{\sqrt{7}}$

b) $\dfrac{6}{\sqrt{9}}$

c) $\dfrac{1}{\sqrt{5}}$

d) $\dfrac{4}{\sqrt{2}} + 3\sqrt{2}$

e) $\dfrac{21}{\sqrt{3}} - \sqrt{27}$

f) $\left(\dfrac{4}{\sqrt{7}}\right)^2$

g) $\sqrt{3}\,(1 + 4\sqrt{3})$

h) $\sqrt{2}\,(3 - \sqrt{2}) + 2(9 + \sqrt{2})$

i) $(2 + \sqrt{5})\,(3 - \sqrt{5})$

j) $(3\sqrt{2} - 1)\,(5 - \sqrt{2})$

k) $(7 + 2\sqrt{3})\,(7 - 2\sqrt{3})$

l) $(9 - 2\sqrt{5})^2$

15 Write each of the following recurring decimals as a fraction expressed in its simplest form.

a) $0.\dot{3}\dot{8}$

b) $0.5\dot{3}\dot{8}$

c) $0.7\dot{3}$

d) $0.5\dot{3}0\dot{2}$

16 The mid-points of the sides of a square of side 20 cm are joined together to form another square. The process is repeated so that a nest of five squares is formed.

Calculate the total length of the perimeters of the five squares, giving your answer in surd form, as simply as possible.

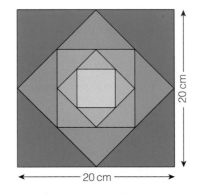

20 cm

20 cm

17 The Indian mathematician Ramanujan discovered that $\left(\dfrac{2143}{22}\right)^{0.25}$ is a close approximation to π.

What is the difference between Ramanujan's value and the value of π on your calculator?

MEI

18 Find the value of the following.

a) $\left(\dfrac{12}{\sqrt{3}}\right)^2$

b) (i) $(3 - \sqrt{7})\,(3 + \sqrt{7})$

(ii) $\dfrac{\sqrt{7}}{3 - \sqrt{7}} - \dfrac{\sqrt{7}}{3 + \sqrt{7}}$

MEI

Mixed exercise 9.6 *continued*

19 a) Write $\sqrt{27} \times \sqrt{32}$ in the form $a\sqrt{6}$ where a is an integer.

b) Simplify $\left(1 + \dfrac{1}{\sqrt{2}}\right)^2$ giving your answer in the form $a + b\sqrt{2}$ where a and b are rational.

MEI

20 A cosmic ray detector is made up of a number of thin layers of glass. The diagram shows a section of the track of a cosmic ray particle as it passes through the detector.

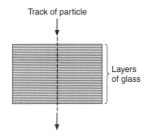

Track of particle

Layers of glass

Each layer of glass is 0.000 023 5 m deep.

a) Write this depth in standard form.

b) The complete detector consists of 1.83×10^3 layers of glass.

The particle travels at a velocity of 2.77×10^8 ms^{-1}.

How long does the particle take to pass through the complete detector?

Give your answer in seconds, in standard form, to an appropriate degree of accuracy.

MEI

Investigation

Investigate for what positive values of x and y, $x^y > y^x$.

Start by taking whole number values of x and y.

Record your results on a sheet of graph paper using, say, a red cross for points where $x^y > y^x$, a grey one for $x^y = y^x$ and a blue one for $x^y < y^x$.

Then go on to other positive values. Describe what you find.

Investigation

What is the value of 0^0?

You know that $x^0 = 1$ and that $0^n = 0$, provided that x and n are not zero.

Use your calculator to find the value of $0.1^{0.1}$. Now repeat for $0.01^{0.01}$ and so on.

What do you find?

Chapter 10

Quadratic equations

> **Before you start this chapter you should:**
>
> ★ be familiar with the work in Chapter 3
>
> ★ be familiar with the work in Chapter 5.

Factorising a quadratic expression

In Chapter 5 you multiplied out expressions involving two brackets, like this:

$$(x + 2)\ (x + 3) = x^2 + 3x + 2x + 6$$
$$= x^2 + 5x + 6$$

The result is a **quadratic** expression because x^2 is the highest power of x.

To factorise a quadratic expression, you have to do the reverse of multiplying out.

Here's one way to factorise a quadratic expression.

> The x^2 must come from multiplying together an x from each bracket

$$x^2 + 6x + 8$$

$$(x + ?)\ (x + ?)$$

> The 8 must come from multiplying together a number from each bracket.
> So these numbers must be either 1 and 8, or 2 and 4

To decide which pair of numbers is correct, look at the middle term, $6x$.
This comes from adding together the two outer terms and the two inner terms.
So the correct pair of numbers must be 2 and 4, as $2x + 4x = 6x$.

One way to set out your work is like this:

$$x^2 + 6x + 8$$
Split up the middle term $= x^2 + 2x + 4x + 8$
Now factorise each pair of terms $= x(x + 2) + 4(x + 2)$
$(x + 2)$ is a common factor $= (x + 2)(x + 4)$

In a simple case like this, you will often be able to go straight to the answer, but you should always check it by multiplying out.

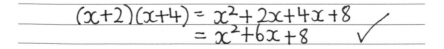

$$(x + 2)(x + 4) = x^2 + 2x + 4x + 8 \checkmark$$
$$= x^2 + 6x + 8 \checkmark$$

Negative terms

Example

Factorise   **a)** $x^2 - 7x + 12$

              b) $x^2 + x - 6$

Do the numbers in each bracket have to be positive or negative? Try to do the factorising yourself before you look at the solutions.

Solution

a) You need to find two numbers whose product is 12 and whose sum is –7. So both numbers must be negative. The numbers are –3 and –4.

$$x^2 - 7x + 12 = x^2 - 3x - 4x + 12$$
$$= x(x - 3) - 4(x - 3)$$
$$= (x - 3)(x - 4)$$

> If you can see the solution straight away, you don't need to write these two lines, but make sure you check by multiplying out

b) You need to find two numbers whose product is –6 and whose sum is 1. So one number must be positive and one negative. The numbers are 3 and –2.

$$x^2 + x - 6 = x^2 - 2x + 3x - 6$$
$$= x(x - 2) + 3(x - 2)$$
$$= (x + 3)(x - 2)$$

The difference of two squares

An expression such as $x^2 - 9$, with no middle term, is called the **difference of two squares**. So that the middle term cancels out, the two numbers in the brackets must be the same, but one positive and one negative.

$$x^2 - 9 = x^2 + 0x - 9 = (x + 3)(x - 3)$$

Perfect squares

A quadratic expression whose factors are both the same is called a **perfect square**,

e.g. $x^2 + 6x + 9 = (x + 3)(x + 3) = (x + 3)^2$

Find some more quadratic expressions which are perfect squares by multiplying out expressions like $(x + 1)^2$, $(x - 2)^2$.

How can you quickly spot a quadratic expression which is a perfect square?

*The statement $x^2 + 6x + 9 = (x + 3)^2$ is an example of an **identity** because it is true for all values of x.*

What is the difference between an equation and an identity?

Give another identity.

Solving quadratic equations

A quadratic equation is an equation in which the highest power of x is x^2.

This is an example of a quadratic equation:

$$x^2 - 2x - 3 = 0$$

It can be written in factorised form like this:

$$(x - 3)(x + 1) = 0$$

You could solve the equation by plotting the graph of $y = x^2 - 2x - 3$ and finding out where it crosses the x axis.

Here are two ways of making a table of values for the graph, the first using the equation $y = x^2 - 2x - 3$, and the second using the factorised form $y = (x - 3)(x + 1)$.

x	-3	-2	-1	0	1	2	3
x^2	9	4	1	0	1	4	9
$-2x$	6	4	2	0	-2	-4	-6
-3	-3	-3	-3	-3	-3	-3	-3
y	12	5	0	-3	-4	-3	0

x	-3	-2	-1	0	1	2	3
$x-3$	-6	-5	-4	-3	-2	-1	0
$x+1$	-2	-1	0	1	2	3	4
y	12	5	0	-3	-4	-3	0

The last row is obtained by multiplying the numbers in the two previous rows

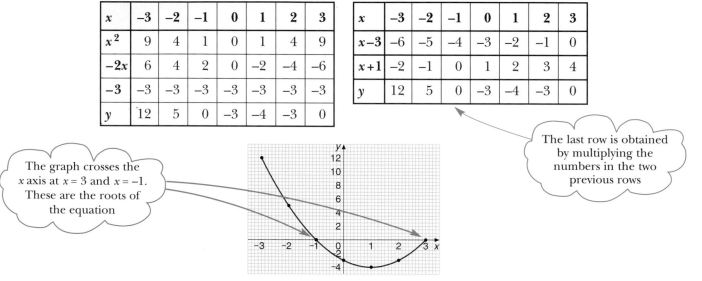

The graph crosses the x axis at $x = 3$ and $x = -1$. These are the roots of the equation

Which way of making the table do you think is easier?

How does factorising the quadratic expression help you to solve the equation?

Instead of drawing the graph, you can solve the equation directly by factorising it, like this:

$$x^2 - 2x - 3 = 0$$

$$(x - 3)(x + 1) = 0$$

Either $x - 3 = 0$ or $x + 1 = 0$

$$x = 3 \text{ or } x = -1$$

If an equation has a common factor, you should take this out before factorising, like this:

$$2x^2 - 12x + 16 = 0$$

$$2(x^2 - 6x + 8) = 0$$

$$2(x - 4)(x - 2) = 0$$

$$x = 4 \text{ or } x = 2$$

Notice that a quadratic equation usually has two roots. Think of a quadratic equation that only has one root.

Exercise 10.1

1 **a)** Find two numbers with sum 7 and product 10.

   b) Hence factorise $x^2 + 7x + 10$.

2 **a)** Find two numbers with sum -4 and product -12.

   b) Hence factorise $x^2 - 4x - 12$.

3 Factorise these quadratic expressions.

   a) $x^2 + 3x + 2$ **b)** $x^2 + 8x + 7$

   c) $x^2 - 5x + 4$ **d)** $x^2 - 8x + 12$

   e) $x^2 - 2x - 3$ **f)** $x^2 + 4x - 5$

   g) $x^2 - 11x + 24$ **h)** $x^2 - 12x + 20$

   i) $x^2 - 16$ **j)** $x^2 + 6x - 16$

   k) $x^2 + 6x + 9$ **l)** $x^2 - 2x + 1$

4 Solve these quadratic equations by factorising.

   a) $x^2 + 4x + 3 = 0$ **b)** $x^2 - 6x + 8 = 0$

   c) $x^2 - 2x - 15 = 0$ **d)** $x^2 - 4 = 0$

   e) $x^2 - 8x + 12 = 0$ **f)** $x^2 + 3x - 10 - 0$

   g) $x^2 - 4x + 4 = 0$ **h)** $x^2 - 5x - 6 = 0$

   i) $x^2 - 25 = 0$ **j)** $x^2 + 8x - 9 = 0$

   k) $x^2 + 10x + 24 = 0$ **l)** $x^2 - 10x + 16 = 0$

   m) $x^2 + 7x - 18 = 0$ **n)** $x^2 + 12x + 36 = 0$

5 Solve these quadratic equations by first taking out a common factor.

   a) $2x^2 + 4x - 16 = 0$ **b)** $3x^2 - 12x + 9 = 0$

   c) $5x^2 + 45x - 50 = 0$ **d)** $\frac{1}{2}x^2 - 2x - 6 = 0$

6 Rearrange these equations so that they are in the form

   $$x^2 + bx + c = 0$$

   Then solve each equation by factorising.

   a) $x^2 + 3x = 4$ **b)** $2 + x - x^2 = 0$

   c) $x(x - 1) = 6$ **d)** $x(x + 5) = 6(x + 2)$

   e) $x = \dfrac{2x + 8}{x}$ **f)** $(x + 3)(x + 4) = 2$

   g) $\dfrac{2x + 3}{3x + 7} = \dfrac{x + 1}{x + 3}$ **h)** $\dfrac{2x - 1}{3x + 2} = \dfrac{x + 4}{x + 2}$

7 The number sequence 2, 6, 12, 20… can be rewritten 1×2, 2×3, 3×4, 4×5…

   a) Write down a formula for the nth term of the sequence.

   b) One term of the sequence is 182. Write down and solve a quadratic equation to find out what number term this is.

8 The length of a swimming pool is 3 m more than its width. The area of the pool is 40 m². Find the length and width of the pool.

Quadratic graphs

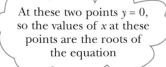 *What happens when you try to solve this quadratic equation by factorising?*

$$x^2 + 6x + 7 = 0$$

Not all quadratic expressions can be factorised. However, some quadratic equations which cannot be solved by factorising do have solutions.

One method of finding approximate roots is to draw a graph and find out where it crosses the *x* axis.

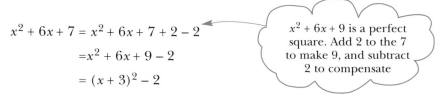

At these two points $y = 0$, so the values of *x* at these points are the roots of the equation

The dotted line is the line of symmetry of the graph

This is the minimum point of the graph

 Read off the values of the roots from the graph above.

How accurate do you think your answers are?

Completing the square

 Look again at the graph above of $y = x^2 + 6x + 7$.

What is the equation of the line of symmetry of the graph?

What are the co-ordinates of the minimum point?

You can find out information like this about a quadratic graph without drawing it, by rewriting the equation of the graph as a perfect square plus a number. This is called the **completed square** form of a quadratic expression.

First, you need to find what number would make $x^2 + 6x$ into a perfect square. You can do this by halving the coefficient of *x* and squaring the result. In this case, half of 6 is 3, and $3^2 = 9$.

$$x^2 + 6x + 7 = x^2 + 6x + 7 + 2 - 2$$
$$= x^2 + 6x + 9 - 2$$
$$= (x + 3)^2 - 2$$

$x^2 + 6x + 9$ is a perfect square. Add 2 to the 7 to make 9, and subtract 2 to compensate

You can find the line of symmetry of the graph by looking at the expression in the bracket. The line of symmetry is $x = -3$. As the minimum point is on this line, it has *x* co-ordinate -3, and its *y* co-ordinate is found from the number outside the bracket, in this case -2. So the minimum point is $(-3, -2)$.

 Explain why the completed square form shows that the minimum value of y must be -2.

Solving quadratic equations by completing the square

By completing the square, you can now find an accurate solution for the quadratic equation at the top of the last page,

$$x^2 + 6x + 7 = 0$$

First, rewrite the equation with the constant term on the right.

$$x^2 + 6x = -7$$

Then find the number needed to complete the square, and add it to both sides of the equation.

$$x^2 + 6x + 9 = -7 + 9$$

Write the left-hand side as a perfect square and then square root both sides.

$$(x + 3)^2 = 2$$

$$x + 3 = \pm\sqrt{2}$$

$$x = -3 \pm\sqrt{2}$$

$$x = -1.586 \text{ or } -4.414$$

If the coefficient of x^2 is not 1, you should divide through by this coefficient first.

Example

Solve the equation

$$2x^2 - 10x + 3 = 0$$

by completing the square.

Solution

$$2x^2 - 10x + 3 = 0$$

$$x^2 - 5x + \frac{3}{2} = 0$$

$$x^2 - 5x = -\frac{3}{2}$$

Halve 5 to get $\frac{5}{2}$, then square to get $\frac{25}{4}$

$$x^2 - 5x + \frac{25}{4} = -\frac{3}{2} + \frac{25}{4}$$

$$\left(x - \frac{5}{2}\right)^2 = \frac{19}{4}$$

$$x - \frac{5}{2} = \pm\sqrt{\frac{19}{4}}$$

$$x = \frac{5}{2} \pm \frac{\sqrt{19}}{2}$$

$$x = 4.679 \text{ or } 0.321$$

The method of completing the square can be generalised to obtain a formula for solving quadratic equations, which you will meet in the next section. Using the formula is much easier, so most people use it rather than completing the square to solve equations. However, as you have seen, completing the square is a very useful technique for finding out about the line of symmetry and the minimum point of a quadratic graph.

Exercise 10.3

1

a) Copy and complete this table of values for the graph
$$y = x^2 - 2x - 2$$

x	–3	–2	–1	0	1	2	3
x^2	9	4					
$-2x$	6	4					
-2	–2	–2					
y	13						

b) Draw the graph of $y = x^2 - 2x - 2$.

c) Use your graph to find approximate solutions to the equation
$$x^2 - 2x - 2 = 0$$

2

a) Draw the graph of $y = 2x^2 + x - 7$ for values of x from –3 to 3.

b) Use your graph to find approximate solutions to the equation
$$2x^2 + x - 7 = 0$$

3

Use a graph to solve the equation
$$1 + 2x - x^2 = 0$$

4

a) Write the quadratic expression
$$x^2 + 4x + 1$$
in the form $(x + a)^2 + b$.

b) Write down the equation of the line of symmetry of the graph of $y = x^2 + 4x + 1$.

c) Write down the co-ordinates of the minimum point of the graph.

5

a) Write the quadratic expression
$$x^2 - 2x + 5$$
in the form $(x + a)^2 + b$.

b) Write down the equation of the line of symmetry of the graph of $y = x^2 - 2x + 5$.

c) Write down the co-ordinates of the minimum point of the graph.

6

Solve each of these quadratic equations by completing the square.

a) $x^2 + 8x - 2 = 0$

b) $x^2 - 6x + 3 = 0$

c) $x^2 - 3x + 1 = 0$

d) $x^2 + 5x - 3 = 0$

e) $2x^2 + 4x - 1 = 0$

f) $2x^2 - x - 2 = 0$

The quadratic formula

The method of completing the square is quite a long-winded way to solve a quadratic equation. However, the method can be generalised to give a formula which can be used instead.

For reference, the generalisation of the method is shown below. See if you can follow the steps. You are not expected to learn this generalisation, only the formula.

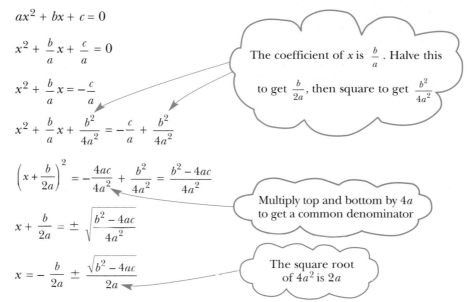

$$ax^2 + bx + c = 0$$

$$x^2 + \frac{b}{a}x + \frac{c}{a} = 0$$

$$x^2 + \frac{b}{a}x = -\frac{c}{a}$$

$$x^2 + \frac{b}{a}x + \frac{b^2}{4a^2} = -\frac{c}{a} + \frac{b^2}{4a^2}$$

The coefficient of x is $\frac{b}{a}$. Halve this to get $\frac{b}{2a}$, then square to get $\frac{b^2}{4a^2}$

$$\left(x + \frac{b}{2a}\right)^2 = -\frac{4ac}{4a^2} + \frac{b^2}{4a^2} = \frac{b^2 - 4ac}{4a^2}$$

Multiply top and bottom by $4a$ to get a common denominator

$$x + \frac{b}{2a} = \pm\sqrt{\frac{b^2 - 4ac}{4a^2}}$$

$$x = -\frac{b}{2a} \pm \frac{\sqrt{b^2 - 4ac}}{2a}$$

The square root of $4a^2$ is $2a$

This is called the quadratic formula. It is usually written like this:

$$x = \frac{-b \pm \sqrt{b^2 - 4ac}}{2a}$$

Always try to factorise the equation first, and only use the formula if it can't be factorised.

Example

Solve the equation $2x^2 + 3x - 1 = 0$, giving the answers to 3 decimal places.

Solution

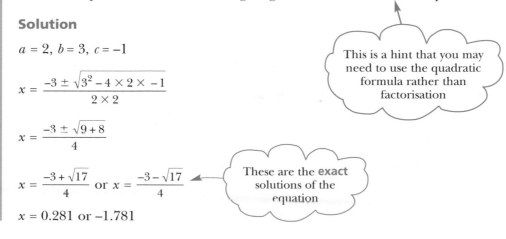

$a = 2$, $b = 3$, $c = -1$

$$x = \frac{-3 \pm \sqrt{3^2 - 4 \times 2 \times -1}}{2 \times 2}$$

$$x = \frac{-3 \pm \sqrt{9 + 8}}{4}$$

$$x = \frac{-3 + \sqrt{17}}{4} \text{ or } x = \frac{-3 - \sqrt{17}}{4}$$

This is a hint that you may need to use the quadratic formula rather than factorisation

These are the **exact** solutions of the equation

$x = 0.281$ or -1.781

Exercise 10.4

1 For each of these equations, write down the values of a, b and c and use the quadratic formula to solve the equation giving your answers to 2 decimal places.

a) $2x^2 - x - 2 = 0$ **b)** $x^2 + 3x + 1 = 0$

c) $x^2 - 4x + 2 = 0$ **d)** $3x^2 + 2x - 2 = 0$

e) $2x^2 - 4x + 1 = 0$ **f)** $5x^2 + x - 2 = 0$

g) $-x^2 + 3x + 1 = 0$ **h)** $4x^2 + 3x - 2 = 0$

i) $3x^2 - 4x - 2 = 0$ **j)** $-2x^2 - x + 4 = 0$

2 Some of these quadratic equations can be solved by factorising, others by using the formula. Solve each equation by an appropriate method.

a) $x^2 - 7x + 12 = 0$ **b)** $x^2 - 7x - 12 = 0$

c) $2x^2 + 10x - 12 = 0$ **d)** $2x^2 - 3x - 4 = 0$

e) $3x^2 + 2x - 4 = 0$ **f)** $5x^2 - 2x - 3 = 0$

g) $4x^2 - 4x + 1 = 0$ **h)** $2x^2 - 6x + 1 = 0$

i) $4x^2 + 7x - 3 = 0$ **j)** $3x^2 + 4x - 15 = 0$

3 Rearrange these equations into the form

$$ax^2 + bx + c = 0$$

and solve them.

a) $x^2 = 1 - 4x$ **b)** $3 - 2x^2 = 6x$

c) $2x(x - 3) = 3(2 - 3x)$ **d)** $(1 - 2x)^2 = 2 - 3x$

e) $(x + 3)(5 - 2x) = 1$ **f)** $(x + 3)^2 = (2x - 1)^2 + 1$

g) $\dfrac{1}{x} + x = 3$ **h)** $\dfrac{2x + 1}{x} = 4x$

i) $\dfrac{x}{2x + 1} = \dfrac{x - 2}{x}$ **j)** $\dfrac{3x + 2}{x - 4} = \dfrac{2x + 1}{x + 2}$

4 This is a right-angled triangle with sides of lengths x, $x + 4$ and $2x + 1$.

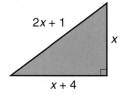

Find the length of each side of the triangle.

5 The surface area of a cylinder is given by the formula

Surface area = $2\pi r^2 + 2\pi rh$

A cylinder has height 10 cm and surface area 250 cm². Find the radius of the cylinder.

6 a) Try to solve this equation using the quadratic formula.

$$x^2 + 2x + 2 = 0$$

Why is it not possible to find solutions?

Exercise 10.4 *continued*

  b) Plot the graph of

$$y = x^2 + 2x + 2$$

     Use the graph to explain why the equation in part a) has no solutions.

  c) How could you use the value of $\sqrt{b^2 - 4ac}$ to find out whether or not a quadratic equation has solutions?

7 **a)** Solve the equation

$$2x^2 - 3x + 1 = 0$$

     by factorising.

  b) Use the quadratic formula to solve the equation in part a).

  c) Explain how you could use the value of $\sqrt{b^2 - 4ac}$ to find out if the solutions of a quadratic equation are rational (i.e. the equation can be solved by factorising).

8 **a)** Solve the equation

$$4x^2 + 12x + 9 = 0$$

     by factorising.

  b) Plot the graph of

$$y = 4x^2 + 12x + 9$$

     Use the graph to explain why the the equation in part a) has only one solution.

  c) Use the quadratic formula to solve the equation in part a).

  d) Explain how you could use the value of $\sqrt{b^2 - 4ac}$ to find out if a quadratic equation has just one solution.

9 For each of the quadratic equations below,

    (i)   work out the value of $b^2 - 4ac$

    (ii) use your answer to (i) to say whether the equation has two irrational solutions, two rational solutions, one rational solution, or no solutions

    (iii) solve the equation, if possible, by an appropriate method.

  a) $x^2 + 4x - 2 = 0$ **b)** $2x^2 + 9x - 5 = 0$

  c) $2x^2 - 5x + 1 = 0$ **d)** $x^2 + 6x + 9 = 0$

  e) $6x^2 - 7x + 2 = 0$ **f)** $x^2 + 3x + 5 = 0$

  g) $4x^2 - 20x + 25 = 0$ **h)** $3x^2 - x - 3 = 0$

  i) $2x^2 - x + 1 - 0$ **j)** $x^2 - 2x - 15 = 0$

10 Rob keeps a record of his score whenever he plays his new computer game. His total score so far after several weeks is 5355 points. One day, he achieves his best ever score of 405 points. He notices that this increases his average score per game by 7 points.

Find the number of games Rob has played.

Finishing off

Now that you have finished this chapter you should be able to:

★ solve a quadratic equation by factorising

★ solve a quadratic equation by using the quadratic formula.

Use the questions in the next exercise to check that you understand everything.

Mixed exercise 10.5

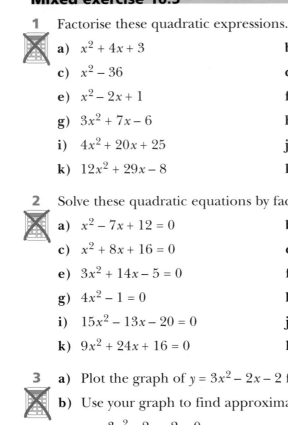

1 Factorise these quadratic expressions.

a) $x^2 + 4x + 3$ 　　　　　　　　　　b) $x^2 + 3x - 10$

c) $x^2 - 36$ 　　　　　　　　　　　　d) $x^2 - 6x + 8$

e) $x^2 - 2x + 1$ 　　　　　　　　　　f) $2x^2 + 9x + 4$

g) $3x^2 + 7x - 6$ 　　　　　　　　　h) $4x^2 - 12x + 5$

i) $4x^2 + 20x + 25$ 　　　　　　　　j) $8x^2 + 6x - 9$

k) $12x^2 + 29x - 8$ 　　　　　　　　l) $9x^2 - 16$

2 Solve these quadratic equations by factorising.

a) $x^2 - 7x + 12 = 0$ 　　　　　　　b) $x^2 + 8x + 12 = 0$

c) $x^2 + 8x + 16 = 0$ 　　　　　　　d) $2x^2 - 7x + 3 = 0$

e) $3x^2 + 14x - 5 = 0$ 　　　　　　f) $4x^2 - 3x - 1 = 0$

g) $4x^2 - 1 = 0$ 　　　　　　　　　h) $6x^2 + 23x + 20 = 0$

i) $15x^2 - 13x - 20 = 0$ 　　　　　j) $6x^2 + 13x - 15 = 0$

k) $9x^2 + 24x + 16 = 0$ 　　　　　l) $12x^2 + 52x - 9 = 0$

3 a) Plot the graph of $y = 3x^2 - 2x - 2$ for values of x from -3 to 3.

　　b) Use your graph to find approximate solutions to the equation

　　　　$3x^2 - 2x - 2 = 0$

4 a) Write the quadratic expression

　　　　$x^2 - 10x + 13$

　　in the form

　　　　$(x + p)^2 + q$

　　b) Write down the equation of the line of symmetry of the graph of $y = x^2 - 10x + 13$.

　　c) Write down the co-ordinates of the minimum point of the graph.

Mixed exercise 10.5 *continued*

5 Use the quadratic formula to solve these equations.

   a) $x^2 + 2x - 5 = 0$ **b)** $x^2 - 3x - 1 = 0$ **c)** $2x^2 + 4x - 3 = 0$

   d) $3x^2 + 8x + 2 = 0$ **e)** $2x^2 - 3x - 3 = 0$ **f)** $5x^2 + 2x - 1 = 0$

   g) $3x^2 + x - 3 = 0$ **h)** $-x^2 + 3x + 5 = 0$ **i)** $2x^2 + 5x - 4 = 0$

   j) $3x^2 - 5x - 4 = 0$ **k)** $-2x^2 - 5x + 1 = 0$ **l)** $6x^2 - x - 3 = 0$

6 Rearrange these equations so that they are in the form

   $$ax^2 + bx + c = 0$$

   and solve them by any appropriate method.

   a) $1 + 4x - 3x^2 = 0$ **b)** $2 - x^2 = 5x$

   c) $\dfrac{2}{x} + x = 3$ **d)** $(2x + 1)(x - 3) = 1$

   e) $\dfrac{1}{x - 1} = 3x$ **f)** $x(3x - 2) = 3(x + 1)$

   g) $\dfrac{x}{x + 1} = \dfrac{2}{x}$ **h)** $\dfrac{1}{x^2} - \dfrac{2}{x} = 3$

   i) $(x + 3)^2 = 1 - x$ **j)** $(2x + 3)^2 - (x + 2)^2 = 3$

   k) $\dfrac{x + 3}{x - 1} = \dfrac{2x + 1}{x + 2}$ **l)** $\dfrac{3x - 1}{2 - x} = \dfrac{x + 1}{x - 4}$

7 The hypotenuse of a right-angled triangle is 25 cm long. There is
   17 cm difference in length between the two shorter sides.

   Find the lengths of the two shorter sides.

8 A cricket ball is thrown from one player to another. After *t* seconds,
   the height, *h*, in metres, of the cricket ball above the ground is given
   by the equation

   $$h = 1 + 6t - 5t^2$$

   a) The ball is thrown when *t* = 0. What height is the ball thrown from?

   b) At what times does the ball reach a height of 2 m?

   c) At what time does the cricket ball hit the ground, assuming it is
   not caught?

9 Tanya's garden is 11 m by 15 m.
   She has a flower bed round three sides of the garden, as shown in
   the diagram. The flower bed is the same width all the way around.
   The area of the lawn is 108 m².

   How wide is the flower bed?

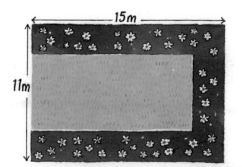

Mixed exercise 10.5 *continued*

10 a) Write $x^2 + 6x + 10$ in the form $(x + a)^2 + b$.

b) Use your answer to explain why the equation $x^2 + 6x + 10 = 0$ has no solution.

MEI

11 Given that $x^2 - 10x + n = (x - m)^2$, find m and n.

MEI

12 a) Factorise this expression.
$$5x^2 - 44x - 9$$

b) Using your answer to part a), solve this equation.
$$5u^4 - 44u^2 - 9 = 0$$

MEI

13 a) Given that $\dfrac{3(x-1)}{2x+3} = \dfrac{1}{x+1}$

prove that $3\left(x - \dfrac{1}{3}\right)^2 = 6\dfrac{1}{3}$.

b) Hence solve $\dfrac{3(x-1)}{2x+3} = \dfrac{1}{x+1}$

giving your answer to 2 decimal places.

MEI

14

The area of this rectangle is numericallly equal to its perimeter.

a) Form and simplify an appropriate equation in x to show this information.

b) Solve the equation to find the dimensions of the rectangle.

15 The two roots of the quadratic equation $ax^2 + bx + c = 0$ are given by the expression

$$x = \frac{-b \pm \sqrt{b^2 - 4ac}}{2a}$$

Show that the sum of the two roots is given by $\dfrac{-b}{a}$.

MEI

Mixed exercise 10.5 *continued*

16 a) This is the graph of

$$y = x^4 - 20x^2 + 40.$$

Use the graph to deduce two facts about the solution to the equation

$$x^4 - 20x^2 + 40 = 0.$$

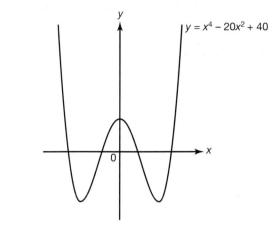

$y = x^4 - 20x^2 + 40$

b) Here is a short extract from a textbook:

> **Equations of the form $x^4 + px^2 + q = 0$ are called biquadratic**
> **equations. They are solved by substituting for x^2 and then**
> **solving the resulting quadratic.**

Substitute z for x^2 to find all the roots of the equation

$$x^4 - 20x^2 + 40 = 0.$$

Give your answers to 2 decimal places.

MEI

17 The dimensions, in centimetres, of a cuboid are x, $x + 2$ and $2x + 1$.

☆ Each side of the cuboid is increased by 2 cm. The volume of the cuboid
☆ increases by 312 cm³.
☆
☆ Find the original dimensions of the cuboid.

Chapter 11

Graphs

Before you start this chapter you should be able to:

★ draw graphs of straight lines

★ make a table of values for an algebraic expression

★ use a table of values to draw the graph of a curve.

Reminder

The line $y = mx + c$ has gradient m and passes through the point c on the y axis.

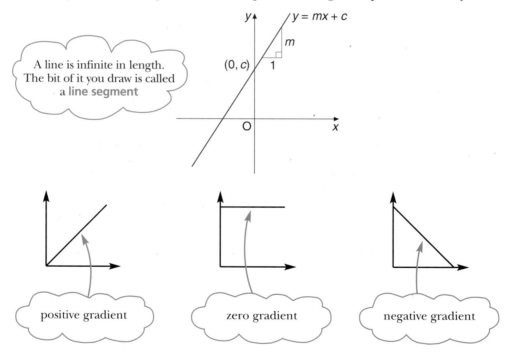

A line is infinite in length. The bit of it you draw is called a **line segment**

positive gradient

zero gradient

negative gradient

To draw the graph of $y = x^2 - 2x - 4$ from $x = -2$ to 4, find out the values of y by making a table.

$(-2)^2$ is 4

$(-2)(-1)$ is 2

x	-2	-1	0	1	2	3	4
x^2	4	1	0	1	4	9	16
$-2x$	4	2	0	-2	-4	-6	-8
-4	-4	-4	-4	-4	-4	-4	-4
y	4	-1	-4	-5	-4	-1	4

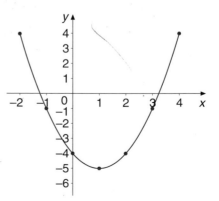

What equations does this graph allow you to solve?

Review exercise 11.1

1 For each of these equations, write down the co-ordinates of the point (or points) where the line crosses the axes.

a) $y = 10$ **b)** $x = 6$ **c)** $y = 3x + 1$

d) $y = x + 2$ **e)** $y = 2x$ **f)** $y = -2x - 2$

2 Write down the equation of each of these lines.

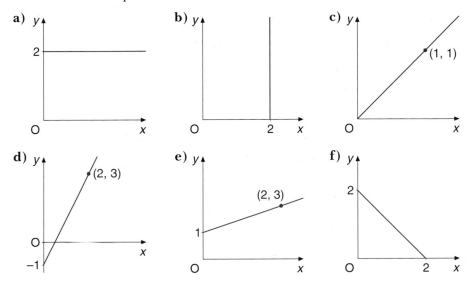

3 **a)** Copy and complete this table for $y = x^2 - 4x - 5$.

x	-1	0	1	2	3	4	5
x^2	1	0			9	16	
$-4x$	4		-4				-20
-5	-5			-5			
y	0						

b) Use the table to draw the graph of $y = x^2 - 4x - 5$ for values of x from -1 to 5.

c) Where does the graph cross the axes?

d) What is x when y is $-\dfrac{1}{2}$?

4 **a)** Construct a table for $y = x^3 + 4x^2 - 3x + 1$ for values of x from -5 to 2.

b) Use the table to draw the graph of $y = x^3 + 4x^2 - 3x + 1$.

c) What are the values of x when

(i) $y = 0$?

(ii) $y = 2$?

Straight line graphs

You will probably find that the work in this section is revision.

Many real-life situations give rise to straight line graphs, such as that in the following example.

Dan runs a delivery service. He has a standing charge and a cost proportionate to the distance. Here is a list of some of his charges.

Miles	Cost
1	£1.80
2	£2.10
3	£2.40
4	£2.70
5	£3.00

How much does he charge per mile?

What is the standing charge?

This can be shown in a graph of cost against distance.

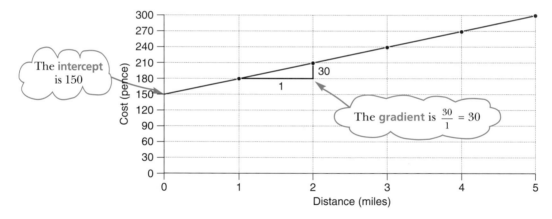

This line has gradient 30 and intercept 150, so its equation is $y = 30x + 150$.

How does this equation relate to Dan's charges?

Parallel and perpendicular lines

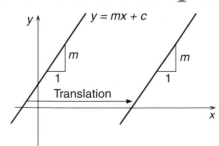

If the line $y = mx + c$ is translated then a parallel line is obtained and it is clear that the gradient of the new line is the same as the gradient of the old line.

Parallel lines have equal gradients.

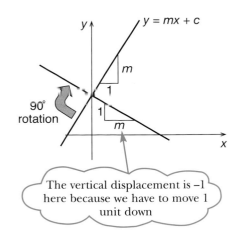

The vertical displacement is –1 here because we have to move 1 unit down

Lines that meet at right angles are called **perpendicular** lines.

If the line $y = mx + c$ is rotated by 90° about a point on the line then a perpendicular line is obtained.

Gradient of new line

$$= \frac{\text{Vertical displacement}}{\text{Horizontal displacement}} = \frac{-1}{m}$$

Thus

Gradient of original line $\times$ Gradient of perpendicular line $= m \times \dfrac{-1}{m} = -1$

The product of the gradients of perpendicular lines is –1.

Example

Find the equation of the line

a) which passes through $(4, 2)$ and is parallel to the line $y = 3x + 6$

b) which passes through $(4, 2)$ and is perpendicular to the line $y = 2x + 5$

Solution

a) The line $y = 3x + 6$ has gradient 3 so the parallel line must also have gradient 3.

The parallel line therefore has the equation	$y = 3x + c$
The parallel line passes through $(4, 2)$ so	$2 = 3 \times 4 + c$
	$2 = 12 + c$
	$-10 = c$
The parallel line has equation	$y = 3x - 10$

b) The line $y = 2x + 5$ has gradient 2 so the perpendicular line must have gradient $\dfrac{-1}{2}$.

The perpendicular line therefore has equation	$y = \dfrac{-1}{2}x + c$
The perpendicular line passes through $(4, 2)$ so	$2 = \dfrac{-1}{2} \times 4 + c$
	$2 = -2 + c$
	$4 = c$
The perpendicular line has equation	$y = \dfrac{-1}{2}x + 4$

Exercise 11.3 *continued*

11 Draw a sketch of each of the following graphs and describe the main features of each graph.

    a) $y = x^2 + 2x - 6$ **b)** $y = 2x^2 - 6x + 7$

    c) $y = -3x^2 + 6x - 5$ **d)** $y = -4x^2 + 12x + 5$

    What can be said about the graph of $y = ax^2 + bx + c$?

12 Draw a sketch of each of the following curves.

    a) $y = (x - 3)(x + 2)$ **b)** $y = 5(x - 1)(x + 2)$

    c) $y = (x - 3)(x - 1)(x + 2)$ **d)** $y = 2(x + 1)(x - 2)(x - 4)$

    Find possible equations for the curves shown in the diagram.

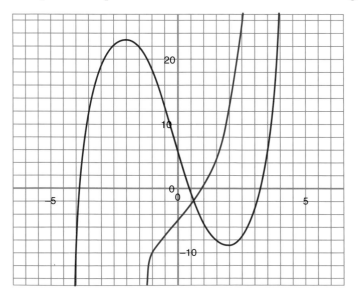

Investigation

Investigate the types of curve that are obtained from equations of the form

    $y = x^3 + px + q$

for different values of p and q.

Find possible equations for the curves shown in the diagram.

Solving equations and inequalities

How would you solve these equations?

$$x^2 - 3x + 2 = 0 \qquad x^3 - 3x^2 + 2 = 0$$

The first one you would solve by factorisation.

For the second one, you could draw a graph of $y = x^3 - 3x^2 + 2$ and find out where $y = 0$ (where it crosses the x axis).

When the line $y = x^3 - 3x^2 + 2$ crosses the x axis, $x^3 - 3x^2 + 2 = 0$.

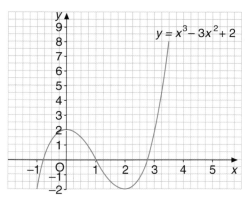

This happens at about $(-0.7, 0)$, $(1, 0)$ and $(2.7, 0)$ and so the solution of $x^3 - 3x^2 + 2 = 0$ is $x = -0.7$, 1 or 2.7.

These values of x are called the **roots** of the equation.

 You can probably only read the roots on this graph to one decimal place. How can you find them more accurately? They are -0.732, 1.000 and 2.732 to 3 decimal places.

You can also use the graph to solve inequalities like $x^3 - 3x^2 + 2 \geqslant 0$. This is true where the graph is above the x axis and so the solution is $-0.732 \leqslant x \leqslant 1.000$ or $x \geqslant 2.732$.

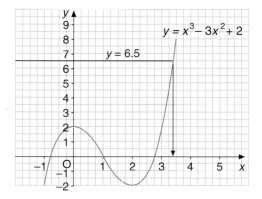

 What are the solutions of $x^3 - 3x^2 + 2 < 0$ and $x^3 - 3x^2 + 2 > 0$?

You can also use the graph above to solve an equation like

$$x^3 - 3x^2 + 2 = 6.5$$

Draw the line $y = 6.5$ on the graph.

You can see that the line $y = 6.5$ crosses the curve at the point $(3.4, 6.5)$.

So the solution of $x^3 - 3x^2 + 2 = 6.5$ is $x = 3.4$. This is the only root because the red line only crosses the curve in this one place.

Notice that the equation $x^3 - 3x^2 + 2 = 6.5$ can also be written as $x^3 - 3x^2 - 4.5 = 0$.

So another way to solve the equation is to draw the graph of $y = x^3 - 3x^2 - 4.5$ and see where it crosses the x axis.

 Are there ever just two roots to a cubic equation?

Exercise 11.4

1 The curve in the graph has equation $y = x^3 - 3x^2 - x + 4$.

Use the graph to estimate the solution of

a) $x^3 - 3x^2 - x + 4 = 0$

b) $x^3 - 3x^2 - x + 4 \geqslant 0$

c) (i) $x^3 - 3x^2 - x + 4 = 2$.   (ii) Simplify this equation.

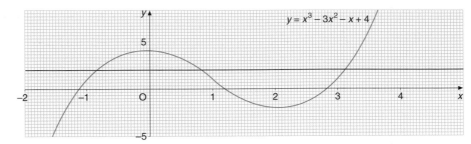

2 a) Copy and complete this table of values for $y = x^2 - 4x + 2$

x	−1	0	1	2	3	4	5
x^2	1			4			
$-4x$		0		−8	−12		
$+2$			2	2			2
y				−2			

b) Use the table to draw the graph of $y = x^2 - 4x + 2$ for values of x from −1 to 5. Draw on it the line $y = 3$.

c) Use your graph to estimate the solution of

(i) $x^2 - 4x + 2 = 0$ (ii) $x^2 - 4x + 2 < 0$

(iii) $x^2 - 4x + 2 = 3$ (iv) $x^2 - 4x + 2 \geqslant 3$

3 a) Copy and complete this table of values for $y = x^3 - 3x + 1$.

x	−2	−1	0	1	2
x^3	−8		0	1	
$-3x$		3		−3	−6
$+1$				1	
y				−1	

b) Draw the graph of $y = x^3 - 3x + 1$ for values of x from −2 to 2.

Draw on it the line $y = 2$.

c) Use your graph to estimate the solution of

(i) $x^3 - 3x + 1 = 0$ (ii) $x^3 - 3x + 1 < 0$

(iii) $x^3 - 3x + 1 = 2$ (iv) $x^3 - 3x + 1 < 2$

d) What extra points would you plot for more accurate answers?

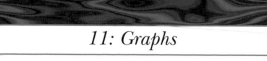
Exercise 11.4 *continued*

4   a)   Copy and complete this table of values for $y = 2x^3 - 9x^2 + 12$.

x	-1.5	-1	0	1	2	3	4	5
$2x^3$	-6.75	-2		2	16			250
$-9x^2$	-20.25			-9		-81		
$+12$	$+12$		12	12			12	
y	-15			5				

   b)   Draw the graph of $y = 2x^3 - 9x^2 + 12$ for values of x from -1.5 to 5.

   c)   Use your graph to estimate the solution of

     (i) $2x^3 - 9x^2 + 12 = 0$ (ii) $2x^3 - 9x^2 + 12 \geqslant 0$

     (ii) $2x^3 - 9x^2 + 12 = 10$ (iv) $2x^3 - 9x^2 + 12 < 10$

5   a)   Copy and complete this table of values for $y = x + \dfrac{1}{x}$.

x	$\dfrac{1}{5}$	$\dfrac{1}{4}$	$\dfrac{1}{3}$	$\dfrac{1}{2}$	1	2	3	4	5
$\dfrac{1}{x}$	5		3		1	$\dfrac{1}{2}$		$\dfrac{1}{4}$	
y	$5\dfrac{1}{5}$		$3\dfrac{1}{3}$			$2\dfrac{1}{2}$		$4\dfrac{1}{4}$	

   b)   Draw the graph of $y = x + \dfrac{1}{x}$ for the range of values of x shown in
the table. (You will need to choose your scale carefully.) Draw on it the
line $y = 3.5$.

   c)   Use your graph to estimate the solution of $x + \dfrac{1}{x} = 3.5$.

   d)   Does the equation $x + \dfrac{1}{x} = 0$ have any roots

     (i) if x is positive

     (ii) if x can take any value?

6   a)   Estimate the solution of the equation $x^3 - 4x - 3 = 0$ graphically,
taking values of x from -2 to 3.

   b)   Use your graph to estimate the solution of the equation $x^3 - 4x - 3 = 4$.

Investigation

When you are drawing graphs, it is always a good idea to check that you have
done it correctly with a graphical calculator.

Use a graphical calculator to check the graphs you have drawn for this exercise.

Then use the trace facility to check your solutions to the equations.

Exercise 12.2

1 Find the length of the arc AB and the area of the shaded sector AOB in each of these circles. Give the answers for perimeters in both cm and m and those for areas in both cm² and m².

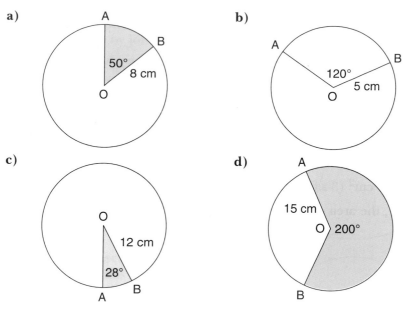

a)

b)

c)

d)

2 Find the missing quantities in the table below.

	Radius (cm)	Angle of sector (°)	Arc length (cm)	Area of sector (cm²)
a)	6	75	?	?
b)	10	?	12	?
c)	?	120	15	?
d)	4	?	?	30
e)	?	150	?	53
f)	?	?	8	25

3 The diagram below shows the area cleared by a windscreen wiper blade.

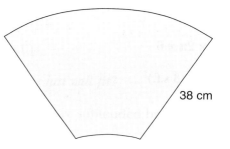

38 cm

The whole wiper arm is 45 cm long and the blade (the part that actually wipes the screen) is 38 cm long. The blade turns through an angle of 72° as it wipes. Find the distance travelled by the tip of the blade in one wipe and also the area wiped by the blade.

Exercise 12.2 *continued*

4 Find the perimeter and area of each of these shapes. (They are not drawn to scale.)

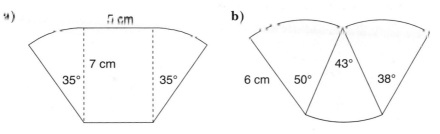

5 The diagram shows a cake with radius 10 cm, which has been cut into two pieces by slicing along a chord AB which subtends an angle of 130° at the centre of the circle.

a) Find the area of the sector AOB.

b) Find the area of the triangle AOB. (Hint: you will need to use trigonometry.)

c) Find the area of the smaller piece of the cake.

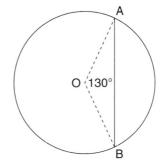

6 The diagram below shows a chain on a bicycle.

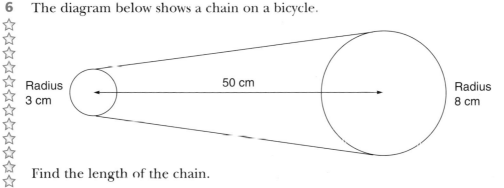

Find the length of the chain.

7 The diagram shows a section of the seating area in a cinema. Each row of seats forms an arc of a circle.

The manager of the cinema wants to know the area of the section. He measures the distances around the edge of the section. The measurements are shown on the diagram.

Find the area of the section.

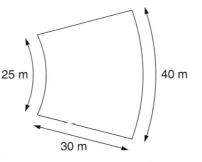

Using nets to construct solid shapes

Look at this diagram. It is the net of a pyramid, A.

How can you make use of a net?

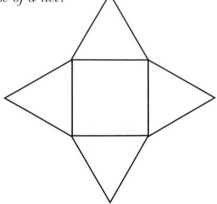

The four triangles are congruent. What does this tell you about the shape of the pyramid?

Here is the net of another pyramid, B.

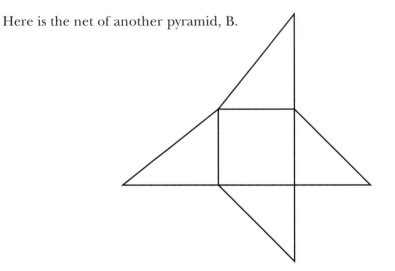

Which triangles in this net are congruent?

Look at the two pyramids below. Which is A and which is B? How can you tell?

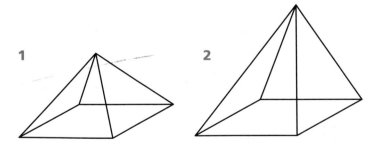

1

2

Plans and elevations

Here are three views of pyramid A.

From on top.

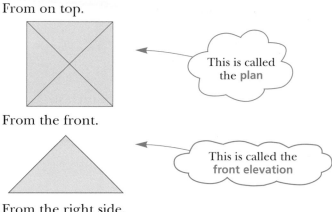

This is called the **plan**

From the front.

This is called the **front elevation**

From the right side.

This is called a **side elevation**

Here are the plan and elevations of pyramid B.
Which is which?

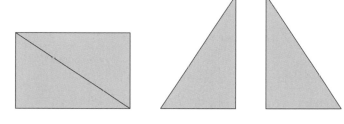

Exercise 12.3

Sketch nets for the following shapes. In each case say which triangle or other shapes in the nets must be congruent.

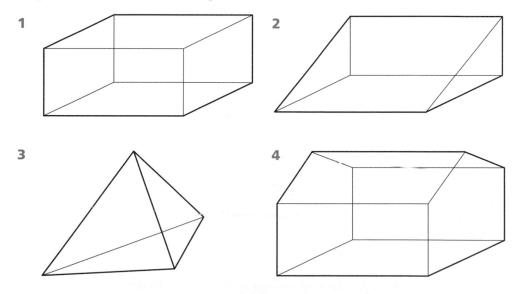

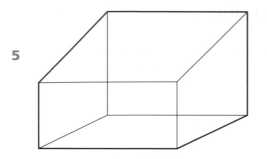

5

Now draw the plan, front elevation and (right) side elevation of each stage.

Volume and surface area of solid shapes

Prisms and cylinders

You are already familiar with the formulae for the volume of a prism

Volume of a prism = Area of cross-section × Length

and a cylinder (a special type of prism)

Volume of a cylinder = $\pi r^2 h$

A formula can be found for the surface area of a cylinder.

If the curved surface of a cylinder is opened out, it becomes a rectangle.

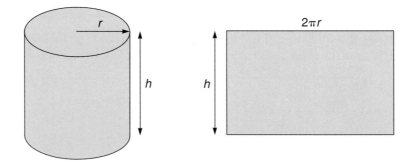

 Why must the length of the rectangle be $2\pi r$?

The area of the curved surface of the cylinder is therefore $2\pi r \times h$.

Curved surface of cylinder = $2\pi rh$

If you need the surface area of the whole cylinder, then you have to add the areas of the two circular ends.

 Write down a formula for the surface area of the whole cylinder.

The surface area of any prism can be found using the formula

**Surface area of a prism = Perimeter of cross-section × Length
+ 2 × Cross-sectional area**

Explain why this formula is valid.

Spheres

The formulae for the surface area and volume of a sphere are given below.
(You do not need to know the proof of these formulae.)

Volume of sphere = $\dfrac{4}{3}\pi r^3$

Surface area of sphere = $4\pi r^2$

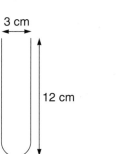

Example

A test tube consists of a cylinder with a
hemisphere at its base. The test tube is
12 cm high and has a diameter of 3 cm.

a) Find the area of material required
   to make one test tube.

b) Find the volume of liquid that the test
   tube can hold when completely full.

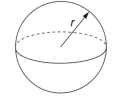

Solution

The radius, r, of both the hemisphere and the cylinder is 1.5 cm

The height of the cylinder is 12 − 1.5 cm = 10.5 cm

a) Area of curved surface of cylinder = $2\pi rh$

$$= 2\pi \times 1.5 \times 10.5$$
$$= 98.96 \text{ cm}^2$$

Area of hemisphere = $\dfrac{1}{2} \times 4\pi r^2$

$$= 2\pi \times 1.5^2$$
$$= 14.14 \text{ cm}^2$$

Total area = 113 cm^2 (3 s.f.)

b) Volume of cylinder = $\pi r^2 h$

$$= \pi \times 1.5^2 \times 10.5$$
$$= 74.22 \text{ cm}^3$$

Volume of hemisphere = $\dfrac{1}{2} \times \dfrac{4}{3}\pi r^3$

$$= \dfrac{2}{3}\pi \times 1.5^3$$
$$= 7.07 \text{ cm}^3$$

Volume of test tube = 81.3 cm^3 (3 s.f.)

Pyramids and cones

 How could you define a pyramid?

The diagram below shows a pyramid with a square base. The surface area of a pyramid can be found by adding together the areas of all the faces. The formula for the volume of a pyramid is given below.

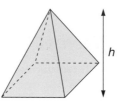

$$\text{Volume of a pyramid} = \frac{1}{3} \times \text{Base area} \times h$$

 Imagine a pyramid whose base is one face of a cube, and whose apex is the centre of the cube. Explain why the formula above must be true for this pyramid.

A cone is a pyramid with a circular base, so the formula for the volume of a cone is the same as the formula for the volume of a pyramid, but using πr^2 for the area of the base.

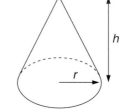

$$\text{Volume of cone} = \frac{1}{3}\pi r^2 h$$

If a cone is opened out, it becomes a sector of a circle. The radius of the circle is the same as the slanted edge, l, of the cone.

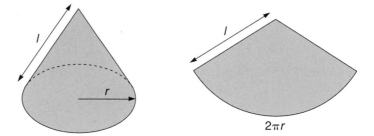

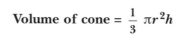 *Why must the length of the curved edge be $2\pi r$?*

What fraction of the whole circle is the sector?

Use your answer to explain why the formula below is valid.

$$\text{Curved surface area of cone} = \pi r l$$

If the whole surface area of the cone is required, the area of the circular base of the cone must be added.

The frustum of a cone

The **frustum** of a cone is the part of a cone left over when a piece is removed by making a cut parallel to the base of the cone.

Example

A plinth for a statue is made in the shape of the frustum of a cone, as shown in the diagram. Find the volume of concrete needed to make the plinth. Give the answer in both cm^3 and m^3.

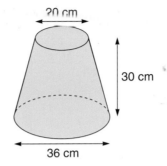

20 cm

30 cm

36 cm

Solution

First you need to find the volume of the whole cone, and then subtract the volume of the small cone which has been removed. To find the height of the whole cone, use similar triangles.

$$\frac{h}{20} = \frac{h+30}{36}$$

$$36h = 20h + 600$$

$$16h = 600$$

$$h = 37.5$$

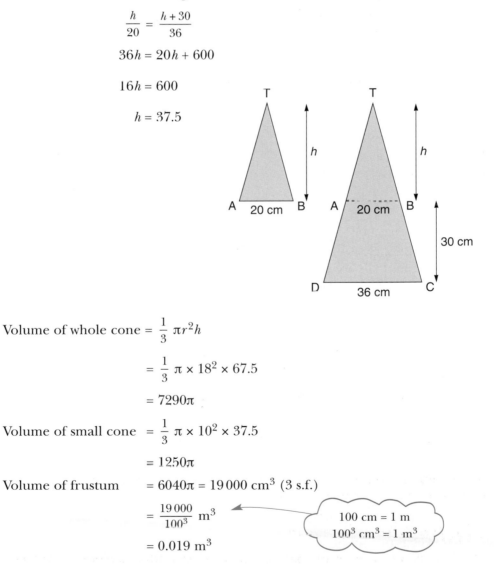

Volume of whole cone $= \frac{1}{3}\pi r^2 h$

$$= \frac{1}{3}\pi \times 18^2 \times 67.5$$

$$= 7290\pi$$

Volume of small cone $= \frac{1}{3}\pi \times 10^2 \times 37.5$

$$= 1250\pi$$

Volume of frustum $= 6040\pi = 19\,000$ cm^3 (3 s.f.)

$$= \frac{19\,000}{100^3} \text{ m}^3$$

100 cm = 1 m
100^3 cm^3 = 1 m^3

$$= 0.019 \text{ m}^3$$

How would you find the surface area of the plinth?

Exercise 12.4

1 Find the volume of each of these prisms and cylinders. Give the answers in both cm³ and m³.

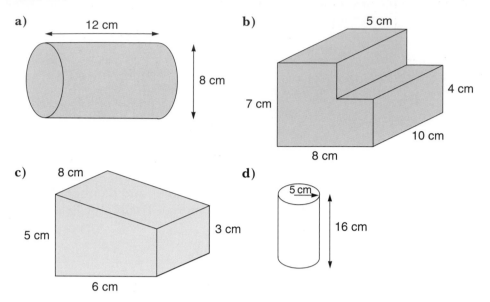

a) 12 cm 8 cm

b) 5 cm 7 cm 4 cm 10 cm 8 cm

c) 8 cm 5 cm 3 cm 6 cm

d) 5 cm 16 cm

2 Find the surface area of each of the prisms and cylinders in question 1.

3 Find the volume and surface area of each of these spheres.

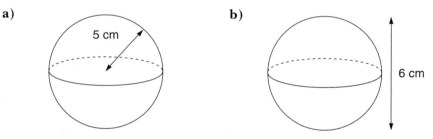

a) 5 cm

b) 6 cm

4 Four tennis balls are stored in a cylindrical container. Each tennis ball has a diameter of 8 cm.

a) Find the surface area of material used to make the container, including the lid.

b) Find the percentage of the available space which is taken up by the tennis balls.

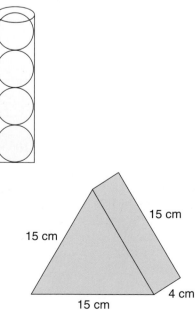

5 A box of chocolates is in the shape of a triangular prism, as shown in the diagram.

a) Find the volume of the box.

b) Sketch the net of the box, and find the area of card needed to make the prism.

15 cm 15 cm 15 cm 4 cm

Exercise 12.4 *continued*

6 Find the volume of each of these pyramids and cones.

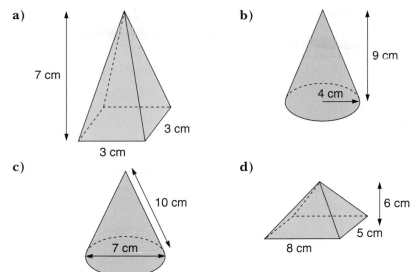

a) 7 cm, 3 cm, 3 cm

b) 9 cm, 4 cm

c) 10 cm, 7 cm

d) 6 cm, 5 cm, 8 cm

7 Find the surface area of each pyramid and cone in question 6.

8 Find the surface area and volume of this frustum of a cone.

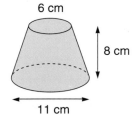

6 cm

8 cm

11 cm

9 An ice-cream cone has radius 3 cm and height 10 cm. A sphere of ice-cream, also with radius 3 cm, is placed in the top of the cone, so that half the sphere is outside the cone, and the other half (which of course gets slightly squashed, but still has the same volume!) is inside the cone.

a) What area of wafer is needed to make the cone?

b) What is the volume of the ice-cream?

c) How much space in the cone is wasted?

10 Special dice are made in the shape of a tetrahedron (each of its four faces is an equilateral triangle). The length of each edge of each die is 2 cm. Find the surface area and volume of each die.

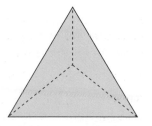

Area and volume of similar shapes

Area of similar shapes

Dave orders a 20-inch pizza to be delivered. When it arrives, the delivery boy explains that the restaurant had run out of 20-inch pizza bases, so he has brought two 10-inch pizzas instead, which Dave can have for the same price.

Dave says this is not fair because one 20-inch pizza is bigger than two 10-inch pizzas.

 Is Dave right? What do you think the pizza restaurant should have offered him?

Look at the diagram below. Both the length and the width of the rectangle on the left have been multiplied by 2, so the area is multiplied by $2 \times 2 = 2^2 = 4$.

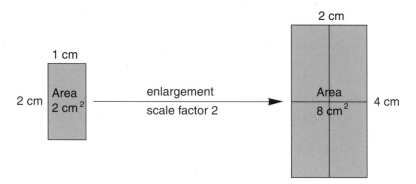

In the same way, if a rectangle is enlarged by a scale factor of 3, the length and the width have both been multiplied by 3, so the area is multiplied by $3^2 = 9$.

These rules are true for any shape, not just rectangles.

> **If a shape is enlarged by a scale factor of x,**
> **the area is multiplied by a factor of x^2.**

 How many pizzas should Dave have been offered?

Volume of similar shapes

A chocolate manufacturer decides to make a special limited edition *Giant Bar* version of its best selling *Jupiter Bar*. The *Giant Bar* will be twice as big in all directions as the standard bar. To decide on a suitable price, the manufacturer needs to know the amount of ingredients that will be needed. The standard *Jupiter Bar* contains 12 g of chocolate, 8 g of caramel and 10 g of biscuit.

To find out the amount of ingredients needed, the manufacturer needs to know something about how the volume of an enlarged solid shape compares with the volume of the original solid shape.

This diagram shows a cuboid enlarged by a scale factor of 2.

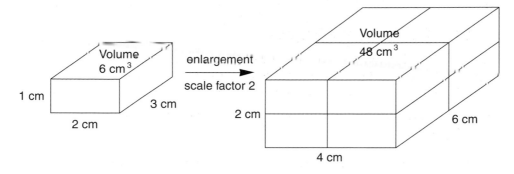

 How many of the original cuboids fit into the enlarged cuboid?

The length, the width and the height have all been multiplied by 2, so the volume is multiplied by $2 \times 2 \times 2 = 2^3 = 8$.

If the original cuboid is enlarged by a scale factor of 3, the length, width and height have all been multiplied by 3, so the area is multiplied by $3^3 = 27$.

**If a solid shape is enlarged by a scale factor of *x*,
the volume is multiplied by a factor of x^3.**

The chocolate manufacturer will therefore need to multiply the ingredients for the standard *Jupiter Bar* by 8 to find the ingredients needed for the *Giant Bar*.

Chocolate needed = $12 \times 8 = 96$ g

Caramel needed = $8 \times 8 = 64$ g

Biscuit needed = $10 \times 8 = 80$ g

Example

A toy car is available in two sizes. The smaller version is 8 cm long. It requires 30 cm^3 of metal to make it and has a surface area for painting of 80 cm^2. The larger version of the car is a scaled-up model of the smaller one, and is 20 cm long.

a) Find the volume of metal required to make the larger car.

b) Find the surface area for painting of the larger car.

Solution

The scale factor of the enlargement = $20 \div 8 = 2.5$

a) The volume is multiplied by 2.5^3

The volume of the large car = $30 \times 2.5^3 = 468.75 \text{ cm}^3$

b) The area is multiplied by 2.5^2

The surface area of the large car $= 80 \times 2.5^2 = 500 \text{ cm}^2$

Exercise 12.5

1   Each pair of shapes shown below are similar. Find the area of the second shape in each diagram.

a)

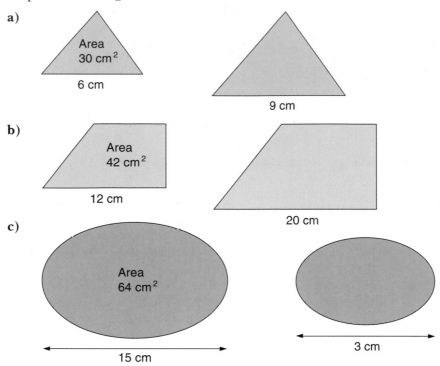

Area
30 cm^2

6 cm

9 cm

b)

Area
42 cm^2

12 cm

20 cm

c)

Area
64 cm^2

15 cm

3 cm

2   Each pair of solid shapes shown below are similar. Find the volume of the second solid in each diagram.

a)

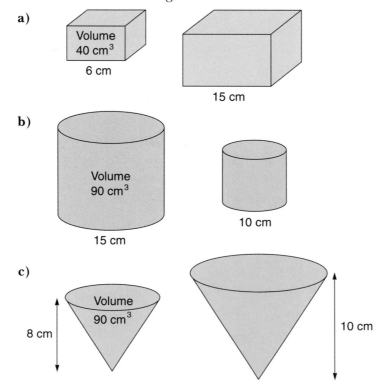

Volume
40 cm^3

6 cm

15 cm

b)

Volume
90 cm^3

15 cm

10 cm

c)

8 cm

Volume
90 cm^3

10 cm

Exercise 12.5 *continued*

3   A museum sells scale model plastic replicas of one of the statues on display. The real statue is 1.5 m tall, and the model is 5 cm tall. 45 cm³ of plastic is needed to make each model. What is the volume of the real statue?

4   Winston is making a scale model of his bedroom, using the scale 1 : 10. He paints the walls of his model bedroom and finds that he uses 50 ml of paint. How much paint would Winston need to paint the walls of his real bedroom? (Assume that the thickness of each coat of paint is the same.)

5   A wedding cake has three tiers which are similar shapes. The widths of each tier are 6", 9" and 11".

    a)   The volume of the smallest cake is 120 cubic inches. What are the volumes of the other two cakes?

    b)   The area to be iced on the smallest cake is 100 square inches. What is the area to be iced on the other two cakes?

6   A children's clothing catalogue includes a sleepsuit in three different sizes.

Newborn	height 55 cm
0–3 months	height 62 cm
3–6 months	height 68 cm

The Newborn size costs £5. What would be fair prices for the other two sizes?

7   Carpet is sold by the square metre. Mrs Williams is buying two pieces of carpet, similar in shape, but different sizes. The larger piece is 6 metres long and costs £225. The smaller piece costs £100. How long is the smaller piece?

8   Lemonade is sold in a bottle which is 24 cm tall and holds 800 ml of lemonade. A larger size bottle is to be made which will be similar to the smaller one but will hold 1500 ml of lemonade. How tall should the new bottle be?

9   Chocolate-coated fudge bars are sold in two different sizes, weighing 100g and 150g. The chocolate coating is the same thickness on both bars. The smaller bar requires 10 cm³ of chocolate to coat it.

    a)   How much does the larger bar require?

    b)   A new size weighing W grams is to be made. Find an expression for the amount of chocolate needed to coat it.

Dimensions of formulae

You have met a large number of formulae for perimeters, areas and volumes. You can tell whether a particular formula is for length, area or volume by considering the number of dimensions in the formula.

The number of dimensions in a formula is the number of measurements of length that are multiplied together in the formula. (Numbers, like 2 or π, do not count as dimensions.)

Formulae for lengths have one dimension, for those area have two and for volume have three.

Examples

$$lwh$$

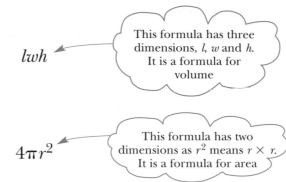

This formula has three dimensions, l, w and h. It is a formula for volume

 What solid shape has this volume?

$$4\pi r^2$$

This formula has two dimensions as r^2 means $r \times r$. It is a formula for area

 This is actually a surface area. What solid shape has this surface area?

$$2(l + h)$$

This formula has one dimension. The l and the h have been added together so they count as one dimension. It is a formula for length

 What shape has this perimeter?

 Draw a table with four columns, headed 'Length', 'Area', 'Volume' and 'None of these'. Check the dimensions of each formula below, then write it in the appropriate column.

   a) $\dfrac{4}{3}\pi p^3$ **b)** $\pi p(p + r)$ **c)** $\dfrac{1}{3} p^2 q$

   d) $p + q + r$ **e)** $pq^2 r$ **f)** πpq^2

   g) πp^2 **h)** $\dfrac{1}{2} pq$ **i)** $\dfrac{1}{3} \pi p^2 q$

   j) $2\pi q(p + q)$ **k)** $2\pi p$ **l)** $pq + pr^2$

   m) pqr **n)** $4\pi p^2$ **o)** $2(pq + qr + pr)$

Finishing off

Use the questions in the next exercise to check that you understand everything.

Mixed exercise 12.6

1 Find the arc length and area of each of these sectors of circles.

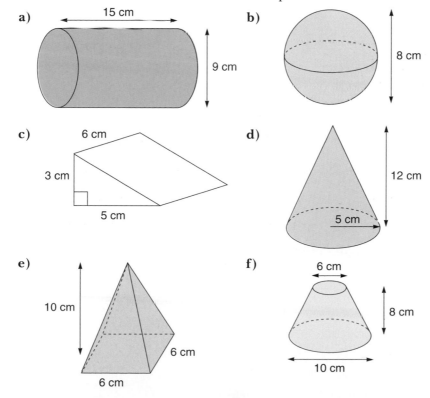

2 Find the volume of each of these solid shapes.

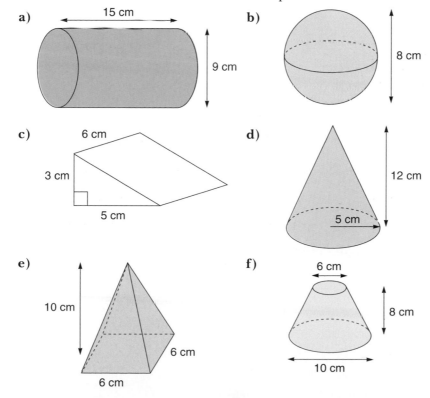

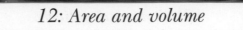
Mixed exercise 12.6 *continued*

3   In this question *a*, *b*, *c* and *d* represent lengths.

   A $\dfrac{ab}{cd}$ B acd C $\sqrt{abc}$ D $\pi ab + vd$ E $\pi a + \dfrac{b+c}{d}$

   Which formula represents

   a) an area,

   b) a volume?   *MEI*

4   One of these expressions gives the
   perimeter of the shape shown, and
   one gives the area.

   A: $\pi a^2 b$ B: πab C: $\pi a^2 b^2$
   D: $\pi(a+b)$ E: πab^2

   Which is the correct expression for

   a) the perimeter,

   b) the area?

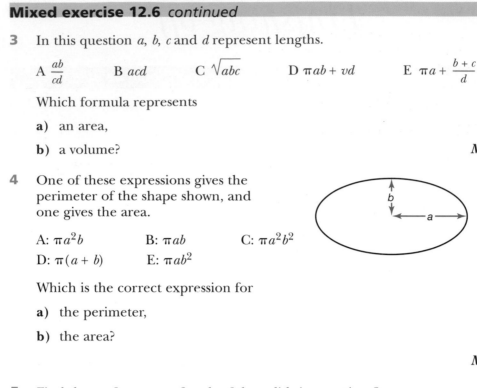

                                                                           MEI

5   Find the surface area of each of the solids in question 2.

6   These three shapes are similar to each other.
   a) Find the area of shape B   **b)** the base length of shape C.

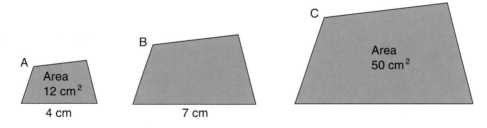

7   These three solid shapes are all similar to each other.
   Find **a)** the volume of shape Q **b)** the height of shape R.

8   **a)** Find the length of the minor
       arc of AB.

   b) Find the area of the shaded
       segment.

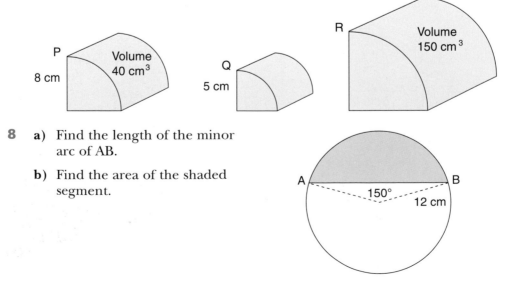

Mixed exercise 12.6 *continued*

9   A spinning top consists of a cone
    and a hemisphere, as shown in the
    diagram.

    a)   Find the volume of the
         spinning top.

    b)   Find the surface area of the
         spinning top.

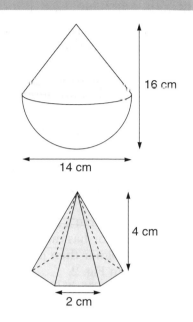

16 cm

14 cm

10 A chocolate is in the shape of a
    pyramid. The pyramid has
    hexagonal base of side 2 cm.
    The height of the pyramid is 4 cm.
    Find the volume of the chocolate.

4 cm

2 cm

11 A set of plastic flower pots comes in three different sizes, small, medium
    and large. They are all similar shapes. The small pot is 8 cm tall, needs an
    area of 280 cm^2 of plastic to make it, and holds 500 cm^3 of soil.

    a)   The medium pot is 11 cm tall. What area of plastic is needed to make
         it, and what volume of soil does it hold?

    b)   The large pot is 15 cm tall. What area of plastic is needed to make it,
         and what volume of soil does it hold?

12 Find the perimeter and area of the shaded region in the diagram below.

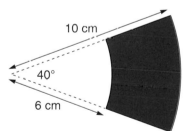

10 cm

40°

6 cm

13 a)   A 60° sector is cut from
         a cylindrical cheese
         of radius 8 cm and
         height 3 cm.

         Calculate the volume
         remaining.

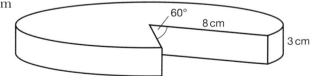

60°
8 cm
3 cm

    b)   A shop sells spherical cheeses in two sizes.
         One has twice the diameter of the other.
         The volume of the larger one is 612 cm^3.

         Calculate the volume of the smaller cheese.

MEI

251

Significant figures

When you round to a chosen number of significant figures, you start counting at the first non-zero digit (from the left).

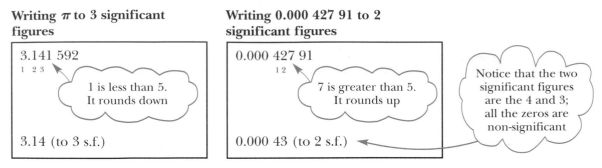

Writing π to 3 significant figures

3.141 592
1 2 3

1 is less than 5. It rounds down

3.14 (to 3 s.f.)

Writing 0.000 427 91 to 2 significant figures

0.000 427 91
        1 2

7 is greater than 5. It rounds up

0.000 43 (to 2 s.f.)

Notice that the two significant figures are the 4 and 3; all the zeros are non-significant

You have to be careful when rounding numbers greater than 1.

When 7952 is rounded to 1 significant figure it becomes 8000. The 8 is the 1 significant figure; the three 0s are all non-significant but they must still be there. If you miss some of them out, you will write 8, 80 or 800 and these numbers are completely different in size from the original 7952.

What do you get when you round 7952 to 2 significant figures? Which digits are significant and which are non-significant?

What do you get when you round 97.6 to 1 significant figure?

Caution

Always round in one stage only, otherwise you may end up with the wrong answer. Take, for example, rounding 0.7649 to 2 decimal places.

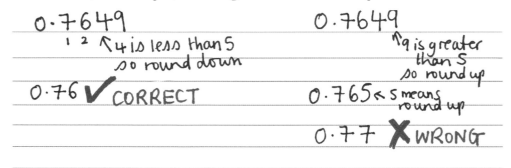

0.7649
     1 2   ↖ 4 is less than 5
           so round down

0.76 ✔ CORRECT

0.7649
        ↖ 9 is greater than 5
           so round up

0.765 ← 5 means round up

0.77 ✘ WRONG

Working with your calculator

Sometimes you need to use your calculator on problems with several stages. Each has its answer which you then use for the next part. You should always keep the current answer on your calculator and work with it, but at the same time you may find it helpful to keep a written record as you go through.

It is useful to use dots to show that there are more figures on your calculator display. When you write 63.4… it means at least 63.4 but less than 63.5.

Giving answers exactly

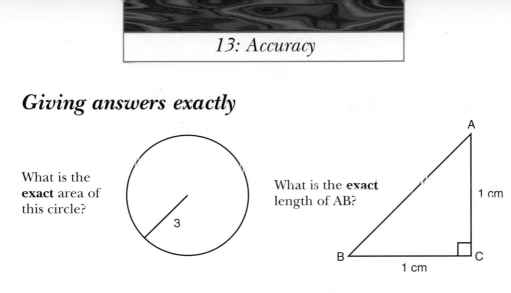

What is the **exact** area of this circle?

3

What is the **exact** length of AB?

A

1 cm

B

1 cm

C

Look at these two questions. In both cases exact values are requested.

The only way this can be done is to use mathematical symbols, like π and $\sqrt{\ }$.

The exact area of the circle is 9π. Even if you gave it as a number to 100 significant figures, it would still be rounded and so not exact. Similarly the exact length of the line AB is $\sqrt{2}$ cm.

Does your calculator display include symbols like π and $\sqrt{\ }$?

Exercise 13.1

1 Write these numbers to the accuracy given.

a) 2.813 6 to 1 decimal place

b) 72.805 9 to 2 decimal places

c) 0.005 67 to 3 decimal places

d) 0.005 67 to 1 significant figure

e) 12.811 to 3 significant figures

f) 412.85 to 3 significant figures

g) 0.000 156 to 2 decimal places

h) 433.9 to 2 significant figures

i) 23.859 to 1 decimal place

j) 6600 to 1 significant figure

2 The number 23.689 is rounded to 23.7. Which of the following are correct descriptions of the rounding and which are incorrect?

a) to 3 decimal places

b) to the nearest $\dfrac{1}{10}$

c) to 3 significant figures

d) to 1 decimal place

e) to 1 significant figure

Exercise 13.1 *continued*

3 A railway company asks the guard to count the number of passengers using a particular train service on each of 20 days. The actual numbers of passengers are as follows:

68	74	92	86	55		78	76	62	54	82
90	77	66	82	59		59	60	70	68	73

a) What is the mean number of passengers per day?

The company tells the guard to record the numbers to the nearest 5.

b) (i) Write down the 20 numbers that the guard tells the company.

(ii) Find the mean of these numbers.

The company then decides to round the guard's figures to the nearest 10, using the rule '5 rounds up', and then to work out the mean.

c) What answer does the company get for the mean?

d) What mistake is the company making?

e) If the company followed this procedure for a large number of trains, what would you expect their error to be?

Errors

Look at this headline. How many people really took part in the protest march? The answer is that no one knows exactly but, if the report is to be believed, the number was nearer 17 000 than 16 000 or 18 000. In other words between 16 500 and 17 500.

You could call the number n and say

$$16\,500 \leqslant n < 17\,500$$

This can be shown on a number line:

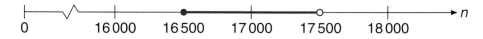

Notice: (i) how the inequality signs are used. By convention the mid-way points round up.

16500 → 17000. It is included.
17500 → 18000. It is not included.

(ii) the symbols used on the number line.
● means the value, in this case 16 500, is included.
○ means the value, in this case 17 500, is not included.
√‾ means there is a break in the scale.

Measure the length, l, of this line in cm, using an ordinary ruler.

How accurate is your answer?

A ruler is marked every $\frac{1}{10}$ of a centimetre, that is every millimetre, and this is the level of accuracy to which you should be able to measure.

Three people measure the line and give these answers:

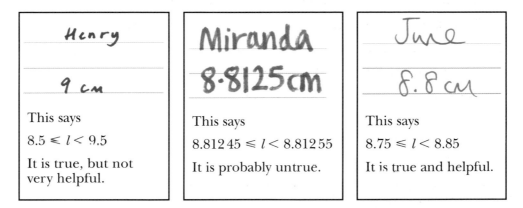

Henry	Miranda	June
9 cm	8·8125 cm	8.8 cm
This says	This says	This says
$8.5 \leqslant l < 9.5$	$8.812\,45 \leqslant l < 8.812\,55$	$8.75 \leqslant l < 8.85$
It is true, but not very helpful.	It is probably untrue.	It is true and helpful.

Whenever you give a measurement, you are also saying something about how accurate you believe it to be.

 *Do you think these measurements are given too accurately, just about right or not accurately enough?*

a) *Janet's weight is 46 kg.*
b) *Raja takes about 2 hours to run a marathon.*
c) *The cost of a typical evening out is £12.65.*

There are other ways of specifying the accuracy of a number you write down.

Error bounds

$t = 7.3 \pm 0.1$ means that t lies between $7.3 - 0.1 = 7.2$

and $7.3 + 0.1 = 7.4$

In this case, 0.1 could also be called the **tolerance**.

The diagram shows how error bounds are indicated on a graph.

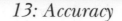

Percentage error

Errors may also be given as percentages. For example 'The number of people was $25\,000 \pm 10\%$'. Since 10% of 25 000 is 2500, this means that the number of people was between

$$25\,000 - 2500 = 22\,500$$
$$\text{and} \quad 25\,000 + 2500 = 27\,500$$

When you work out a percentage error, always base your calculation on the true value (if you know it) as in the next example.

Example

Veronica does an experiment to find the value of g, the acceleration due to gravity. The true value is 9.81 ms^{-2}; Veronica's result is 10.32 ms^{-2}.

Find **a)** the error and **b)** the percentage error, in Veronica's result.

Solution

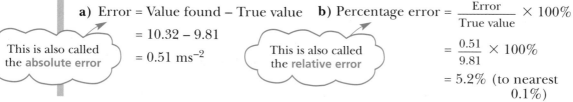

a) Error = Value found − True value   **b)** Percentage error = $\dfrac{\text{Error}}{\text{True value}} \times 100\%$

This is also called the **absolute error**

$$= 10.32 - 9.81$$
$$= 0.51 \text{ ms}^{-2}$$

This is also called the **relative error**

$$= \frac{0.51}{9.81} \times 100\%$$
$$= 5.2\% \text{ (to nearest } 0.1\%)$$

Sometimes the accuracy of a number is not clear from the way you say or write it. How accurate are the numbers in these statements?

a) *The rope is 30 m long.*
b) *The aeroplane is 45 minutes late.*

Exercise 13.2

1 Write algebraic statements, using inequalities and the letters indicated, to describe what you understand by these statements.

    a) There were 600 people at the rally (n)

    b) The thickness of the book is 4 cm (t)

    c) The tunnel will cost £4 billion (c)

    d) The quantity of lead present in the sample was 0.000 042 g (l)

    e) Jane is 99 years old (j)

    f) The number is 1.414... (x)

2 State the maximum error you expect in these measurements.

    a) The length is 25.42 cm.

    b) The thickness is 0.072 mm.

    c) The journey takes 6 hours.

    d) The mass is 4.613 g.

    e) The estimated cost is £2000.

Exercise 13.2 *continued*

3   Four of these descriptions of a length *l* are equivalent, but three are not. Which ones are equivalent?

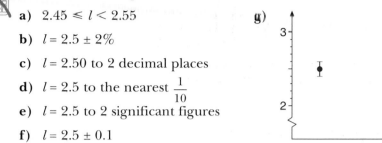

a) $2.45 \leqslant l < 2.55$

b) $l = 2.5 \pm 2\%$

c) $l = 2.50$ to 2 decimal places

d) $l = 2.5$ to the nearest $\dfrac{1}{10}$

e) $l = 2.5$ to 2 significant figures

f) $l = 2.5 \pm 0.1$

g)

4   In an experiment Boris finds the concentration of a chemical to be 19.8 grams per litre. The true value is 18.0. Find

a) the error in Boris's result   b) the percentage error in his result.

5   Janet measures the height of a table to be 69 cm. The true value is 75 cm. Find

a) the error in Janet's measurement   b) the percentage error.

6   A scientist carries out an experiment to find the density of a substance. She states her result as '4.29 grams per cubic centimetre'. This value is too high; her error is 10%. What is the true value?

7   Selina and Leon both do the same experiment to measure a quantity, *P*. Selina's result is 99 units and Leon's is 118.8 units; both of these results may be up to 10% in error (but no more).

a) Show that one of these results must be greater than the true value of *P* and one less than it.

b) State the range of possible values of *P* in the form $\ldots \leqslant P \leqslant \ldots$.

Accumulating errors

What is the area of this trapezium?

Using the formula

$$A = \frac{1}{2}(a + b)h$$

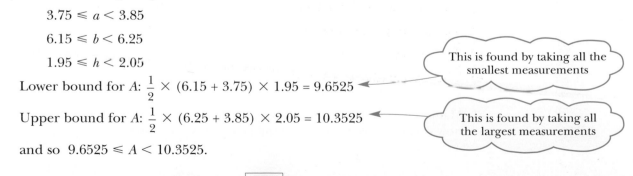

gives $\dfrac{1}{2} \times (6.2 + 3.8) \times 2.0 = 10 \text{ cm}^2$ for the area.

How accurate is this answer?

Look at the range of possible values of the measurements:

$3.75 \leqslant a < 3.85$

$6.15 \leqslant b < 6.25$

$1.95 \leqslant h < 2.05$

Lower bound for *A*: $\dfrac{1}{2} \times (6.15 + 3.75) \times 1.95 = 9.6525$

This is found by taking all the smallest measurements

Upper bound for *A*: $\dfrac{1}{2} \times (6.25 + 3.85) \times 2.05 = 10.3525$

This is found by taking all the largest measurements

and so $9.6525 \leqslant A < 10.3525$.

The error involved in estimating A to be 10 can be slightly more than 3.6%. Explain how this figure is obtained. This is bigger than the possible percentage error in any of the measurements. Why?

In the example of the trapezium the smallest possible measurements gave the smallest possible area, and vice versa, but this is not always the case.

Example

On a field trip a geologist finds a small piece of rock which he thinks could be a meteorite. He uses his available equipment to make these measurements.

Mass = 1.6 grams (to nearest 0.1 g)

Volume = 0.3 cubic centimetres (to nearest 0.1 cm^3)

Between what values does its density lie?

Solution

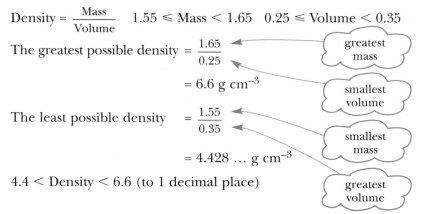

Density = $\dfrac{\text{Mass}}{\text{Volume}}$ $1.55 \leqslant \text{Mass} < 1.65$ $0.25 \leqslant \text{Volume} < 0.35$

The greatest possible density = $\dfrac{1.65}{0.25}$

= 6.6 g cm^{-3}

The least possible density = $\dfrac{1.55}{0.35}$

= 4.428 … g cm^{-3}

4.4 < Density < 6.6 (to 1 decimal place)

greatest mass

smallest volume

smallest mass

greatest volume

Exercise 13.3

1   In each of these calculations, the numbers have been rounded to the accuracy shown. State the range of values that the answers may take. If an answer is not exact, give it to 3 significant figures.

a) 2.45 + 2.86 + 3.3 + 6.052   b) 5.8 − 5.6

c) 21 × 29   d) $\dfrac{14.2}{7.1}$

e) $\dfrac{125 \times 31.4}{22}$ f) $\dfrac{18.6 - 18.3}{5.22 - 5.19}$

2   Sections of a railway line are measured to the nearest metre as either 200 m or 80 m.

What are the upper and lower bounds on the total length of 15 sections, consisting of eight 200 m sections and seven 80 m sections?   ***SEG***

3   Alka and Manoj are going on holiday. They have four suitcases which they weigh to the nearest kg on their bathroom scales as: 15 kg, 10 kg, 9 kg, 7 kg. Their total baggage allowance is 40 kg.

a) State the range of possible values of the total weight of their cases.

b) Is it possible that they are not overweight?

c) Manoj takes out a pair of boots which he weighs to be 3 kg. Are they now certain to be within the limit? Explain your answer.

Exercise 13.3 *continued*

4   Mary goes for a walk. The distance is 10 km to the nearest 1 km and it takes her 90 minutes, to the nearest 10 minutes.

Find the range of possible values of the following quantities.
(If an answer is not exact, give it to 3 significant figures.)

a)   the time she takes, in seconds

b)   the distance she walks, in metres

c)   her average speed in

   (i) metres per second   (ii) kilometres per hour.

5   Correct to 3 decimal places, $a = 2.236$.

a)   For this value of a write down

   (i)   the upper bound

   (ii) the lower bound.

Correct to 3 decimal places, $b = 1.414$.

b)   Calculate

   (i)   the upper bound for the value of $a + b$

   (ii) the lower bound for the value of $a + b$.

Write down all the figures on your calculator display for parts c) and d) of this question.

c)   Calculate the lower bound for the value of ab.

d)   Calculate the upper bound for the value of $\dfrac{a}{b}$.

London

6   Roger needs to give his cat, Meffy, some pills but first he has to weigh Meffy. He stands on his bathroom scales holding Meffy; the reading is 88 kg. He then puts Meffy down and the reading becomes 85 kg. Both readings are correct to the nearest 1 kg (the accuracy of the scales).

a)   What are the lower and upper bounds for Meffy's weight?

b)   The correct dose is given in this table.

How many tablets should Roger give Meffy?

Exercise 13.3 *continued*

7 Simon is one of the timers at an amateur athletics event. For the 200 m race the start is some distance from the finish. Simon starts his stop watch when he sees the smoke from the starting pistol; this can be anything up to 0.2 seconds after the race has actually begun. He stands on the finishing line and stops the watch when the runner goes by with an accuracy of ± 0.05 seconds.

a) Simon gives Maria a time of 26.42 seconds. What is the range of times she could actually have taken?

b) Show the range of Maria's possible times on a number line.

c) Simon is timing the third place in each of the 6 heats of the event. The four runners with the fastest times will go through to the next round. He gives the times for the other runners as: Adowa 25.50, Felicity 26.90, Amy 27.47, Tessa 26.65, Karabi 26.52.

For each runner, state whether she was definitely in the four fastest, might have been or was definitely not.

Rough calculations

You often need to make rough calculations. Two situations are particularly important.

● You want to check that a figure is roughly right. This could, for example, be a bill you are being asked to pay, or it could be an answer on your calculator.

● You want to estimate a quantity, like the number of potatoes in a typical sack, where an exact answer may be meaningless.

To carry out a rough calculation, round all the numbers so that they become easy to work with.

Example   Find the rough total of £9.99, £6.95, £11.99 and £4.50.

Solution   £9.99 —— is about ➤ £10.00

£6.95 —— is about ➤ £ 7.00

£11.99 —— is about ➤ £12.00

£4.50 —— is about ➤ £ 4.50

£33.50

Notice that you could have rounded £4.50 to £5.00. In that case the answer would have been £34; that is still a good approximation for the actual total of £33.43.

You must be very careful if subtraction is involved, as in the case of

$$\frac{28.4 \times 321.8}{18.62 - 18.39}$$

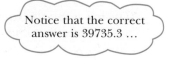

Notice that the correct answer is 39735.3 …

The top line is straightforward: $30 \times 300 = 9000$.

The bottom line requires more thought. Rounding $18.62 \to 19$ and $18.39 \to 18$ would give: $19 - 18 = 1$ and $\frac{9000}{1} = 9000$, which is nothing like the right answer.

The problem is that the difference between 18.62 and 18.39 is small compared to the size of the numbers; it is just 0.23. Rounding $18.62 \to 18.6$ and $18.39 \to 18.4$ is better. That gives $\frac{9000}{0.2} = 45\,000$, which is much closer.

It is often helpful to write numbers in standard form before doing a rough calculation.

Example

John works out $\dfrac{2\,341\,921\,611 \times 0.005\,846\,32}{112463}$

on his calculator.
His answer is 1217.433…
John does not believe his answer.
Find an approximate answer. Is John's answer wrong?

Solution

Approximate answer is $\dfrac{2 \times 10^9 \times 6 \times 10^{-3}}{1 \times 10^5}$

$$= 12 \times 10^{9-3-5}$$

$$= 12 \times 10^1$$

$$= 120$$

John's answer is clearly wrong.

If you have to estimate a quantity you will usually use rough figures from the very start. Here is Owen's estimate for the cost of a week's driving holiday in the Scottish Highlands for 2 people.

	EXPENSES ON HOLS	
TRAVEL	7 days @ 200 miles a day @ 30p a mile $7 \times 200 \times £0.30 =$	£420
NIGHTS	7 nights @ £40 a night $\qquad 7 \times £40 \quad =$	£280
MEALS	7 days for 2 people at £20 $\quad 7 \times 2 \times £20 =$	£280
SPENDING	£150 each $\qquad\qquad\qquad =$	£300
	TOTAL	£1280
	ROUGH ESTIMATE £1300	

Exercise 13.4

1 Carl has done the following sums on a calculator. In each case his answer is given beside it. Some of his answers are right and some are wrong.

(i) Do a rough calculation to check whether Carl's answer is reasonable.

(ii) If you think Carl's answer is wrong, use your calculator to find the right answer, giving it to 3 significant figures.

a) $26.79 \times 512.305 - 62.81 \times 54.3$ 65400 (nearest 100)

b) $\dfrac{210.3 + 489.1}{2165.91 - 2131.62}$ 20.4 (1 d.p.)

c) $2.1^3 \times 2.9^4 \times 1.04^5$ 796.923 ...

d) $\sqrt{(132^2 + 85^2)}$ 217

e) $117\frac{1}{2}$ % of £263.99 + £517.45   £918.19 (nearest 1 d.p.)

f) $2 \times \pi \times 11.1 \times 6.3 + 2 \times \pi \times 11.1^2$ 1210 (3 sig. figs)

g) $3.79 \times \sin 85.1°$ −1.036 (3 d.p.)

h) $\dfrac{3 \times 13 + 7 \times 14 + 6 \times 15 + 4 \times 16}{3 + 7 + 6 + 4}$ 14.55

i) $14\,978\,000\,000 \times 365 \times 24 \times 3600$ 4.7×10^{17} (2 sig. figs)

j) $\dfrac{1.989 \times 10^{33}}{9.108 \times 10^{-24}}$ 218×10^8 (3 sig. figs)

2 Estimate

a) the number of passengers on a reasonably full mainline train with 8 carriages

b) the number of words in this book

c) the number of seconds, in total, the people in your mathematics group have been alive

d) the mass of your hand

e) the cost of a dinner party for 6 people.

3 The moon appears to be about the same size as one of these circles held at arm's length. You can find out which one by experiment on a moonlit night, or you can cheat by looking in the answers at the back of the

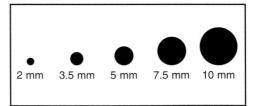

2 mm   3.5 mm   5 mm   7.5 mm   10 mm

book. The distance of the moon from Earth is known to be about a quarter of a million miles. The density of the moon is believed to be about 3.3 grams per cubic centimetre.

a) Use this information to estimate the mass of the moon in kg.

The sun appears to be the same size as the moon. The sun is 93 million miles from the earth. The mass of the sun is known to be 2×10^{30} kg.

b) Estimate the density of the sun.

c) Why is the density of the sun less than that of the moon?

Finishing off

> **Now that you have finished this chapter you should be able to:**
>
> ★ round a number to a given number of decimal places or significant figures
> ★ write the error bounds for a number
> ★ work out the effect of accumulating errors
> ★ carry out rough calculations
> ★ estimate quantities.

Use the questions in the next exercise to check that you understand everything.

Mixed exercise 13.5

1 Write the following numbers to the accuracy specified.

   a) 0.001 567 to 3 decimal places

   b) 24 900 to the nearest thousand

   c) 5293 to 2 significant figures

   d) 0.061 446 to 3 significant figures

   e) $\sqrt{3}$ to 4 decimal places

2 The number 0.041 95 is rounded to 0.042. Which of the following are correct descriptions of the rounding and which are incorrect?

   a) to 2 decimal places

   b) to the nearest one thousandth

   c) to 2 significant figures

3 State the maximum error you expect in the following measurements.

   a) The length is 25 cm ± 4%.

   b) The mass is 2.31 kg.

   c) The estimated cost is £120.

4 A number is given as $0.002\ 14 \pm 5 \times 10^{-6}$.

   State

   a) the number of decimal places

   b) the number of significant figures to which the number is given.

5 State the error in each of these approximations, giving your answers

      i) to 2 significant figures   ii) as a percentage of the true value.

   a) π is taken to be $\sqrt{10}$ **b)** π is taken to be $\frac{22}{7}$

   c) 2^{10} is taken to be 1000   **d)** $\sqrt{2}$ is taken to be 1.4

   e) $\sin 53°$ is taken to be $\frac{4}{5}$.

Mixed exercise 13.5 *continued*

6 The measurements on this rectangle are correct to the accuracy given. Find the least and greatest values of **a)** the perimeter and **b)** the area of the rectangle.

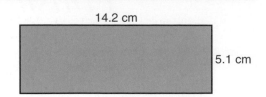

14.2 cm

5.1 cm

7 The formula

$$x = \frac{10}{a - b}$$

is used to calculate a value of x from measured values of a and b. Louise measures a as 5.1 and b as 3.4. What should Louise quote as the maximum possible true value of x?   ***MEI***

8 ABCD is a rectangle. The length of AB is 6.3 cm measured to the nearest millimetre.

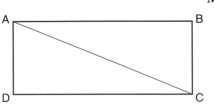

a) Complete the inequality

.... $\leqslant$ AB < ....

The diagonal AC is 7.6 cm measured to the nearest millimetre.

b) Calculate the upper and lower bounds for the length of the side BC.

c) Give the length of BC to an appropriate degree of accuracy.   ***MEG***

9 Ama uses her calculator to find the value of

$$x = \frac{23.526 + 23.319}{3.526 - 3.319}$$

Her answer is 26.8 to 1 decimal place.

Carry out a rough calculation to check whether this is reasonable. If Ama's answer is wrong, state what it should be.

10 Estimate how long your hair would be if you had never had it cut and the ends had not frayed.

11 The British Isles can be regarded as a triangle of base 500 km and perpendicular height 850 km. The population of the British Isles is approximately 55 million.

Estimate

a) the area, in m², of the British Isles

b) the average area, in m², that each inhabitant of the British Isles has to live in, expressing your answers in standard form to an appropriate degree of accuracy.

12 The trunk of an average tree of a particular species has radius 40 cm and height 6.4 m and may be regarded as cylindrical.

a) Calculate the volume, in cubic centimetres, of the average tree trunk. Express your answer in standard form correct to 3 significant figures.

The tree trunk is to be turned into matchsticks which have a square cross section of side 3 mm and are 35 mm long.

Mixed exercise 13.5 *continued*

b) Calculate the volume, in cubic centimetres, of one of these matchsticks. Express your answer in standard form.

c) How many of these matchsticks can be made from the tree truck if there is no wastage? Give your answer in standard form, correct to 2 significant figures.

13

Fred is 9 years old and is doing a maths experiment measuring a tin can.
He measures its diameter as 6 cm correct to the nearest centimetre.
He measures its circumference as 18 cm correct to the nearest centimetre.

His teacher tells him that circumferece ÷ diameter will give him the 'magic number' π.

Work out the upper bound for π based on these data.

MEI

14

Distances on motorway signs are given to the nearest mile.
Anil's speedometer gives speeds to the nearest 5 miles per hour.
His speedometer shows a constant speed of 65 miles per hour.

Work out the upper bound for his time to travel between the two services.

MEI

Mixed exercise 13.5 *continued*

15 Lien and Lok are using a clinometer to find the height of a tower.

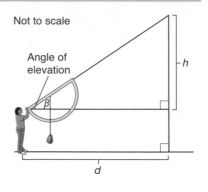

They use the formula

$$h = d \tan ß.$$

To measure *d*, Lien paces the distance. She finds it is exactly 25 of her paces. She measures one of her paces as 90 cm to the nearest 10 centimetres.

Lok measures the angle of elevation, ß, as 51° to the nearest degree.

Calculate the lower bound for *h*. Give the units of your answer.

MEI

16 Gaynor cuts a cake into six sectors, making the cuts in the order shown in the diagram. She tries to make all the pieces equal but in practice the angles for the first five are 60° ± 10%.

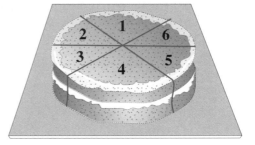

a) What are the least and greatest angles for each of the first five pieces?

b) What are the least and greatest angles for the last piece?

c) Express your answers to part b) as a possible percentage error.

d) When Angus cuts a cake into six pieces, the angles for the first five are 60° ± *p*%. Prove that the angle for the last piece is 60° ± 5*p*%.

Chapter 14

Manipulating expressions

Before you start this chapter you should be able to:

★ multiply out brackets

★ factorise expressions

★ add, subtract, multiply and divide fractions

★ solve linear equations.

Reminder

Multiplying out brackets

> Each term in the bracket is multiplied by $3a$

- $3a(2a + 3b) = 3a \times 2a + 3a \times 3b$

$$= 6a^2 + 9ab$$

- $(x + 2)(2x - 3) = 2x^2 - 3x + 4x - 6$

> Each term in the second bracket is multiplied by each term in the first bracket

$$= 2x^2 + x - 6$$

Factorising

- $2p^2 - 6pq = 2p(p - 3q)$

> 2 and p are factors of both terms

Fractions

- $\dfrac{2}{3} + \dfrac{1}{4} = \dfrac{8}{12} + \dfrac{3}{12} = \dfrac{11}{12}$

- $\dfrac{3}{5} \times \dfrac{1}{6} = \dfrac{\cancel{3}}{5} \times \dfrac{1}{\cancel{6}_2} = \dfrac{1}{10}$

- $\dfrac{7}{5} \div \dfrac{5}{6} = \dfrac{7}{5} \times \dfrac{6}{8} = \dfrac{7}{5} \times \dfrac{\cancel{6}^3}{\cancel{8}_4} = \dfrac{21}{20}$

Linear equations

Example

Solve   **a)** $\dfrac{3 - 2x}{4} = 2$ **b)** $5x - 3 = 2x + 9$

Solution

> Multiply both sides by 4

a) $\dfrac{3 - 2x}{4} = 2$

$3 - 2x = 8$

> It is easier to deal with a positive x term

$3 = 8 + 2x$

$-5 = 2x$

$x = -2.5$

b) $5x - 3 = 2x + 9$

$5x = 2x + 12$

$3x = 12$

$x = 4$

> Collect the x terms on one side and the numbers on the other

Use the questions in the next exercise to check that you remember these topics.

Review exercise 14.1

1 Multiply out the brackets.

a) $3(x+2y)$ b) $5(3p-2q)$

c) $4(2r+3s-t)$ d) $x(y+z)$

e) $a(a-b)$ f) $3c(2d-3e)$

g) $2p(p+2q-3r)$ h) $3ab(2a-3b+4c)$

2 Factorise these expressions.

a) $4a+6b$ b) $pq-pr$

c) x^2-2xy d) $2rs+s^2-s$

e) $3cd+6c^2+9c$ f) $2a^2b-3ab^2$

g) $4p^2qr+8pq^2r$ h) $9x^3y^2-12x^2y^2$

i) $5pq-10p^2q$ j) $10f^2g-15fgh+25fg^2$

3 Multiply out the brackets.

a) $(x+3)(y-2)$ b) $(a+4)(a+1)$

c) $(p-5)(p+2)$ d) $(x-4)^2$

e) $(a-3)(a-4)$ f) $(z+3)(z-3)$

g) $(2p+1)(q-3)$ h) $(2x+3)(x-2)$

i) $(3a+4)(2a+1)$ j) $(4c-3)(3c+5)$

4 Multiply out the brackets and simplify.

a) $3(2a+1)-2(a-3)$ b) $2p(q+2)+4q(2p-3)$

c) $(x+1)(x-3)-(x+2)(x-1)$ d) $(2y-1)^2+(y+2)^2$

5 Work these out.

a) $\frac{1}{3}+\frac{2}{5}$ b) $\frac{3}{4}-\frac{1}{6}$ c) $\frac{5}{8}+\frac{2}{3}$ d) $\frac{5}{7}-\frac{2}{5}$

e) $\frac{4}{9}+\frac{5}{6}$ f) $\frac{11}{12}-\frac{3}{8}$ g) $\frac{2}{3}\times\frac{6}{7}$ h) $\frac{3}{5}\times\frac{5}{9}$

i) $\frac{3}{4}\div\frac{9}{10}$ j) $\frac{5}{6}\div\frac{3}{8}$ k) $\frac{4}{5}\times\frac{7}{12}$ l) $\frac{8}{15}\div\frac{7}{10}$

6 Solve these equations.

a) $2x+3=10$ b) $\frac{x}{3}-1=4$

c) $5-4x=12$ d) $\frac{1-3x}{4}=4$

e) $2x+1=x+6$ f) $3x-2=5x+4$

g) $4x-1=6-x$ h) $2(3x-1)=3(x+4)$

i) $\frac{2x+1}{2}=\frac{3-2x}{5}$ j) $(x-2)(x+3)=(x+1)^2$

k) $\frac{6}{x-1}=5$ l) $\frac{2x-1}{3-2x}=3$

m) $\frac{2}{1-x}=\frac{5}{3x+1}$ n) $\frac{2x-3}{x+1}=\frac{4x+5}{2x+1}$

Algebraic fractions

Simplifying fractions

Numerical fractions can sometimes be simplified, or cancelled down.

e.g. $\dfrac{12}{16} = \dfrac{3}{4}$ ← Divide both the top and the bottom by 4

Sometimes algebraic fractions can be simplified in a similar way.

e.g. $\dfrac{x^2}{xy} = \dfrac{x}{y}$ ← Divide both the top and the bottom by x

Here is some work in which George has cancelled down some fractions.

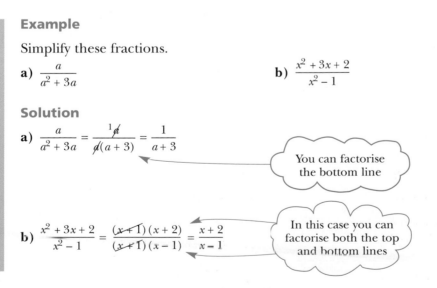

$$\frac{y}{y+2} = \frac{y^1}{y+2} = \frac{1}{2} \quad \text{✗}$$

$$\frac{3x^2+2x}{2x^2+5x} = \frac{3x^2+2x}{2x^2+5x} = \frac{3+2}{2+5} = \frac{5}{7} \quad \text{✗}$$

Why is George's work wrong?

(You may find it helpful to substitute numbers for y and x.)

What should he have done in each question?

When you can factorise the top line or the bottom line (or both) you may be able to cancel down the fraction.

Example

Simplify these fractions.

a) $\dfrac{a}{a^2 + 3a}$

b) $\dfrac{x^2 + 3x + 2}{x^2 - 1}$

Solution

a) $\dfrac{a}{a^2 + 3a} = \dfrac{{}^1\!\cancel{a}}{\cancel{a}(a + 3)} = \dfrac{1}{a + 3}$

You can factorise the bottom line

b) $\dfrac{x^2 + 3x + 2}{x^2 - 1} = \dfrac{(x+1)(x + 2)}{(x+1)(x - 1)} = \dfrac{x + 2}{x - 1}$

In this case you can factorise both the top and bottom lines

Multiplying algebraic fractions

You multiply two numerical fractions like this.

You multiply algebraic fractions in the same way.

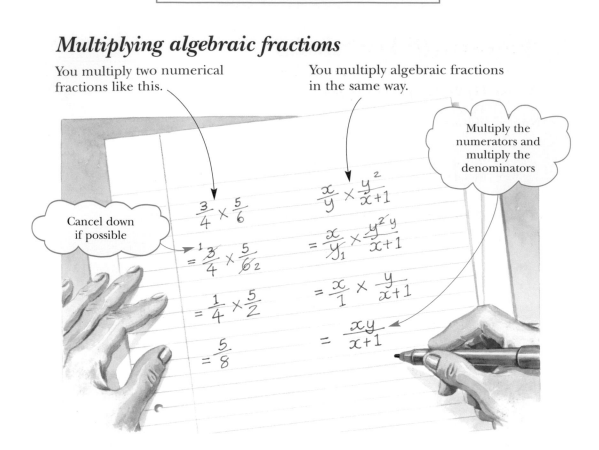

Cancel down if possible

Multiply the numerators and multiply the denominators

$$\frac{3}{4} \times \frac{5}{6}$$

$$= \frac{{}^{1}\cancel{3}}{4} \times \frac{5}{\cancel{6}\,_2}$$

$$= \frac{1}{4} \times \frac{5}{2}$$

$$= \frac{5}{8}$$

$$\frac{x}{y} \times \frac{y^2}{x+1}$$

$$= \frac{x}{\cancel{y}_1} \times \frac{y^2 y}{x+1}$$

$$= \frac{x}{1} \times \frac{y}{x+1}$$

$$= \frac{xy}{x+1}$$

Dividing algebraic fractions

You divide two numerical fractions like this.

You divide algebraic fractions in the same way.

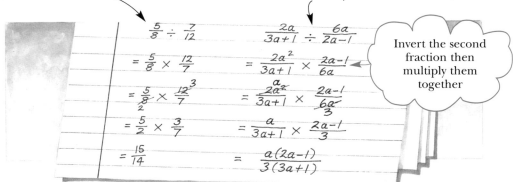

Invert the second fraction then multiply them together

$$\frac{5}{8} \div \frac{7}{12}$$

$$= \frac{5}{8} \times \frac{12}{7}$$

$$= \frac{5}{\cancel{8}_2} \times \frac{\cancel{12}^3}{7}$$

$$= \frac{5}{2} \times \frac{3}{7}$$

$$= \frac{15}{14}$$

$$\frac{2a}{3a+1} \div \frac{6a}{2a-1}$$

$$= \frac{2a^2}{3a+1} \times \frac{2a-1}{6a}$$

$$= \frac{2\cancel{a^2}^{a}}{3a+1} \times \frac{2a-1}{\cancel{6a}_3}$$

$$= \frac{a}{3a+1} \times \frac{2a-1}{3}$$

$$= \frac{a(2a-1)}{3(3a+1)}$$

Example

Simplify   **a)** $\dfrac{p}{q^2} \times \dfrac{q^5}{p+1}$ **b)** $\dfrac{d+1}{d} \div \dfrac{d+2}{d^2-d}$

Solution

a) $\dfrac{p}{\cancel{q^2}} \times \dfrac{\cancel{q^5}^{\,q^3}}{p+1} = \dfrac{p}{1} \times \dfrac{q^3}{p+1} = \dfrac{pq^3}{p+1}$

b) $\dfrac{d+1}{d} \div \dfrac{d+2}{d^2-d} = \dfrac{d+1}{d} \times \dfrac{d^2-d}{d+2} = \dfrac{d+1}{\cancel{d}} \times \dfrac{\cancel{d}(d-1)}{d+2}$

$$= \frac{(d+1)(d-1)}{d+2} = \frac{d^2-1}{d+2}$$

Exercise 14.2

1 Simplify these fractions, where possible.

a) $\dfrac{x}{3x}$

b) $\dfrac{y^2}{y^3}$

c) $\dfrac{2a^2}{4a}$

d) $\dfrac{6py}{9q^2}$

e) $\dfrac{s^2 + 2s}{st}$

f) $\dfrac{c + d}{2c + d}$

g) $\dfrac{2g - 6}{4g}$

h) $\dfrac{4x}{2x - xy}$

i) $\dfrac{6y^2z - 3yz}{9yz^2}$

2 Simplify these fractions, where possible.

a) $\dfrac{x + 2}{x^2 + x - 2}$

b) $\dfrac{a + 1}{a^2 - 2a + 1}$

c) $\dfrac{p^2 - 3p}{p^2 - 5p + 6}$

d) $\dfrac{c^2 + 4c + 3}{2c^2 - c - 1}$

e) $\dfrac{2t^2 - 6t + 4}{t^3 - 3t^2 + 2t}$

f) $\dfrac{2b^2 + b - 3}{2b^2 - b - 3}$

3 Write these as a single fraction, simplifying if possible.

a) $\dfrac{2}{3} \times \dfrac{4}{5}$

b) $\dfrac{3}{4} \times \dfrac{8}{9}$

c) $\dfrac{5}{6} \div \dfrac{1}{3}$

d) $\dfrac{7}{8} \div \dfrac{5}{12}$

e) $\dfrac{x}{2} \times \dfrac{2x}{3}$

f) $\dfrac{3a}{b} \times \dfrac{a}{2b}$

g) $\dfrac{3}{y} \div \dfrac{4}{y^2}$

h) $\dfrac{c^2}{2d} \div \dfrac{4c}{3d^2}$

i) $\dfrac{2p^2}{q} \times \dfrac{q + 1}{p}$

4 Write these as a single fraction, simplifying if possible.

a) $\dfrac{z + 1}{z} \div \dfrac{2}{z}$

b) $\dfrac{3s^3}{2t} \div \dfrac{6s^5}{t^2}$

c) $\dfrac{(2a)^2}{b} \times \dfrac{b + 1}{3a}$

d) $\dfrac{2p + 1}{p} \times \dfrac{3p}{4p + 2}$

e) $\left(\dfrac{x}{2y}\right)^2 \div \dfrac{2x}{y}$

f) $\dfrac{a^3}{b^2} \div \dfrac{a^5}{b^4}$

5 a) A cuboid made of solid lead has dimensions $\dfrac{a}{2}$ m, $\dfrac{a}{3}$ m and $\dfrac{2a}{3}$ m. Find an expression for the volume of the cuboid.

b) The cuboid is melted down and some small cylinders of lead are made from it. Each cylinder has radius $\dfrac{a}{50}$ cm and height b cm.

Find an expression for the number of cylinders that can be made.

c) How many cylinders can be made if $b = 3a$?

Adding and subtracting algebraic fractions

When you add or subtract numerical fractions, you start by finding a common denominator.

e.g. $\frac{1}{6} + \frac{3}{4} = \frac{2}{12} + \frac{9}{12} = \frac{11}{12}$

In the same way, when you add or subtract algebraic fractions you start by finding a common denominator. You should use the simplest algebraic expression that is a multiple of both denominators.

Example

Simplify   **a)** $\frac{2}{x} + \frac{3}{x^2}$ **b)** $\frac{b-1}{b} - \frac{b}{b+1}$ **c)** $\frac{p}{6q} + \frac{p+1}{8pq}$

Solution

a) The simplest expression that is a multiple of both x and x^2 is x^2.

b) The simplest expression that is a multiple of both b and $b+1$ is $b(b+1)$.

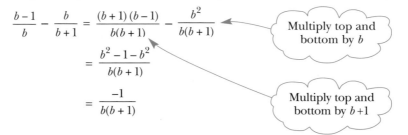

c) The lowest common multiple of 6 and 8 is 24.

The simplest expression which is a multiple of both q and pq is pq.

So the common denominator is $24pq$.

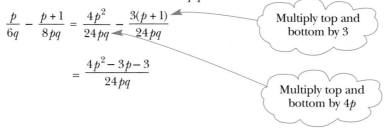

Exercise 14.3

1 Write each of these as a single fraction and simplify if possible.

a) $\dfrac{2}{3} + \dfrac{1}{4}$ **b)** $\dfrac{4}{5} - \dfrac{1}{3}$

c) $\dfrac{2}{7} + \dfrac{3}{5}$ **d)** $\dfrac{w}{3} + \dfrac{2w}{5}$

e) $\dfrac{3y}{4} - \dfrac{2y}{7}$ **f)** $\dfrac{a+1}{2} + \dfrac{3a-2}{4}$

g) $\dfrac{2c-1}{4} - \dfrac{c-2}{3}$ **h)** $\dfrac{3p-2}{6} - \dfrac{1-p}{8}$

i) $\dfrac{5x+6y}{5} - 2x$

2 Write each of these as a single fraction and simplify if possible.

a) $\dfrac{3}{a} + \dfrac{1}{2a}$ **b)** $\dfrac{4}{z} + \dfrac{3}{z^2}$

c) $\dfrac{1}{a} - \dfrac{2}{b}$ **d)** $\dfrac{3}{p} - \dfrac{2}{p+1}$

e) $\dfrac{4}{x+1} + \dfrac{2}{x-2}$ **f)** $\dfrac{3y}{y+1} - \dfrac{2y}{y-1}$

g) $\dfrac{2a-1}{a+2} + \dfrac{1-3a}{2a+1}$ **h)** $\dfrac{3p+1}{q-1} - \dfrac{2p-1}{q+3}$

i) $\dfrac{2w-z}{w+z} + \dfrac{3w+z}{z-2w}$ **j)** $\dfrac{2}{a} - \dfrac{3}{a-1} + \dfrac{1}{a+1}$

3 a) Write $\dfrac{x}{x+1} + \dfrac{x-2}{x+2}$ as a single fraction.

b) Hence solve the equation $\dfrac{x}{x+1} + \dfrac{x-2}{x+2} = 2$

4 a) Write $\dfrac{2}{x} - \dfrac{1}{x-1}$ as a single fraction.

b) Hence solve the equation $\dfrac{2}{x} - \dfrac{1}{x-1} = \dfrac{1}{x+3}$

5 Simplify these fractions.

(Hint: factorise the denominator of each fraction first.)

a) $\dfrac{1}{x^2+3x+2} + \dfrac{1}{x^2+x} - \dfrac{1}{x^2+2x}$

b) $\dfrac{1}{a^2-1} - \dfrac{1}{2a^2+3a+1} - \dfrac{1}{2a^2-a-1}$

Rearranging a formula

In this section you revise the work on rearranging formulae that you covered in Chapter 5.

Reminder

- When you rearrange a formula you must do the same to each side of it, just as you do when you are solving an equation.

- Think about the order of operations on x in the formula. You must 'undo' them in reverse order.

- Isolate squared and square root terms before dealing with them.

Example

Make x the subject of these formulae.

a) $\dfrac{ax + b}{c} = d$

b) $\dfrac{p}{q - x} = r$

c) $r(x^2 + s) = t$

d) $\sqrt{\dfrac{x}{w}} + y = z$

Solution

a) $\dfrac{ax + b}{c} = d$

Multiply both sides by c

$ax + b = cd$

Subtract b from both sides

$ax = cd - b$

$x = \dfrac{cd - b}{a}$

Divide both sides by a

b) $\dfrac{p}{q - x} = r$

$p = r(q - x)$

Get rid of the fraction by multiplying both sides by $q - x$

$\dfrac{p}{r} = q - x$

$\dfrac{p}{r} + x = q$

$x = q - \dfrac{p}{r}$

If you have a negative x term, add it to both sides so that you are working with a positive x term

c) $r(x^2 + s) = t$

$x^2 + s = \dfrac{t}{r}$

$x^2 = \dfrac{t}{r} - s$

Isolate the x^2 term before square rooting

$x = \sqrt{\dfrac{t}{r} - s}$

d) $\sqrt{\dfrac{x}{w}} + y = z$

$\sqrt{\dfrac{x}{w}} = z - y$

Isolate the square root term before squaring

$\dfrac{x}{w} = (z - y)^2$

Notice the use of brackets

$x = w\,(z - y)^2$

Formulae in which the new subject appears more than once

Suppose you want to make x the subject of the formula

$$ax - b - cx + d$$

Notice that there are two x terms in the formula. To make x the subject, you need first to collect the x terms together. It is a bit like solving an equation such as

$$5x - 1 = 3x + 7$$

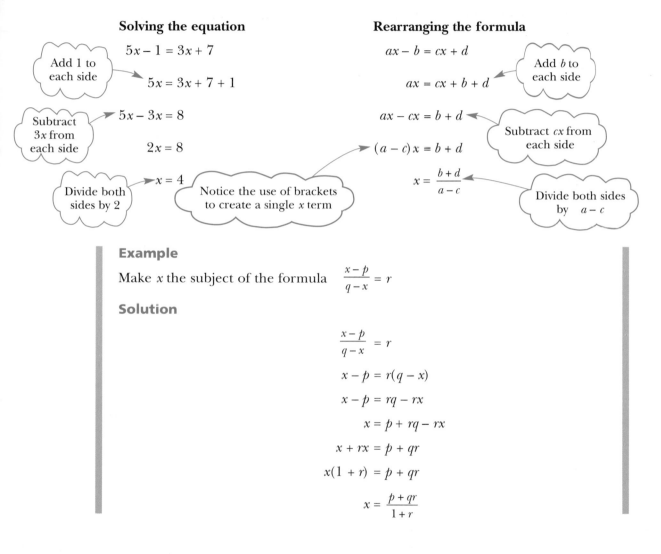

Solving the equation

$$5x - 1 = 3x + 7$$

Add 1 to each side

$$5x = 3x + 7 + 1$$

Subtract $3x$ from each side

$$5x - 3x = 8$$

$$2x = 8$$

Divide both sides by 2

$$x = 4$$

Notice the use of brackets to create a single x term

Rearranging the formula

$$ax - b = cx + d$$

Add b to each side

$$ax = cx + b + d$$

Subtract cx from each side

$$ax - cx = b + d$$

$$(a - c)x = b + d$$

$$x = \frac{b + d}{a - c}$$

Divide both sides by $a - c$

Example

Make x the subject of the formula $\dfrac{x - p}{q - x} = r$

Solution

$$\frac{x - p}{q - x} = r$$

$$x - p = r(q - x)$$

$$x - p = rq - rx$$

$$x = p + rq - rx$$

$$x + rx = p + qr$$

$$x(1 + r) = p + qr$$

$$x = \frac{p + qr}{1 + r}$$

Exercise 14.4

1 Make x the subject of each of these formulae.

a) $wx + y = z$

b) $s - x = t$

c) $\dfrac{x}{a} - b = c$

d) $\dfrac{y}{x} = z$

e) $\dfrac{p - x}{q} = r$

f) $\dfrac{r}{s - x} = t$

g) $\dfrac{x^2 + a}{b} = c$

h) $\sqrt{cx - d} = e$

i) $p - \sqrt{\dfrac{x}{q}} = r$

j) $\dfrac{f}{(x - h)^2} = g$

k) $\dfrac{w}{\sqrt{x + y}} = z$

l) $a - \dfrac{b}{x^2} = c$

2 Make x the subject of each of these formulae.

a) $ax + b = cx + d$

b) $px - q = qx$

c) $xy + z = y - xz$

d) $\dfrac{cx + d}{e} = x$

e) $\dfrac{x - a}{b} = \dfrac{x + b}{c}$

f) $\dfrac{x + p}{x - q} = p$

g) $\dfrac{x}{s} + \dfrac{x}{t} = r$

h) $\dfrac{a}{x} + \dfrac{b}{ax} = b$

i) $\sqrt{\dfrac{x - y}{x + w}} = z$

j) $\dfrac{x + c}{x + d} = \dfrac{x - d}{x + 2c}$

k) $\dfrac{\sqrt{x^2 + p}}{x} = p$

l) $(ax + b)^2 = (bx + a)^2 + a^2$

3 Consider the formula

$S = \pi r^2 + \pi r \sqrt{r^2 + h^2}$

a) Make h the subject of the formula.

b) Given that r and h are lengths, determine whether S is an area or a volume.

4 The formula $\dfrac{1}{R} = \dfrac{1}{R_1} + \dfrac{1}{R_2}$ is used to find resistance in an electric circuit.

a) Make R the subject of the formula.

b) Make R_1 the subject of the formula.

5 The cylinder and the cuboid shown both have the same height, h.

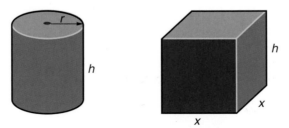

a) Find an expression for the surface area of the cuboid.

b) Find an expression for the surface area of the cylinder.

c) The two surface areas are equal. Find an expression for h in terms of r and x.

Finishing off

Use the questions in the next exercise to check that you understand everything.

Mixed exercise 14.5

1 Write each of these as a single fraction, and simplify where possible.

a) $\dfrac{4a}{9b} \times \dfrac{3b}{2a^2}$

b) $\dfrac{p+1}{p} \times \dfrac{2p^2}{5}$

c) $\dfrac{x^2+2x}{y} \div \dfrac{x+2}{y+1}$

d) $\dfrac{(2z)^2}{z-1} \div \dfrac{3z}{z^2-1}$

e) $\dfrac{1}{x} + \dfrac{2}{x+1}$

f) $\dfrac{2}{a} - \dfrac{1}{a^2}$

g) $\dfrac{3}{ab} + \dfrac{1}{2ac}$

h) $\dfrac{3}{x+2} - \dfrac{2}{2x-1}$

i) $\dfrac{y}{y+1} - \dfrac{y+3}{y-1}$

j) $\dfrac{2p-1}{q+2} + \dfrac{3-2p}{q-1}$

2 a) Write $\dfrac{2x-1}{x+2} + \dfrac{3x+2}{x+1}$ as a single fraction.

b) Hence solve the equation $\dfrac{2x-1}{x+2} + \dfrac{3x+2}{x+1} = 5$

3 Make x the subject of each of these formulae.

a) $\dfrac{x}{a} - b = c$

b) $\dfrac{p-qx}{r} = p$

c) $\dfrac{c}{x-d} = e$

d) $rx + s = sx - r$

e) $\dfrac{x^2+w}{z} = y$

f) $a - \sqrt{\dfrac{x}{b}} = b$

g) $\dfrac{p}{x-q} = \dfrac{q}{p+x}$

h) $\left(\dfrac{y}{z-x}\right)^2 = z$

i) $\sqrt{m - \dfrac{n}{x}} = n$

j) $\dfrac{f}{g-x} = \dfrac{g+x}{h}$

4 This formula gives the energy E of a moving object:

$$E = mgh + \tfrac{1}{2}mv^2$$

a) Make m the subject of the formula.

b) Make v the subject of the formula.

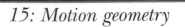

Enlargement

To describe an enlargement you need to state

- the **scale factor**
- the centre of enlargement.

Here, A_1B_1 is 3 times as long as AB, so the scale factor is 3.

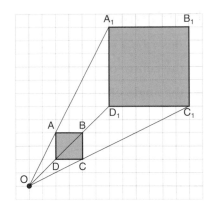

The ratio $OA : OA_1$ also gives the scale factor.

Finding an enlargement

Extend A_1A and B_1B until they meet at O. This is the centre of enlargement.

The scale factor is $\dfrac{A_1B_1}{AB}$ or $\dfrac{OA_1}{OA}$ (etc.).

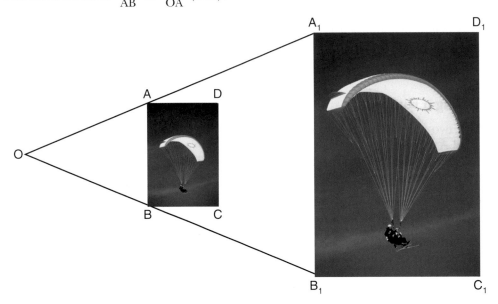

The geometry of transformations

Working with transformations will help you to understand the ideas that underlie much of geometry. Before going on to the next exercise, think about the following problems.

How many pairs of corresponding points is it essential to join to find an axis of symmetry? a centre of rotation? a translation vector? a centre of enlargement? Why is it a good idea to join an extra pair?

In which transformations do
a) lengths   b) angles   c)   areas
remain the same?
In which are lines in the objects always parallel to their images?

Which types of transformation have congruent objects and images?
Which types of transformation have similar objects and images?

Exercise 15.2

1 Describe the transformations which map A on to each of P, Q, R, S and T.

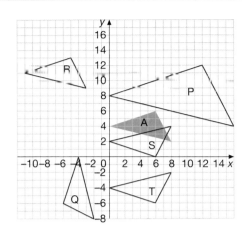

2 Take axes $-1 \leqslant x \leqslant 9$ and $-5 \leqslant y \leqslant 5$.

The triangle L had co-ordinates (1, 3), (3, 1) and (8, 4).

Find, by drawing, the co-ordinates of

a) the reflection of L in the line $y = 2$

b) the image of L under the translation $\binom{3}{-5}$.

3 Take axes $-2 \leqslant x \leqslant 15$ and $-2 \leqslant y \leqslant 10$.

a) Draw triangle A with vertices at (1, 3), (1, 1) and (4, 1).

b) Enlarge A by a scale factor of 3 about the origin to obtain B.

c) Translate B by vector $\binom{2}{-4}$ to get C.

d) Describe fully the transformation that maps A on to C.

4 Take axes $-4 \leqslant x \leqslant 10$ and $-6 \leqslant y \leqslant 6$.

Draw triangle ABC with vertices at (1, 1), (4, 1) and (1, 2). Draw images under

a) rotation through 90° anticlockwise about O and label this image $A_1B_1C_1$

b) enlargement centre O, scale factor 2 and label your image $A_2B_2C_2$

c) reflection in $y = -1$ and label your image $A_3B_3C_3$.

5 Take axes $-6 \leqslant x \leqslant 6$ and $-4 \leqslant y \leqslant 4$.

Draw triangle ABC with vertices at (2, 2), (5, 2) and (5, 4).

a) Draw the image under rotation through 180° about O and label this image $A_1B_1C_1$.

b) Reflect $A_1B_1C_1$ in the line $x = 0$ and label this $A_2B_2C_2$.

c) Describe the transformation that maps ABC on to $A_2B_2C_2$.

d) Describe the transformation that maps $A_2B_2C_2$ on to ABC.

Mixed exercise 15.5 *continued*

6 The diagram shows two successive reflections in two parallel mirror lines.

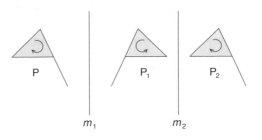

The object P is reflected to P_1 in mirror line m_1, and then P_1 is reflected to P_2 in mirror line m_2. The distance between m_1 and m_2 is x.

a) Give a full description of the single transformation which maps P to P_2.

b) Investigate what happens when the original object is

(i) between m_1 and m_2,   (ii) to the right of m_2.

c) Investigate what happens if the order of the reflections is reversed.

d) Investigate two successive reflections in two non-parallel mirror lines.

7 The diagram shows a trapezium labelled Q.

Three transformations are defined:

M is a reflection in the x axis.

T is a translation with vector $\begin{pmatrix} 2 \\ 4 \end{pmatrix}$.

D is a reflection in the line $y = x$.

a) On a copy of the diagram draw and label:

(i) **M**(Q)

(ii) **TM**(Q)

(iii) **DTM**(Q).

b) Describe the *single* transformation which maps Q onto **DTM**(Q).

SEG

8 In the diagram M is the mid-point of the chord AB.

a) Where is the line of symmetry of the figure?

b) Explain why the three sides of the triangle AOM are the same as the three sides of triangle BOM.

c) State the size of angle AMO.

d) Complete the sentence

"The line from the centre of the circle to the mid-point of the chord is ...".

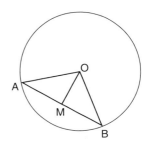

Mixed Exercise 15.5 *continued*

9   The diagram shows a cuboid C. The co-ordinates of its eight vertices are given.

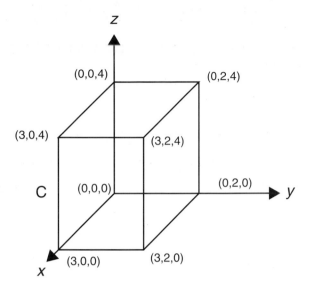

a)   Find the volume and the surface area of C.

E is an enlargement, centre $(0, 0, 0)$, scale factor 3.

b)   Write down the co-ordinates of the eight vertices of E(C).

c)   Find the volume and the surface area of E(C).

d)   By what factor is the volume of C increased when it is enlarged?

e)   By what factor is the surface area of E increased?

10   The transformation R is a rotation through $90°$ clockwise about the point O.
The object is an isosceles right-angled triangle I. R is applied to the object
and then to successive images so that a square is produced as shown.

a)   Can the square be generated using R^2?

What about using R^3?

b)   Describe the rotations and the triangle needed to
generate a regular pentagon, hexagon and general
polygon.

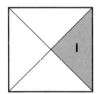

c)   How many different angles of rotation
will generate a regular polygon of
n sides in this way?

Investigation

Draw the triangle with vertices $(1, 1)$, $(4, 1)$, $(3, 2)$ in the middle of a piece of
graph paper.

a)   Investigate whether it is possible to use it to draw a tesselation that covers
the whole sheet of graph paper (with no gaps except at the edges), using

(i)   only translations
(ii)   only rotations (any angles, any centres)
(iii) only reflections (any mirror lines).

b)   Where the answers are No, what pairs of transformations do you need?

Chapter 16

Equations

Before you start this chapter you should be able to:

★ solve linear equations

★ solve linear simultaneous equations and realise that solving these equations is equivalent to finding the point of intersection of two lines

★ solve quadratic equations using factorisation and the quadratic equation formula

★ solve inequalities

★ use equations to solve problems.

Use this exercise to check that you remember how to solve the various types of equations.

Review exercise 16.1

1
 a) $5x - 3 = 42$
 b) $17 - 3x = 32$
 c) $8x + 3 = 18 - 2x$
 d) $7(3x - 2) + 4 = 20 + 6x$
 e) $5(y + 3) - 7 = 2(3y - 1)$
 f) $15 - 3x = 35 + 2x$
 g) $\dfrac{x + 3}{5} + \dfrac{5x - 3}{8} = 6$
 h) $\dfrac{2y - 3}{5} - \dfrac{y - 1}{8} = 2$

2
 a) $3x - 2y = 5$
 $x + 3y = 9$
 b) $5x + 3y = 11$
 $3x + 4y = 0$
 c) $2x + 7y = 2$
 $5x - 3y = 46$
 d) $5x + 3y = 25$
 $y = x + 3$

3
 a) $x^2 + 5x - 14 = 0$
 b) $y^2 - 7y = 30$
 c) $x(x + 7) = 44$
 d) $y^2 - 11y + 24 = 0$

4
 a) $3x^2 + 7x - 26 = 0$
 b) $2x^2 - 9x + 7 = 0$
 c) $4x^2 - 9x - 9 = 0$
 d) $8x^2 - 14x + 3 = 0$
 e) $x(3x - 2) = 8$
 f) $(2x - 5)(3x + 1) = 39$

5
 a) $\dfrac{12}{2x - 1} = 4$
 b) $\dfrac{24}{5x - 2} = 3$
 c) $\dfrac{x + 9}{x - 1} = \dfrac{x + 15}{x}$
 d) $\dfrac{2x + 3}{x - 3} = x - 1$

6 Solve these inequalities.
 a) $3x + 4 > 13$
 b) $1 - 4x \leqslant 9$
 c) $4x - 1 \geqslant x + 11$
 d) $3 - 2x > 1 - 5x$
 e) $4(2x - 1) \leqslant 3(6 - x)$
 f) $\dfrac{2x}{3} \geqslant \dfrac{x + 2}{4}$

Review exercise 16.1 *continued*

7   A theatre has three types of seats: stalls, dress circle and balcony.

The theatre has *s* seats in the stalls. The number of seats in the dress circle is 20 less than the number of seats in stalls. The number of seats in the balcony is three times the number of seats in the dress circle.

a)   Write down expressions involving *s* for

   (i)   the number of seats in the dress circle

   (ii) the number of seats in the balcony.

The price of a seat in the stalls is £3, the price of a seat in the dress circle is £4, and the price of a seat in the balcony is £2.

b)   On a day when the theatre is full, the theatre receives a total of £840 for the seats.

Write down an equation that must be satisfied by *s*. Solve this equation and hence find the total number of seats in the theatre.

8   Nicholas goes for an outing on his bicycle. After leaving home he rides for two hours at a speed of *v* m.p.h.

After a short rest for a chocolate bar he starts riding again and now cycles for 90 minutes at a speed which is 4 m.p.h. faster than his first speed.

In total, Nicholas travels a distance of 55 miles.

Write down an equation that must be satisfied by *v* and solve this equation.

9   At a sweet shop Mercury chocolate bars cost *m* pence and Venus bars are 6p more expensive.

Sharon buys four Mercury bars and nine Venus bars. Sharon's purchases cost £3.27 in total.

a)   Write down and solve an equation that must be satisfied by *m*.

b)   Hence find the cost of buying two Mercury and three Venus bars.

10 John has a red container and a blue container. The red container initially contains 28 litres of water, and the blue container initially contains 4 litres of water.

V litres of water are now added to each container. The volume of water in the red container is now three times the volume in the blue container.

Write down and solve an equation to find the value of *V*.

11 I can buy two packets of crisps and one bottle of cola for 92p or three packets of crisps and two bottles of cola for £1.57.

If crisps cost *x* pence per packet and cola costs *y* pence per bottle, write this information as a pair of simultaneous equations and solve them to find *x* and *y*.

Hence find the cost of buying four packets of crisps and three bottles of cola.

Intelligent search

Alison simplifies the equation by multiplying through by 3 to obtain

$$2\pi r^3 + 48\pi r^2 = 900$$

Using her scientific calculator, Alison starts by using an **integer search** to determine the two integers between which r must lie.

When $r = 1$ $2\pi r^3 + 48\pi r^2 = 2\pi \times 1^3 + 48\pi \times 1^2 = $ 157.1

When $r = 2$ $2\pi r^3 + 48\pi r^2 = 2\pi \times 2^3 + 48\pi \times 2^2 = $ 653.5

When $r = 3$ $2\pi r^3 + 48\pi r^2 = 2\pi \times 3^3 + 48\pi \times 3^2 = $ 1526.8

When $r = 2$ the value of $2\pi r^3 + 48\pi r^2$ is too small but when $r = 3$ the value of $2\pi r^3 + 48\pi r^2$ is too big. The value of r must therefore lie in the interval $2 < r < 3$.

Alison continues by noting that the value of $2\pi r^3 + 48\pi r^2$ is much closer to the target value when $r = 2$ than when $r = 3$, so she decides to use $r = 2.3$ as her next value in her trial and improvement solution.

> **Notation**
> 'r lies in $(2, 3)$' is a useful shorthand for the statement 'r lies in the interval $2 < r < 3$'
>
> 'r lies in $[2, 3]$' is a useful shorthand for the statement 'r lies in the interval $2 \leqslant r \leqslant 3$'

r	$2\pi r^3 + 48\pi r^2$	Comments
2	653.5	
3	1526.8	r lies in $(2, 3)$
2.3	874.2	r lies in $(2.3, 3)$
2.4	955.4	r lies in $(2.3, 2.4)$
2.33	898.1	r lies in $(2.33, 2.4)$
2.34	906.2	r lies in $(2.33, 2.34)$
2.335	902.2	r lies in $(2.33, 2.335)$

> 874.2 is closer to 900 than 955.4 is, so I'll try $r = 2.33$ as the next value

> I still don't know whether $r = 2.33$ or 2.34 correct to 2 decimal places. I shall use $r = 2.335$ to decide

Alison concludes by saying she knows that the solution lies in the interval $(2.33, 2.335)$ and that any number in this interval rounds down to 2.33 when it is written to 2 decimal places.

The radius is therefore 2.33 cm (correct to 2 decimal places).

Interval bisection

Brian decides to rearrange the equation

$$16\pi r^2 + \tfrac{2}{3}\pi r^3 = 300$$

by subtracting 300 from each side to obtain

$$16\pi r^2 + \tfrac{2}{3}\pi r^3 - 300 = 0$$

Then he uses his graphic calculator to draw a graph of $y = 16\pi r^2 + \tfrac{2}{3}\pi r^3 - 300$

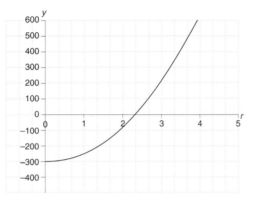

From the graph he sees that the positive solution of $16\pi r^2 + \tfrac{2}{3}\pi r^3 - 300 = 0$ lies in the interval $(2.2, 2.4)$.

He continues his search for the value of r using the method of **interval bisection**, where at each stage the interval is halved by considering the value of $16\pi r^2 + \tfrac{2}{3}\pi r^3 - 300$ at its mid-point.

	Mid-point $= m$	$16\pi m^2 + \tfrac{2}{3}\pi m^3 - 300$
r is in $(2.2, 2.4)$	2.3	−8.61
r is in $(2.3, 2.4)$	2.35	4.77
r is in $(2.3, 2.35)$	2.325	−1.96
r is in $(2.325, 2.35)$	2.3375	1.40
r is in $(2.325, 2.3375)$	2.33125	−0.29
r is in $(2.33125, 2.3375)$	2.334375	0.55
r is in $(2.33125, 2.334375)$		

When r is 2.2 or 2.3 the value of $16\pi r^2 + \tfrac{2}{3}\pi r^3 - 300$ is negative but when r is 2.4 the value is positive. So r must be in $(2.3, 2.4)$

At this stage Brian realises that if r is in $(2.33125, 2.334375)$, then r must equal 2.33 correct 2 decimal places.

Decimal search

Like Alison, Camilla uses an integer
search to discover that the value of r
lies between 2 and 3.

She continues by using a spreadsheet
to conduct a **decimal search** for the
value of r.

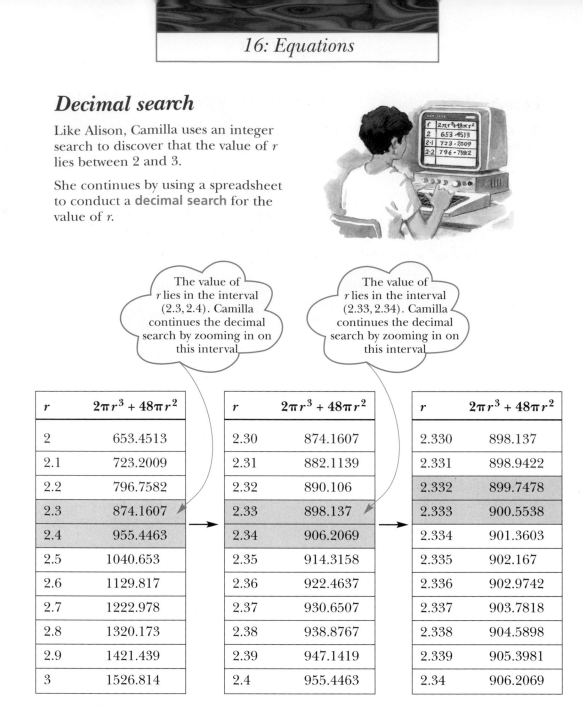

The value of
r lies in the interval
$(2.3, 2.4)$. Camilla
continues the decimal
search by zooming in on
this interval

The value of
r lies in the interval
$(2.33, 2.34)$. Camilla
continues the decimal
search by zooming in on
this interval

r	$2\pi r^3 + 48\pi r^2$
2	653.4513
2.1	723.2009
2.2	796.7582
2.3	874.1607
2.4	955.4463
2.5	1040.653
2.6	1129.817
2.7	1222.978
2.8	1320.173
2.9	1421.439
3	1526.814

r	$2\pi r^3 + 48\pi r^2$
2.30	874.1607
2.31	882.1139
2.32	890.106
2.33	898.137
2.34	906.2069
2.35	914.3158
2.36	922.4637
2.37	930.6507
2.38	938.8767
2.39	947.1419
2.4	955.4463

r	$2\pi r^3 + 48\pi r^2$
2.330	898.137
2.331	898.9422
2.332	899.7478
2.333	900.5538
2.334	901.3603
2.335	902.167
2.336	902.9742
2.337	903.7818
2.338	904.5898
2.339	905.3981
2.34	906.2069

r is therefore in the interval $(2.332, 2.333)$, so the value of r is 2.33 correct to
2 decimal places.

*What are the advantages and disadvantages of each of the three methods used to
find the radius of the pencil case?*

Exercise 16.2

In questions 1 to 4, find the positive value of x that satisfies the equation, and give your answer correct to 2 decimal places.

1 $x^3 + 5x = 96$ **2** $4x^3 + x^2 = 20$

3 $x^3 = 3x + 20$ **4** $x^4 = 20 + 5\sqrt{x}$

5 A cuboid is to be constructed to have a capacity of 2 litres. The base is to be square and the height is to be 5 cm greater than the width of the base.

Find the dimensions of the cuboid, giving your answer correct to the nearest millimetre.

6 A baby's toy is to be made as shown in the diagram. It consists of a cone and a hemisphere joined together. The height of the cone is 3 cm more than the diameter of the hemisphere. The volume of the toy is to be 200 cm³.

Determine, correct to the nearest millimetre, the radius of the hemisphere.

7 **a)** Mark invests £3000 in a savings account which pays 4% per annum compound interest. Determine the value of his savings after

   (i) 2 years   (ii) 4 years   (iii) n years.

b) Claire invests £2000 in a savings account that pays 4% per annum compound interest and £1000 in another account that pays 6.5% per annum compound interest.

Explain why, after x years, her savings will be worth

   $$2000 \times 1.04^x + 1000 \times 1.065^x$$

After how long will Claire's savings be worth £5000?

Where two graphs cross

? *How would you solve the equation $x^2 = x + 5$?*

You could draw the graph of $y = x^2 - x - 5$ and see where it crosses the x axis.

Another way is to draw the graph of $y = x^2$ and the line $y = x + 5$ and see where they cross.

You can see from the graph that the roots of $x^2 = x + 5$ (or $x^2 - x - 5 = 0$) are about $x = -1.8$ and $x = 2.8$.

? *Check the roots from the graph by using the quadratic formula $x^2 - x - 5 = 0$.*

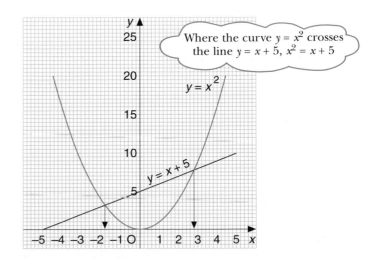

Where the curve $y = x^2$ crosses the line $y = x + 5$, $x^2 = x + 5$

$y = x^2$

$y = x + 5$

If you need to solve another quadratic equation, such as $x^2 + 2x - 10 = 0$, you could rearrange it as $x^2 = -2x + 10$.

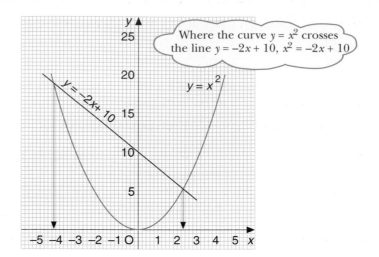

> Where the curve $y = x^2$ crosses the line $y = -2x + 10$, $x^2 = -2x + 10$

Now all you need to do is add the line $y = -2x + 10$ to the graph of $y = x^2$ above.

You can see from the graph that the roots of $x^2 = -2x + 10$ are about $x = -4.3$ and $x + 2.3$.

You can also use this graph to solve quadratic inequalities. Between $x = -4.3$ and $x = 2.3$ the graph of $y = x^2$ is below the line $y = -2x + 10$.

So the solution of $x^2 \leqslant -2x + 10$ is $-4.3 \leqslant x \leqslant 2.3$.

Everywhere else, the graph of $y = x^2$ is above the line $y = -2x + 10$.

So the solution of $x^2 > -2x + 10$ is $x < -4.3$ or $x > 2.3$.

When do you use the '…or equals' signs $\geqslant$ and $\leqslant$, and when the strict inequality signs $>$ and $<$?

Use the graph on the previous page to solve the inequalities

   $x^2 \leqslant x + 5$ *and* $x^2 > x + 5$.

Exercise 16.3

1   Draw the graph of $y = x^2$ for values of x from -3 or 3.

For each of the equations add a single line to your graph and so estimate the solution of the equation, giving your answers to 1 decimal place.

a) $x^2 = 2x + 5$ **b**) $x^2 = 10 - x$ **c**) $x^2 = 4x - 4$

2   Draw the graphs of $y = x^3$ and $y = x^2 + 5x$ for $-2 \leqslant x \leqslant 3$ on the same axes.

a) Find the values of x at the points of intersection of these graphs.

b) State the equation you solved in part a).

Exercise 16.3 *continued*

3   Draw the graphs of $y = x^3$ and $y = -x^2 + 5x$ for $-3 \leqslant x \leqslant 2$ on the same axes.

   a)   Find the values of x at the points of intersection of these graphs.

   b)   State the equation you solved in part a).

4   Draw the graph of $y = x^3$ for $-3 \leqslant x \leqslant 3$.

   a)   Add a labelled graph to estimate the solution of $x^3 = x^2 - 4$.

   b)   Are there likely to be any other roots? Justify your answer.

5   Draw the graphs of $y = \dfrac{12}{x}$ and $y = x + 5$ for $-12 \leqslant x \leqslant 12$ on the same axes.

   Notice that there is no value of $\dfrac{12}{x}$ when $x = 0$.

   a)   Find the values of x at the points of intersection of these graphs.

   b)   State the equation you solved in part a). Can it be written as a quadratic equation?

6   Draw the graphs of $y = \dfrac{1}{x^2}$ and $y = x + 4$ for $-4 \leqslant x \leqslant 4$ on the same axes.

   Notice that there is no value of $\dfrac{1}{x^2}$ when $x = 0$.

   a)   Find the values of x at the points of intersection of these graphs.

   b)   State the equation you solved in part a). Can it be written as a quadratic equation?

7

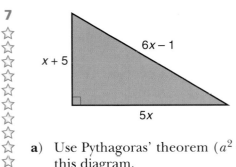

   a)   Use Pythagoras' theorem ($a^2 + b^2 = h^2$) to write an equation in x from this diagram.

   b)   Solve the equation graphically and so work out the actual dimensions of the triangle.

   c)   Is there another way of solving the equation?

8   Draw the graphs of $y = x^2$, $y = 2x + 5$ and $y = 10 - x$, all on the same axes. Use them to estimate the solutions of the inequalities.

   a) $x^2 \leqslant 2x + 5$ b) $x^2 < 2x + 5$

   c) $x^2 \leqslant 10 - x$ d) $x^2 > 10 - x$

The equation of a circle

The diagram shows a circle whose centre is the origin and whose radius is 5. The point P (x, y) lies on the circle.

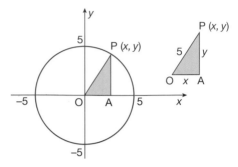

When Pythagoras' theorem is applied to the right-angled triangle OAP, the equation

$$x^2 + y^2 = 5^2$$

is obtained.

$x^2 + y^2 = 25$ is the equation of the circle with centre $(0, 0)$ and radius 5.

Find the equation of the circle with centre $(0, 0)$ and radius 8.

Find the equation of the circle with centre $(0, 0)$ and radius 25.

Find the equation of the circle with centre $(0, 0)$ and radius r.

James is trying to find the points where the line $y + x = 7$ meets the circle with centre the origin and radius 5.

James knows that the equation of the circle is

$$x^2 + y^2 = 5^2$$

or

$$x^2 + y^2 = 25$$

He also knows that finding the points of intersection of the circle and the line is the same as trying to find values of x and y that satisfy *both* the equations $y + x = 7$ and $x^2 + y^2 = 25$.

James therefore realises that he is trying to solve the simultaneous equations

$$x + y = 7$$
$$x^2 + y^2 = 25$$

He decides to start by rewriting the first equation in a form that gives x in terms of y.

He then substitutes $7 - y$ for x in the second equation.

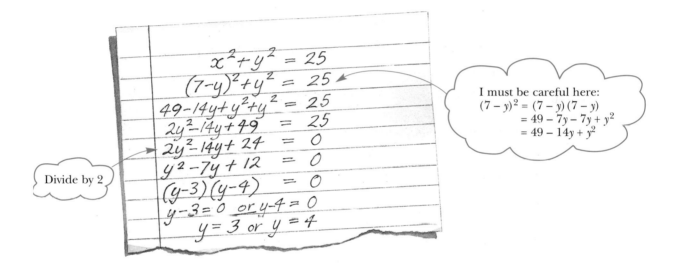

Finally, James remembers to find the x values and the points of intersection of the line and the circle.

When $y = 3$: $x = 7 - y = 4$
When $y = 4$: $x = 7 - y = 3$
Points of intersection are $(3, 4)$ and $(4, 3)$

Exercise 16.4

1 Draw the circle $x^2 + y^2 = 4$ and the line $y = x$. Use the same scales for both axes. Use your graph to find the co-ordinates of the points of intersection, to 1 decimal place.

2 Draw the circles $x^2 + y^2 = 1$ and $x^2 + y^2 = 9$. Use the same scales for both axes. Now draw the line $y = 1$. Use your graph to find the co-ordinates of the points where the line meets the circles, giving the answers to 1 decimal place where appropriate.

In questions 3 to 10, solve the simultaneous equations.

3 $x + y = 12$
$y = x^2$

4 $x - y = 3$
$4x - y^2 = 0$

5 $x + y = 9$
$x^2 + y^2 = 41$

6 $x - 2y = 3$
$2x^2 - y^2 = 94$

7 $p + q = 5$
$p^2 - q^2 = 15$

8 $x - 3y = 8$
$y = x^2 - 26$

9 $y - 2x = 6$
$y + x^2 = 9$

10 $x + 2y = 9$
$y^2 = 16x$

11 The 'L' shape in the diagram has a perimeter of 40 cm and an area of 27.75 cm^2.

Determine the values of x and y.

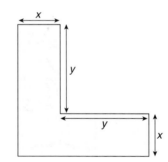

12 a) Draw the circle $x^2 + y^2 = 25$ and the line $x + y = 7$. Use the same scales for both axes. Use your graph to find the co-ordinates of the points where they intersect.

b) On the same graph draw the line $x + y = -7$. Where does this cross the circle?

c) Now draw lines joining $(-7, 0)$ to $(0, 7)$ and $(7, 0)$ to $(0, -7)$. Write down the co-ordinates of the points where these two lines cross the circles.

d) What shape do the four lines make?

e) What shape do you get if you join up all the points of intersection?

13 a) Write down the equation of the circle with centre $(0, 0)$ and radius 10.

b) Find the points of intersection of this circle with the line $y + 7x = 50$.

14 Find where the line $3x + 4y = 25$ meets the circle $x^2 + y^2 = 25$.

☆
☆ Interpret your answer geometrically.

15 The diagram shows the ellipse
☆ $x^2 + 4y^2 = 100$ and the line $14y - x = 50$.
☆

Find the co-ordinates of the points of intersection of the ellipse and the line.

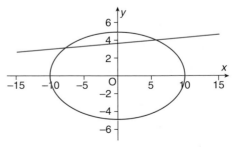

Finishing off

When you have finished this chapter you should be able to:

★ use trial and improvement to solve an equation to a required level of accuracy

★ use the intersection of graphs to find approximate solutions to equations

★ solve simultaneous equations where one equation is linear and one is quadratic

★ recognise the equation $x^2 + y^2 = r^2$ as the equation of a circle of radius r and centre the origin.

Use the equations in the next exercise to check that you understand everything.

Mixed exercise 16.5

1 Solve these equations.

a) $37 - 3x = 10$

b) $5(2x - 3) + 6x = 48 - 2x$

c) $\dfrac{3x - 5}{8} = 2$

d) $\dfrac{20}{11 - 2x} = 5$

e) $\dfrac{5x - 2}{3} - \dfrac{2(x + 4)}{11} = 9$

2 Solve these equations.

a) $x^2 + 7x - 30 = 0$

b) $3x(x + 2) = 2x^2 + 10x + 5$

c) $3x^2 = 5x + 22$

d) $(5x - 1)(x + 2) = (x - 1)(7x + 10)$

e) $\dfrac{3x - 5}{x + 1} = \dfrac{x + 5}{x - 1}$

3 Find, correct to 2 decimal places, the solutions of these equations.

a) $3x^2 + 11x - 12 = 0$

b) $3x(x - 2) = 3x + 1$

4 Solve these pairs of simultaneous equations.

a) $3x - 2y = 25$
   $x + 3y = 1$

b) $4x + 3y = 5$
   $6x - 5y = -2$

c) $y = 3x - 5$
   $2x + y = 5$

d) $x + 3y = 28$
   $y^2 - x = 0$

5 a) Draw the graph of $y = x^2 - 5x$ for values of x between -2 and 7.

b) Making your method clear, use your graph to solve the equations

   (i) $x^2 - 5x = 8$

   (ii) $x^2 - 5x + 3 = 0$

c) By drawing another line on your diagram, find the solutions of the equation

$$\dfrac{x^2 - 5x}{x - 4} = 2$$

Mixed exercise 16.5 *continued*

6 Solve the simultaneous equations

$2x + y = 5$

$y^2 + 6x = 19$

7 Use a trial and improvement method to find, correct to 2 decimal places, the solution of the equation

$x^5 = 60 - 3x$

8 Find the points of intersection of the line $y = 3x + 6$ with the curve $y = 3x^2$.

9 An ornament is to be made in the shape of a cylinder of length 10 cm and radius r cm, and at both ends of the cylinder there is to be a hemisphere of radius r cm. The volume of the ornament is to be 800 cm^3.

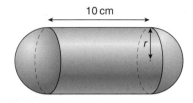

Write down an equation that must be satisfied by r and use a trial and improvement method to determine the value of r, giving your answer correct to 2 decimal places.

10 a) Draw the graph of $y = x^3 - 5x^2$ for $-2 \leqslant x \leqslant 7$.

b) Use the graph to find all the solutions of these equations.

(i) $x^3 - 5x^2 = 15$

(ii) $x^3 - 5x^2 + 10 = 0$

c) By drawing another line on the diagram, solve the equation

$x^3 - 5x^2 - 4x + 10 = 0$

11 Solve the simultaneous equations

$3x - 2y = 8$

$xy = 8$

12 Solve these inequalities.

a) $3x - 2 > 5 - x$ **b)** $\dfrac{x+1}{2} + \dfrac{2x-1}{3} \leqslant 4$

13 The perimeter of a rectangle is 20 cm and its area is 22 cm^2. Find the length and width of the rectangle.

Mixed exercise 16.5 *continued*

14 A company makes compact discs (CDs).

The total cost, P pounds, of making n compact discs is given by the formula

$$P = a + bn$$

where a and b are constants.

The cost of making 1000 compact discs is £58 000.

The cost of making 2000 compact discs is £64 000.

a) Calculate the values of a and b.

The company sells the compact discs at £10 each.

The company does not want to make a loss.

b) Work out the minimum number of compact discs the company must sell.

Edexcel

15 Two students, Anya and Karim are finding the points of intersection of various circles and straight lines.

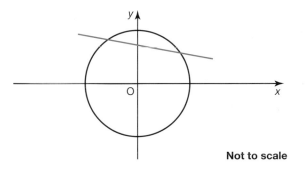

Not to scale

a) Anya is finding the intersections of the straight line $3y + x = 5$ with the circle $x^2 + y^2 = 25$.

Use an algebraic method to find the points of intersection.

b) Karim is finding the intersections of $y = x - 9$ with $x^2 + y^2 = 25$.
He (correctly) finds that in doing this he has to solve the equation $x^2 - 9x + 28 = 0$.

What can you say about the intersections that Karim is trying to find?
Give your reasons.

MEI

Mixed exercise 16.5 *continued*

16 Water absorbs light passing through it.

The percentages of light passing through d metres of water is given by

$100(0.65)^d$.

Use trial and improvement to find the depth of this lake.
In a certain lake, only 1% of the light reaches the bottom.
Show all your trials and their outcomes.
Give your answer to the nearest metre.

MEI

17 In this question one unit represents 1 km.

A navigation buoy is situated at the point $(0, 0)$ and its light can be seen
from any point that is within 5 km of the buoy.

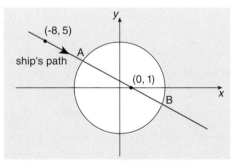

The points from which the light can just be seen form the circle with
equation $x^2 + y^2 = 25$.

A ship, travelling in a straight line at a speed of 10 km/h passes through
the points $(-8, 5)$ and $(0, 1)$ in that order.

a) Find the equation of the straight line representing the ship's path.

b) Write down a pair of simultaneous equations whose solutions represent
the point A, where the buoy can first be seen from the ship, and the
point B, from which is is last seen.

c) Solve the simultaneous equations to determine the co-ordinates of
A and B.

d) Determine the length of time for which the buoy can be seen from
the ship.

Chapter 17

Similarity and congruence

Similarity

The image produced by an enlargement is the same shape as the object but a different size: the object and image are said to be **similar**.

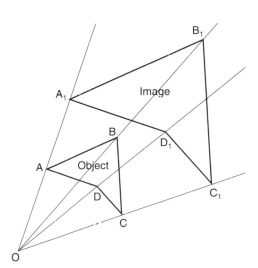

With an enlargement, the object and image have other properties too.

For example, each line joining a point on an object A, and its image, A_1, passes through the centre of enlargement, O, and corresponding lines AB and A_1B_1 are parallel.

The object and image are said to be **similarly situated**.

Two shapes can be similar without being similarly situated.

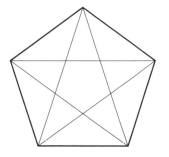

The diagram shows a regular pentagon with its diagonals.

Check that you can find 30 triangles in this figure. How many different shapes of triangles are there?

For each shape of triangle find a pair of triangles that are similarly situated (i.e. are the object and image of an enlargement) and a pair of triangles that are not similarly situated.

Exercise 17.1

1 Prove that these pairs of triangles are similar. Then copy and complete the statement below each figure. (Lines marked with arrows are parallel.)

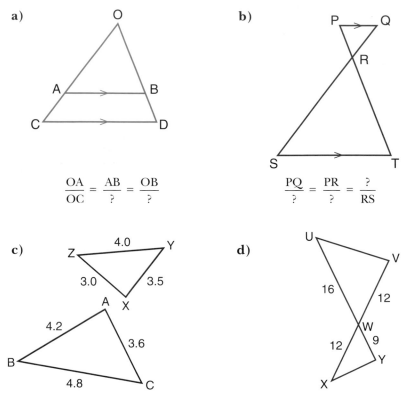

a)

$$\frac{OA}{OC} = \frac{AB}{?} = \frac{OB}{?}$$

b)

$$\frac{PQ}{?} = \frac{PR}{?} = \frac{?}{RS}$$

c)

$$\angle A = \angle ?$$

d)

$$\angle V = \angle ?$$

2 Use similar triangles to find the lengths p, q, r, s.

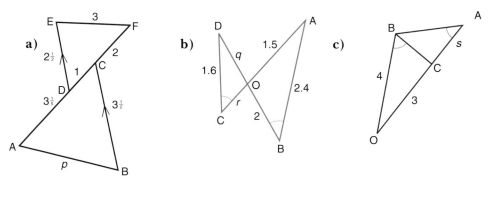

a)

b)

c)

3 Find the perpendicular height x of this right-angled triangle, and hence find the area of the triangle.

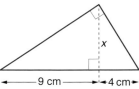

Exercise 17.1 *continued*

4   The diagram shows the side of a
house with a garage attached.
Beyond the garage is a path and
boundary fence. How high above
the ground is the lowest point of
the house wall that can be
reached using a straight ladder?

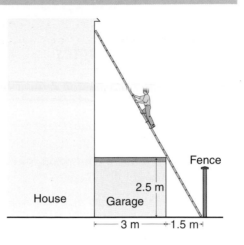

5   The diagram shows a framework
for supporting the overhead wire
on an electric railway.
OC = OD = 8 m, OB = AB = 5 m,
CD = 3 m, and AB is parallel to CD.
Find the length of CA.

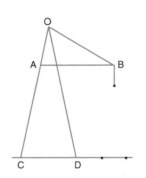

6   Use similar triangles to prove that the line joining the mid-points of two
sides of a triangle is parallel to and half as long as the third side.

7   The summit, S, of Triangle Mountain is at an altitude of 3900 m.
A straight horizontal tunnel, AB, has been cut through the mountain.
This tunnel is at an altitude of 2700 m and is 8 km long.
A second tunnel, CD, is proposed.
It will be straight and parallel to AB, at an altitude of 900 m.

Assuming that SAC and SBD are straight, how long will the new tunnel be?

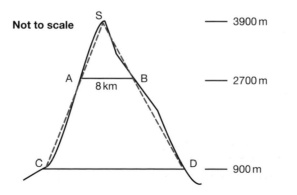

MEI

Congruence

Congruent triangles

Use a ruler and compasses to draw a triangle ABC with AB = 5 cm, BC = 6 cm and CA = 4 cm.

Is it possible to draw two different triangles using this information?

Use a ruler, protractor and compasses to draw a triangle PQR with PQ = 5 cm, ∠PQR = 35° and QR = 7 cm.

Is it possible to draw two different triangles using this information?

Use a ruler, protractor and compasses to draw a triangle STU with ST = 5 cm, ∠UST = 30° and ∠UTS = 75°.

Is it possible to draw two different triangles using this information?

Use a ruler, protractor and compasses to draw a triangle VWX with ∠VWX = 70°, ∠WVX = 50° and ∠WXV = 60°.

Is it possible to draw two different triangles using this information?

Two triangles are **congruent** if they are alike in every respect: the three sides of the first triangle must be the same as the three sides of the second triangle, and the three angles of the first triangle must be the same as the three angles of the second triangle.

Is it possible for similar triangles to be congruent?

The examples below give three ways of showing that a pair of triangles are congruent.

① All three sides are equal. (This is abbreviated to 'side, side, side' or SSS.)

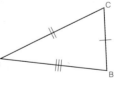

② Two pairs of sides and the **included** angles are equal. (Abbreviation 'side, angle, side' or SAS.)

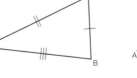

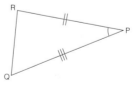

③ Two pairs of angles and one pair of **corresponding** sides are equal. (Abbreviation AAS.)

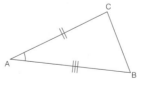

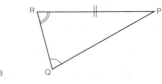

Example

A developer describes a triangular plot of land ABC to his surveyor by telephone, saying, 'Angle A is 40°, side AB 74 m and side BC is 53 m. Please calculate the area for me.'

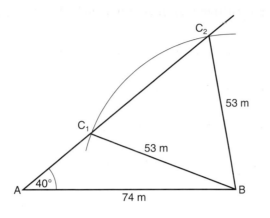

The surveyor attempts to draw a plan of the plot of land:

She quickly realises that there are two possible triangles, ABC_1 and ABC_2 that satisfy the information given by the the developer and that these two triangles are not congruent and have different areas.

This example illustrates why it is essential to use the **included** angle in ③ above.

There is a useful special case when two pairs of sides and a non-included angle will prove congruence. This is when the angle is a right angle. For example, suppose that $\angle P = 90°$, $PQ = 7$ and $QR = 9$.

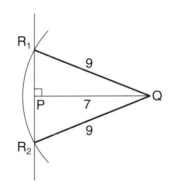

Drawing the triangle again gives two possibilities for the position of R; R_1 and R_2 on the diagram.

Use Pythagoras' theorem to calculate the lengths of PR_1 and PR_2.

What can be said about the triangles PQR_1 and PQR_2?

This gives a fourth way of showing that two triangles are congruent.

④ Both triangles are right-angled, the hypotenuses are equal and one other pair of sides are equal. (Abbreviation RHS.)

Once you have been shown that two triangles are congruent you may deduce the following facts:

- corresponding pairs of sides and angles are equal

- other corresponding lengths (for example altitudes) are equal

- the areas of the triangles are equal.

Using congruent triangles to prove geometrical results

Example

A parallelogram is defined as a quadrilateral with opposite pairs of sides parallel. Prove that opposite pairs of sides are also equal.

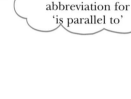

Diagram

ABCD is a parallelogram with AB parallel to DC and BC parallel to AD. Diagonal AC is drawn.

Proof

In triangles ABC, CDA

∠BAC = ∠DCA (alternate angles AB // DC)

∠ACB = ∠CAD (alternate angles, BC // AD)

AC is common to both triangles.

> This is the standard abbreviation for 'is parallel to'

Therefore the triangles are congruent (AAS).

Therefore AB = CD and BC = DA (corresponding pairs of sides).

 What other well-known property of a parallelogram can be deduced using the same triangles?

Example

Prove that the two tangents drawn from a point to a circle are equal in length.

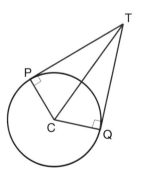

Diagram

The tangents from T touch the circle at P and Q, C is the centre of the circle, and CT is drawn.

Proof

In triangles CPT, CQT

∠CPT = CQT = 90° (angle between radius and tangent)

CP = CQ (radii)

CT is common.

Therefore the triangles are congruent (RHS).

Therefore TP = TQ (corresponding sides of congruent triangles).

 Deduce also that CT *bisects both* ∠PTQ *and* ∠PCQ.

Congruence and transformations

When a triangle is reflected in a mirror line, rotated about a point or translated, the image looks to be the same size and shape as the original triangle. The object and image appear to be congruent. But appearances can be deceptive: a mathematician must be absolutely convinced of the truth of a statement and this requires a formal proof.

Proof

Look at the diagram which shows a triangle ABC and its image A'B'C' after a reflection in the mirror line.

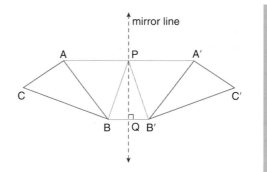

The triangles ABC and A'B'C' *look* as if they are congruent. Can it be proved?

Yes, it can: start by looking at triangles PQB and PQB'.

> PQ is common
> $\angle$ PQB = $\angle$ PQB' (reason :   )
> BQ = B'Q (reason :   )

So the triangles are congruent (SAS) and we can deduce that

> PB = PB'   and $\angle$ BPQ = $\angle$ B'PQ

What are the reasons that should go into the brackets above to explain why $\angle$ PQB = $\angle$ PQB' and why BQ = B'Q?

Now look at $\angle$APB and $\angle$A'PB'.

> $\angle$A'PB' = 90° − $\angle$ B'PQ
>   = 90° − $\angle$ BPQ (since we already know that $\angle$ BPQ = $\angle$ B'PQ)
>   = $\angle$ APB

Now look at triangles PAB and PA'B'.

> PA = PA' (reason :   )
> $\angle$ APB = $\angle$ A'PB' (reason :   )
> PB = PB' (reason :   )

So the triangles are congruent (SAS) and, in particular, AB = A'B'.

What are the reasons that should go into these brackets?

We have now proved that AB = A'B'.

You can repeat the same argument to prove that AC = A'C' and then again to prove that BC = B'C'.

The triangles ABC and A'B'C' are now certain to be congruent (SSS).

The triangle ABC *is translated on to the triangle* A'B'C'.

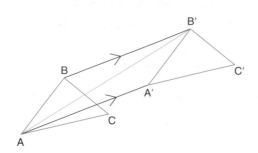

Prove that triangles ABB' *and* B'A'A *are congruent.*

What can be deduced about AB *and* A'B' *?*

Explain why the triangles ABC *and* A'B'C' *must be congruent.*

The triangle ABC *is rotated about the point* O *through an angle* α *to obtain triangle* A'B'C'.

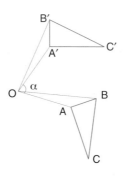

Explain why angles AOB *and* A'OB' *are equal.*

Explain why triangles AOB *and* A'OB' *are congruent.*

Explain why triangles ABC *and* A'B'C' *are congruent.*

The images under translations, reflections and rotations of a triangle are exactly the same size and shape as the object triangle.

What can be said about the images under translations, reflections and rotations of a polygon? Explain your answer by splitting the polygon into triangles.

Two figures that are exactly the same size and shape are said to be congruent.

The image of a figure under a translation, reflection or rotation is congruent to the object.

An object is enlarged. Is the image congruent to the object?

Congruence and constructions

Peter has found the following instructions in a book.

'To draw the perpendicular bisector of a line segment AB:

① *Draw an arc with centre A and radius greater than half of AB.*
② *Draw another arc, with centre B and the same radius, cutting the first arc at points P and Q.*
③ *Draw the line joining P and Q: this is the perpendicular bisector of A and B.'*

He follows the instructions to produce this diagram:

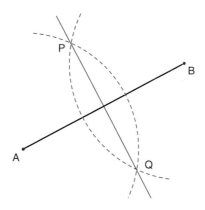

He asks his maths teacher, Miss Edmunds, to explain why these instructions must produce the perpendicular bisector of AB.

Miss Edmunds redraws the diagram and then asks Peter to answer some questions:

1 Why are AP and BP equal?
Why are AQ and BQ equal?

2 Explain why triangles APQ and BPQ are congruent.
What can you now say about ∠ APQ and ∠ BPQ?

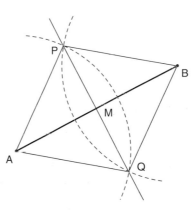

3 What can you tell me about AP and BP?
What can you tell me about ∠ APM and ∠ BPM?
What can you deduce about triangles APM and BPM?

4 What do you now know about the lines AM and BM? What does this tell you about the point M?
What can you now tell me about ∠ AMP and ∠ BMP?

5 What do you now know about the line PQ?

What answers should Peter give to these questions?

How do Miss Edmunds' questions help you to construct a formal proof that the line PQ is the perpendicular bisector of AB?

Exercise 17.2

Look at these constructions.

1 **a)** An angle bisector.

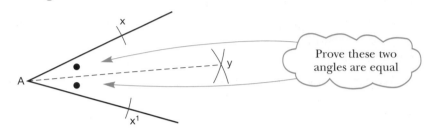

b) The perpendicular from a point Q on a line M.

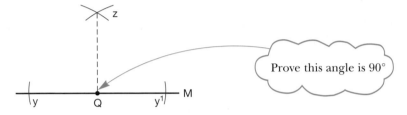

c) The perpendicular from a point P to a line L.

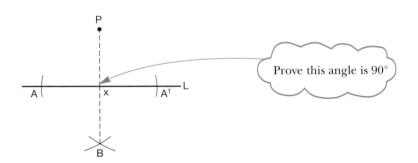

In each case draw the construction for yourself to make sure you see what is happening.
Then draw in lines to make suitable congruent triangles.
Then use your congruent triangles to prove that the construction works.

Exercise 17.3

1 In each case, decide whether triangles ABC, XYZ drawn with the following properties are congruent. If so, state which case of congruency applies.

a) AB = XY, BC = ZX, CA = YZ   **b)** AB = ZX, ∠B = ∠Y, ∠A = ∠Z

c) AB = XY, ∠A = ∠Y, ∠B = ∠X   **d)** AB = YZ, BC = ZX, ∠B = ∠Z

e) AB = XY, BC = YZ, ∠B = ∠Z   **f)** AB = ZX, BC = YX, CA = YZ

g) ∠B = ∠Z = 90°, AC = YZ, BC = XY

2 ABC is an isosceles triangle with AB = AC, and AD is the perpendicular from A to BC. Without assuming any other properties of isosceles triangles, prove that triangles ABD, ACD are congruent. Deduce that

a) ∠B = ∠C   **b)** D is the midpoint of BC   **c)** AD bisects ∠BAC.

Exercise 17.3 *continued*

3   A rectangle is defined as a parallelogram in which one angle is a right angle. Without assuming any other properties of rectangles prove that the diagonals of a rectangle are equal.

4   The diagonals of a quadrilateral are perpendicular and bisect each other. What can you deduce about the quadrilateral?

5   The diagram shows the straight edge and compasses construction of bisector of angle ABC.

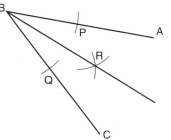

Prove that triangles BPR and BQR are congruent.

Hence explain how you know that the line BR bisects angle ABC.

6   A book contains these instructions.

'AB *is a line segment and* C *is a point which is not on the line* AB.

   ① *Draw a circle with centre* A *and radius* AC.

   ② *Draw a circle with centre* B *and radius* BC.

   ③ *Let* D *be the point of intersection (other than* C*) of the two circles.*

   ④ *Draw the line* CD.'

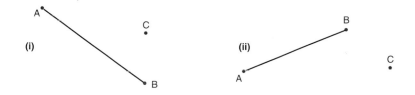

(i)   **(ii)**

a)   Copy the diagrams below and use these instruction to produce the line CD in each case.

b)   What relationship is there between the initial line AB and the constructed line CD in each case?

c)   Use congruent triangles to justify this relationship.

d)   What type of quadrilateral is ACBD?

7   AB is a line segment and C is a point on the line segment.

Devise a straight edge and compasses method of constructing a line through C which is perpendicular to the line AB.

Explain why your construction works.

8   A circle has centre C, PQ is a chord of the circle and M is the mid-point of PQ. The diameter of the circle that passes through M is drawn.

Use congruent triangles to prove that this diameter is perpendicular to PQ.

Exercise 17.3 *continued*

9 ABCD is a square and triangles XAB, YBC are both equilateral, with X inside and Y outside the square. Use triangles ABC, XBY to prove that XY equals the length of a diagonal of the square.

10 ABC is a triangle in which AB is longer than AC. The bisector of ∠A meets the perpendicular bisector of BC at K, the perpendicular from K to AB meets AB at P, and the perpendicular from K meets AC produced at Q. Prove that

   a) KP = KQ   **b)** KC = KB   **c)** BP = CQ.

11 In the diagram, AB = AC and AM is perpendicular to BC.

   By proving that triangles ABM and ACM are congruent, show that angle ABC = angle ACB.

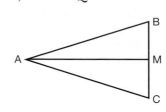

MEI

12 In the quadrilateral ABCD, AB is parallel and equal to DC. The diagonals AC and BD meet at a O.

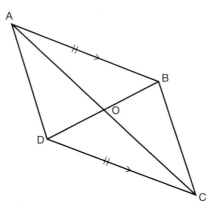

Use congruent triangles to prove that O is the mid-point of AC and BD.

MEI

13 Two straight lines RS and TV bisect each other at X.

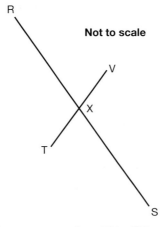

Not to scale

Use congruent triangles to prove that RT = VS.

MEI

Exercise 17.3 *continued*

14 A geometry book contains these instructions.

'AB *is a line segment and* C *is a point which is not on the line* AB.

① *Draw an arc with centre* C *and radius which is large enough to cross* AB *at a point* D.
② *Draw an arc with centre* D *and radius* CD *to meet* AB *at the point* E.
③ *Draw an arc with centre* D *and radius* CE *to meet the first arc at* F.
④ *Draw the line* CF.'

The diagram below shows the result of following these instructions.

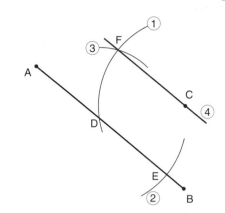

What relationship does there appear to be between the initial line AB and the constructed line CF?

Use congruent triangles to prove this relationship.

Drawing triangles

To draw a triangle accurately, you need to know at least three facts about the length of its sides and the size of its angles. You need a ruler, compasses and a protractor.

Drawing a triangle given one side and two angles

Follow these steps to draw a triangle ABC with side AB = 6 cm long, angle BAC = 62° and angle ABC = 47°.

① Draw and label the side AB (6 cm long).

② Put your protractor at end A of the line and mark off angle BAC.
Draw the line.

③ Do the same for angle ABC. Make sure the lines cross.

④ The point where the lines cross is point C.

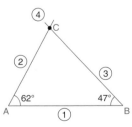

Drawing a triangle given the lengths of all three sides

Follow these steps to draw a triangle with sides of length 8 cm, 6 cm and 5 cm.

① Draw a line 8 cm long. (You could use any of the sides to start the triangle.)

② Open your compasses to a length of 6 cm. Put the point of the compasses on one end of the 8 cm line. Use the compasses to draw an arc (part of a circle) above the line.

③ Now open the compasses to a length of 5 cm. Put the point of the compasses on the other end of the 8 cm line. Draw another arc to cross the first arc. (If you find that you did not draw the first arc far enough, you will have to go back and make it longer.)

④ The point where the arcs cross is the third corner of the triangle. Join this point to both ends of the 8 cm line, and the triangle is complete.

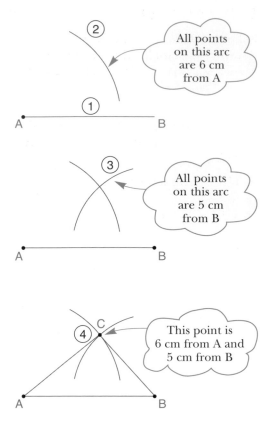

Drawing a triangle given two sides and the angle between them

Follow these steps to make an accurate drawing of triangle ABC, with side AB 7 cm long, side AC 5 cm long, and angle CAB 54°.

① Draw the line AB 7 cm long.

② Put the protractor at A and mark off the angle CAB. Draw a line.

③ Mark point C on the line 5 cm from A.

④ Join B to C to complete the triangle.

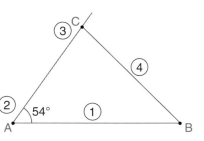

Drawing a triangle given two sides and an angle not between them

Follow these steps to make an accurate drawing of triangle ABC, with side AB 4 cm long, side AC 7 cm long and angle ABC 110°.

① Draw the line AB 4 cm long. (The first line you draw must be the one with the given angle at one end of it.)

② Use a protractor or angle measurer to mark off an angle of 110° at B, and draw a line. (Make the line longer than you think it needs to be.)

③ Open your compasses to a length of 7 cm. Put the point of the compasses at A. Draw an arc so that it crosses the line you have just drawn from B. Mark point C where the arc crosses the line.

④ Join C to A to complete the triangle.

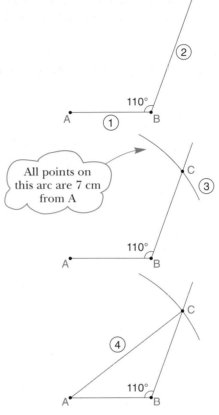

All points on this arc are 7 cm from A

Exercise 17.4

1 **a)** Make an accurate drawing of each of these triangles.

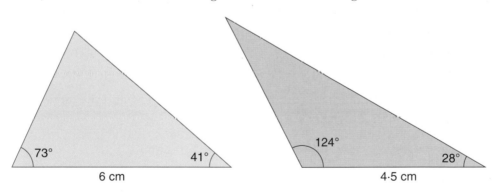

73°   41°   6 cm

124°   28°   4·5 cm

b) Measure the lengths of the other two sides of each triangle. Mark them on your drawings.

2 Make a rough sketch and then an accurate drawing of each of these triangles. On each accurate drawing, measure and label the lengths of the sides that were not given.

a) Triangle ABC with AB = 7 cm, angle ABC = 46° and angle BAC = 62°.

b) Triangle PQR with PQ = 5 cm, angle PQR = 108° and angle PRQ = 31°.

(Hint: work out angle QPR first.)

Exercise 17.4 *continued*

3 Make accurate drawings of triangles with sides as follows. On each drawing, measure and mark on the sizes of all the angles.

    a) 3 cm, 5 cm, 6 cm   **b)** 4.5 cm, 8 cm, 9 cm

    c) 4 cm, 5.2 cm, 6.8 cm   **d)** 7.1 cm, 3.2 cm, 8.4 cm.

4   **a)** Try to draw a triangle with sides 7 cm, 4 cm and 2 cm.

    b) Explain why it is not possible to draw this triangle.

5 In each part of this question three lengths are given. Some of these can form the sides of a triangle, others cannot. Without trying to draw the triangles say which can be drawn and which cannot.

    a) 3 cm, 6 cm, 8 cm   **b)** 4 cm, 3 cm, 9 cm

    c) 2.5 cm, 4.1 cm, 6.8 cm   **d)** 5.3 cm, 6.4 cm, 11.1 cm

    e) 4.2 cm, 5.7 cm, 9.9 cm

6 Make a rough sketch and then an accurate drawing of each of these triangles.

    a) Triangle DEF with DE = 8 cm, EF = 3 cm and angle DEF = 57°.

        Measure and mark on your diagram the length of side DF.

    b) Triangle XYZ with XY = 4 cm, XZ = 5.6 cm and angle YXZ = 135°.

        Measure and mark on your diagram the length of side YX.

7 Make a rough sketch and then an accurate drawing of each of these triangles.

    a) Triangle FGH with FG = 5 cm, FH = 6 cm and angle FGH = 54°.

        Measure and mark on your diagram the length GH and the angle GFH.

    b) Triangle LMN with MN = 3.8 cm, LN = 5.6 cm and angle LMN = 94°.

        Measure and mark on your diagram the length LM and the angle LNM.

8 You now know how to draw a triangle if you are given

    ● all three sides but no angles

    ● two sides and the angle between them

    ● two sides and an angle not between them

    ● one side and two angles.

Could you draw a triangle if you were given all three angles but no sides? Explain your answer.

Exercise 17.4 *continued*

9 **a)** Choose a suitable scale and make an accurate scale drawing of each of the triangular sails shown below.

   b) Measure on your drawings the angles marked *p*, *q*, *r* and *s*.

   c) Measure on your drawings the sides marked *a*, *b*, *c* and *d* and use your scale to work out the real lengths.

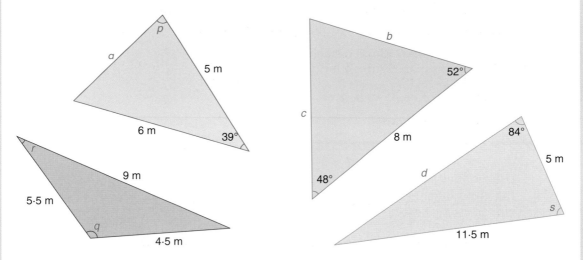

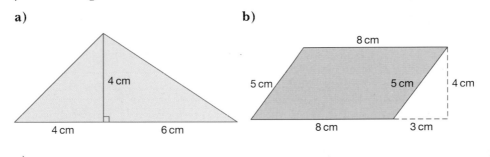

10 Make accurate drawings of the following shapes, and measure the angles you are not given.

   a)   **b)**

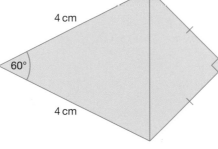

   c)

Locus

A *locus* (plural *loci*) is the set of points which satisfy a given condition or set of conditions. Every point of the locus must satisfy all the conditions, and every point which satisfies all the conditions must be included in the locus. Here all loci are in two dimensions.

- The locus of points a fixed distance *r* from a fixed point C is the circle with radius *r* and centre C.

- The locus of points whose distance from C is less than *r* is the interior of this circle.

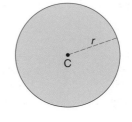

- The locus of points a fixed distance from a straight line is a pair of lines parallel to the given line.

- The red curve gives the locus of points a fixed distance from a line segment.

 What is the difference between a line and a line segment?

- The locus of points equidistant from two fixed points is the perpendicular bisector of the line joining these points.

- The locus of points equidistant from two non-parallel lines is the pair of bisectors of the angle formed by these lines.

 What is the angle between the two angle bisectors?

Locus of equidistant points

Exercise 17.5

1 Draw triangle ABC with AB = 4 cm, AC = 7 cm and ∠BAC = 58°.

a) Draw the locus of points equidistant from AB and AC (or these lines extended).

b) Draw the locus of points equidistant from B and C.

Mark on your diagram the two points P, Q which are equidistant from B and C and also equidistant from AB and AC. Measure the distance PQ.

2 When the Walton family go down to the beach they sit in an area where they are at least 20 m away from the car park, not more than 30 m from the café door, and more than 5 m from the high tide mark. On a scale drawing, shade the area within which they sit.

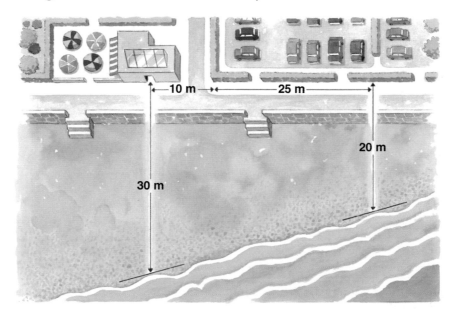

3 There are three secondary schools in Heretown. Toplea School is 7 miles from Yoosterby High and 9 miles from Frankly Comprehensive. Yoosterby and Frankly are 12 miles apart, and the railway station is halfway along the straight road joining them.

Gill and Len want to move house. They want Toplea to be the nearest secondary school and Len would like to be within 3 miles of the station. Show on a scale drawing the locus of points in an ideal position for the new house.

4 Two parties, A and B, set off from a base camp on an exploratory survey travelling at the same speed, A on a bearing of 048° and B on a bearing of 136°. A vehicle carrying supplies sets off from the camp at the same time as A and B.

a) Draw an accurate diagram showing the route the supply vehicle should follow if it is always equal distances from A and B.

The supply vehicle is to keep as near to A and B as possible.

b) Should the supply vehicle travel faster or slower than A?

c) Find the ratio of the supply vehicle's speed to A's speed. (Give your answer in the form *k* : 1.)

Finishing off

Now that you have finished this chapter you should be able to:

★ recognise similarity and prove similarity of triangles

★ use properties of similar shapes in calculations

★ recognise congruence and prove congruence of triangles

★ use congruent triangles to prove geometrical results

★ carry out ruler and compasses constructions and understand why they work

★ construct triangles and other 2-D shapes

★ draw simple loci.

Use the questions in the next exercise to check that you understand everything.

Mixed exercise 17.6

1

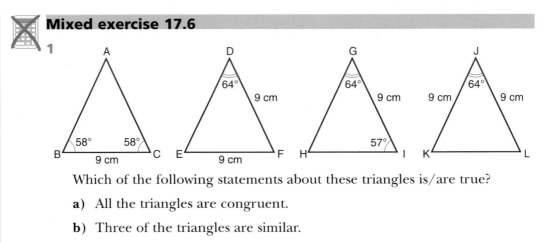

Which of the following statements about these triangles is/are true?

a) All the triangles are congruent.

b) Three of the triangles are similar.

c) Triangles ABC and JKL are congruent.

d) Triangles DEF and GHI are similar but not congruent.

e) Triangles ABC and JKL are similar but not congruent.

2

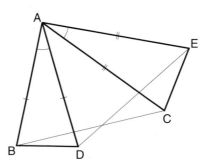

ABD and ACE are similar isosceles triangles with a common vertex A.
Prove that BC = DE.

Mixed exercise 17.6 *continued*

3   Craig used the following method to find the width of a straight canal.
He placed a stake at B directly opposite a tree A on the opposite bank of
the canal. He walked 10 metres along the canal to point C where he
placed another stake.
He walked another 2 metres to point D. He then walked at right angles to
the canal until he reached a point E directly in line with A and C.

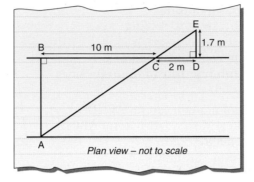

Plan view – not to scale

a) Explain clearly why triangle ABC is similar to triangle EDC.

b) Given that the distance DE = 1.7 metres, find the width AB of the canal.

MEI

4   In the diagram, PQ = PS and
PR = PT. Angle RPT = angle SPQ.

a) Show that triangles PRQ and
PTS are congruent.

b) Hence show that PS bisects
angle QST.

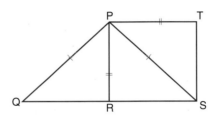

London

5   These triangles are congruent.

a) What is the value of *x*?

b) What is the length, *y*?

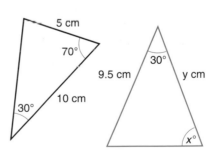

NEAB

6   Given the information in
the diagram

a) prove that triangles XAD,
XCB are similar;

b) prove that ∠ ABC and ∠ ADC
are supplementary (i.e. add
up to 180°).

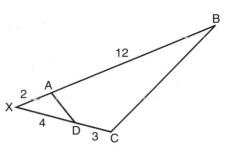

Mixed exercise 17.6 *continued*

7   Lines AP, BQ, CR are drawn inside triangle ABC so that the marked angles are equal.

   Prove that triangles ABC, PQR are similar.

   Investigate what happens if the lines are drawn outside triangle ABC.

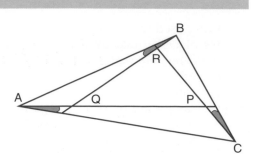

8   A parallelogram can be defined as a quadrilateral with one pair of opposite sides equal and parallel.

   The diagonals of a quadrilateral ABCD bisect each other. Must quadrilateral ABCD always be a parallelogram? Justify your answer carefully.

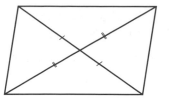

MEI (adapted)

9   Draw a scale diagram with scale 1 cm to 1 km showing the positions of two oil rigs, A and B, which are 7 km apart with B on bearing 210° from A.

   Ships are asked to keep out of the region less than 2 km from oil rig B.

   a) Shade that part of the diagram which represents the region less than 2 km from B.

   A boat sails so that it is always the same distance from A as it is from B.

   b) On the diagram draw the route taken by the boat.

   The 7 km distance has been rounded to the nearest kilometre.

   c) (i) Write down the minimum distance it could be.

   (ii) Write down the maximum distance it could be.   *London*

10   Scale: 1 cm to 10 cm

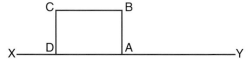

   The diagram represents a box which is to be moved across a floor XY.
   AD = 30 cm and AB = 20 cm.

   First the box is rotated about the point A so that BC becomes vertical.
   Then the box is rotated about the new position of the point B so that CD becomes vertical.

   a) Make a scale drawing of the diagram above (scale 1 cm to 10 cm) and draw on it the locus of the point C.

   b) Calculate the maximum height of C above the floor. Give your answer correct to one decimal place.

   (A measurement from the scale drawing is unacceptable.)   *London*

Investigation

Investigate sets of conditions which ensure that two quadrilaterals are

a) similar   b) congruent.

Chapter 18

Probability

Before you start this chapter you should:

★ know that probability is measured on a scale from 0 (impossible) to 1 (certain)

★ be able to calculate the probabilities of an event happening and not happening

★ know the meaning of the terms fair and at random

★ be able to use data to estimate probabilities

★ be able to use probability to estimate the number of times an event can be expected to occur.

Reminder

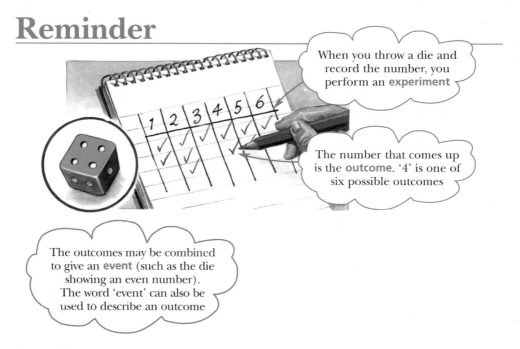

When you throw a die and record the number, you perform an **experiment**

The number that comes up is the **outcome**. '4' is one of six possible outcomes

The outcomes may be combined to give an **event** (such as the die showing an even number). The word 'event' can also be used to describe an outcome

Example

A fair die is thrown.

a) What is the probability that it comes up 5?

b) What is the probability that it does not come up 5?

c) The die is thrown 300 times. How many times would it be expected to come up 5?

Solution

a) Probability = $\dfrac{\text{Number of favourable outcomes}}{\text{Number of possible outcomes}}$

> There is one favourable outcome, the number 5

 P means Probability

P (die comes up 5) = $\dfrac{1}{6}$

> There are six possible outcomes, the numbers 1, 2, 3, 4, 5 and 6

b) P (die does not come up 5) = 1 – P (die comes up 5)

$$= 1 - \dfrac{1}{6}$$

$$= \dfrac{5}{6}$$

> You could have said there are five favourable outcomes (1, 2, 3, 4 and 6) out of six possible outcomes (1, 2, 3, 4, 5 and 6)

c) Expected number of 5s = $\dfrac{1}{6} \times 300$

$$= 50$$

Most times you would not get exactly fifty 5s from 300 throws. You would usually get between forty and sixty.

Notice that you can only use the definition

$$\text{Probability} = \dfrac{\text{Number of favourable outcomes}}{\text{Number of possible outcomes}}$$

when all the outcomes are equally likely (equiprobable).

Think of an experiment where the possible outcomes are not equally likely.

Sometimes it is helpful to show the outcomes in a list or in a table. The table below shows the outcomes when you throw two fair dice; the outcomes are given as totals.

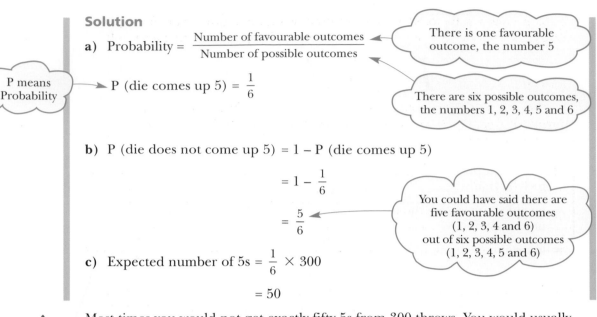

Die 1

		1	2	3	4	5	6
	1	2	3	4	5	6	7
	2	3	4	5	6	7	8
Die 2	3	4	5	6	7	8	9
	4	5	6	7	8	9	10
	5	6	7	8	9	10	11
	6	7	8	9	10	11	12

You can see that the probability of getting a total of 7 is given by

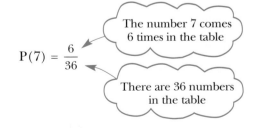

> The number 7 comes 6 times in the table

P(7) = $\dfrac{6}{36}$

> There are 36 numbers in the table

 What is the probability of getting a total of 10 when two dice are thrown?

What about a total of 1?

There are many situations where you cannot work out a probability from theory and so have to estimate it on the basis of data, as in the next example.

Example

Most beech trees have green leaves but a few occur naturally with copper (purple) leaves. The table below shows the results of counts of the different sorts in two woods.

Wood	Green-leaf trees	Copper-leaf trees
Great Spinney	75	5
Norman Copse	38	2

Use the results from each wood separately and from the two together to obtain three estimates of the probability that a randomly selected tree has copper leaves.

Solution

Great Spinney (80 trees):

Estimated probability $= \dfrac{5}{80} = \dfrac{1}{16} = 0.0625$

> In a situation like this, the fraction $\dfrac{5}{80}$ is sometimes called the **relative frequency**

Norman Copse (40 trees):

Estimated probability $= \dfrac{2}{40} = \dfrac{1}{20} = 0.05$

Altogether (120 trees)

Estimated probability $= \dfrac{7}{120} = 0.583$

 Which of the three estimates do you think is likely to be the most accurate?

 Jasmine says, 'When the two are taken together you should get the average value
$\dfrac{(0.0625 + 0.05)}{2} = 0.056\,25$'.

 Explain the mistake in her reasoning.

Review exercise 18.1

1 Classify each of these events as impossible, unlikely, likely or certain:

a) getting a 7 on a throw with an ordinary die

b) it snowing in Birmingham during next January

c) a cat catching a mouse somewhere tomorrow

d) you living to the age of 100.

2 When this spinner is spun, the side that it lands on is the outcome.

 a) How many possible outcomes are there?

b) What is the probability of getting

    (i) green?

    (ii) yellow?

    (iii) not red?

3 A set of snooker balls is made up of one each of white, yellow, green, brown, blue, pink, and black, and 15 red balls.

All the balls are put into a bag and one is taken out at random.

What is the probability that it is

a) red?

b) white?

c) green, brown or yellow?

d) not white?

4 a) Copy and complete this table, showing the possible outcomes when you throw a die and a coin.

	1	2	3	4	5	6
Head		H,2				
Tail				T,4		

b) What is the probability of getting

    (i) an even number?

    (ii) a head and an even number?

    (iii) a tail and a number greater than 4?

Review exercise 18.1 *continued*

5 Here are the possible outcomes from tossing a coin and spinning a spinner, which is an equilateral triangle with colours red, blue and green.

a) Is each outcome equally likely?

b) Find the probability of getting

(i) red (ii) a tail and blue

(iii) a head and not green.

	Red	Blue	Green
Head	H,R	H,B	H,G
Tail	T,R	T,B	T,G

6 John kept a record of the minimum night-time temperatures last January.

```
                        JANUARY

  Su             -10   6    5   13    6   20   -1   27
  Mo             -12   7    4   14    6   21   -4   28
  Tu    5    1   -10   8   -1   15    5   22   -2   29
  W     2    2   -15   9    0   16    5   23   -3   30
  Th    0    3    -1  10   -1   17    2   24    4   31
  F    -4    4     2  11    3   18    3   25
  Sa   -6    5     8  12    4   19   -1   26
```

Use the figures to estimate the probability that on a night chosen at random next January the minimum temperature will be

a) below freezing (0°C)

b) above freezing

c) above –2°C.

7 A certain commonly prescribed tablet causes an upset stomach in some patients. Data are collected from a number of doctors' practices to investigate this.

Practice	Number of prescriptions issued	Number of patients reporting upset stomach
A	50	6
B	45	4
C	30	5

a) Use these data to estimate the probability that a patient will have an upset stomach.

b) Estimate the probability that a patient will not have an upset stomach.

c) What reasons could be given to support the suggestion that these figures are not accurate?

d) In one Health Authority 1500 prescriptions are issued for these tablets. How many people are likely to report an upset stomach?

Review exercise 18.1 *continued*

8 A family has three children.

  a) Complete the table, showing its possible composition of boys and girls.

  b) Using this table, find the probability that

3 boys	BBB
2 boys, 1 girl	BBG, BGB, GBB
1 boy, 2 girls	
3 girls	

(Each entry is in the order of age)

  (i) there are no boys

  (ii) there are more boys than girls.

  c) What assumption did you need to make in order to be able to do part **b**)?

9 **a)** Copy and complete this diagram showing the possible totals when two fair dice are thrown.

  b) What is the probability of totals of:

  (i) 12
  (ii) not 12
  (iii) 7
  (iv) 4 or 6?

Second die

6						
5						
4			7	8		
3			6			
2			5			
1	2	3	4			
	1	2	3	4	5	6

First die

  c) In part **a)** the dice are described as 'fair'. What does this word mean in this situation?

Mutually exclusive events

A die is thrown once.

The outcome could be 3.   The outcome could be 2.

It cannot be both 3 and 2 at the same time.

If the outcome is 3, this prevents the outcome being 2. If it is 2, then 3 cannot happen.

This means P(3 and 2) = 0.

The two outcomes are **mutually exclusive**. Either one of them prevents the other.

Indeed, all six outcomes for a die are mutually exclusive. Any one of them occurring prevents the others.

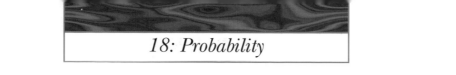

To find the probability of one **or** other of mutually exclusive outcomes, you just add the individual probabilities.

So, for the die $P(2 \text{ or } 3) = P(2) + P(3) = \frac{1}{6} + \frac{1}{6} = \frac{2}{6} = \frac{1}{3}$

In general, if the events A, B, C, ... are mutually exclusive, then

$$\mathbf{P(A \text{ or } B \text{ or } C \text{ or } ...) = P(A) + P(B) + P(C) + ...}$$

Example

The colours of 100 paper hats are red (40), mauve (10), yellow (30) and green (20). The hats are put in Christmas crackers. Each cracker has just one hat.

One of the crackers is chosen at random.

What is the probability that it will contain

a) a red hat?   **b)** a yellow hat?   **c)** a red or yellow hat?

d) a hat which is neither red nor yellow?

Solution

The four different outcomes are mutually exclusive. For example, getting a red hat means you cannot get a yellow hat.

So the probabilities can be added.

   a) $P(\text{red}) = \dfrac{40}{100} = 0.4$

   b) $P(\text{yellow}) = \dfrac{30}{100} = 0.3$

   c) $P(\text{red or yellow}) = P(\text{red}) + P(\text{yellow}) = 0.4 + 0.3 = 0.7$

   d) $P(\text{neither red nor yellow}) = 1 - P(\text{red or yellow})$
   $$= 1 - 0.7 = 0.3$$

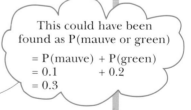

This could have been found as P(mauve or green)
= P(mauve) + P(green)
= 0.1   + 0.2
= 0.3

**It is often helpful to think of mutually exclusive events as
'either, or' situations. Add probabilities in these cases.**

Exercise 18.3 *continued*

6   Brian enjoys swimming.

If it is a sunny day the probability that he swims is 0.9.

If the day is not sunny, the probability that he swims is 0.65.

The probability that tomorrow will be sunny is 0.8.

a) Draw a tree diagram to illustrate this information.

b) Calculate the probability that Brian will not swim tomorrow.

MEG

7   A town council keeps records of whether or not it is raining at 8 p.m. every day for one year. The results are summarised in the table below which gives the number of days each month it was not raining, and was raining.

Month	No rain	Rain	Month	No rain	Rain	Month	No rain	Rain
Jan	11	20	May	21	10	Sept	21	9
Feb	14	14	June	24	6	Oct	21	10
Mar	15	16	July	26	5	Nov	16	14
Apr	14	16	Aug	24	7	Dec	16	15

The Council are trying to book an Australian pop group for an open air concert, starting at 8 p.m., one day next year.

a) Estimate the probability that it will be raining at the start of the concert if:

   (i)   it is held in September

   (ii) it is held some time in May, June, July or August

   (iii) it could be held any time in the year.

b) The Council want to offer the group the period covering the greatest number of months for which the overall probability that it will not be raining is greater than 0.75. Which months should they choose?

c) The data were grouped into months. A local politician says this was silly: 'We could have been much more certain if we had kept it day by day.' Is he right?

8   A poultry breeder is developing a new breed of chicken in which, as chicks, the hens are speckled and the cockerels plain coloured. (This will make it easy to sex the chicks when they are newly hatched.)

The table refers to the chicks in the most recent batch. All chicks are either speckled or plain.

	Hens	Cockerels
Speckled	66	18
Plain	4	62

a) A chick is speckled. Estimate the probability that it is a hen.

b) A chick is a hen. Estimate the probability that it is speckled.

c) At this stage the breeder classifies all speckled chicks as hens and all plain chicks as cockerels. Estimate the probability of a chick being incorrectly classified.

Finishing off

> **Now that you have completed this chapter you should be able to:**
>
> ★ calculate and estimate probability
> ★ calculate probabilities for mutually exclusive events
> ★ calculate probabilities for independent events
> ★ draw tree diagrams and use them to calculate probabilities
> ★ work with conditional probabilities.

Use the questions in the next exercise to check that you understand everything.

Mixed exercise 18.4

1   When Alan and Bill play snooker Alan wins with probability 0.65.

   a)   What is the probability that Bill wins?

   If Alan and Bill play two games of snooker, find the probability that

   b)   Alan wins both games

   c)   Alan wins one game and Bill wins the other.

2   Mrs Jones buys three tulip bulbs at random from a large bucket which contains 30% red-flowering bulbs and 70% yellow-flowering bulbs.

   Draw a tree diagram to illustrate all the different purchases that Mrs Jones could make.

   Find the probability that she buys

   a)   three red-flowering bulbs

   b)   three bulbs which will produce flowers of the same colour

   c)   two yellow-flowering bulbs and one red-flowering bulb.

3   All female chaffinches have the same pattern of laying eggs.

   The probability that any female chaffinch will lay a certain number of eggs is given in the table below.

Number of eggs	0	1	2	3	4 or more
Probability	0.1	0.3	0.3	0.2	0.1

   a)   Calculate the probability that a female chaffinch will lay less than three eggs.

   b)   Calculate the probability that two female chaffinches will lay a total of two eggs.

London

Mixed exercise 18.4 *continued*

4   Some parts of a garden are dry and some damp, while some parts of the garden are sunny and some shady. The tables below show the number of Foxglove seedlings planted in each part of the garden and the number of these plants which grew to the flowering stage.

Number planted in	Sunny conditions	Shady conditions
Dry conditions	24	30
Damp conditions	45	18

Number growing to flowering stage in	Sunny conditions	Shady conditions
Dry conditions	15	24
Damp conditions	27	12

Use this information to decide where Foxglove seedlings should be planted so that they have the greatest chance of growing to the flowering stage.

Show how you decide.   *MEI*

5   The month in which each student at a sixth-form college was born is recorded.

Month	Jan	Feb	Mar	Apr	May	Jun	Jul	Aug	Sep	Oct	Nov	Dec	Total
Number of birthdays	28	25	25	30	34	31	33	22	29	23	28	32	340

a) Estimate the probability that a student chosen at random was born between November and February (inclusive).

b) What is the probability that a student chosen at random was not born during the months July or August?

c) There are usually more births in May than in other months.

   (i)   Are these figures consistent with that pattern?

   (ii) Someone is selected at random from a pop concert.
         Would you be right to say that the probability of that person being born in May is exactly $\frac{1}{10}$?

6   Light bulbs are tested by passing a high voltage through them until they fail.

The light bulb passes the test if it lasts more than a certain time.

a) Why should a sample of light bulbs from a batch be tested to see whether the batch is acceptable rather than testing the whole batch?

b) In a sample of 100 bulbs, 3 fail.

   (i)   Estimate the probability that a bulb taken from this batch will pass.

   (ii) A sample of 200 bulbs from the same batch gives P(pass) = 0.98. Give the best estimate of P(fail) for this batch.

Mixed exercise 18.4 *continued*

7   On Mondays, Wednesdays and Fridays, Laura and some of her friends have lunch in a particular café.

If Laura arrives at 12:30 for lunch, there is a probability of 0.7 that she is first to arrive.

One week, Laura arrives at 12:30 for lunch on all three days.

a) Find the probability that Laura will be first to arrive on all three days.

b) Find the most likely number of days in this week on which Laura will be first to arrive.

Show the calculations you do to justify your conclusion.

MEI

8

a) Wayne and Donna each have five cards lettered A, B, C, D and E.

Both sets of cards have been placed face down on the table.

They each pick up one of their cards at random.

(i)   What is the probability that they both pick up a card lettered B?

(ii) What is the probability that they both pick up a card with the same letter?

b) Colin and Dipak are playing a series of games each of which one of them must win.

The probability that Colin wins the first game is 0.6.

For further games the probability that Colin wins is: 0.8 if he won the previous game; 0.3 if he lost the previous game.

(i)   Calculate the probability that Dipak wins the first two games.

(ii) Calculate the probability that, in three games, Colin wins two and Dipak one.

MEG

Mixed exercise 18.4 *continued*

9   In the game of tennis a player has two serves.

If the first serve is successful the game continues.

If the first serve is not successful the player serves again. If this second serve is successful the game continues.

If both serves are unsuccessful the player has served a 'double fault' and loses the point.

Gabriella plays tennis. She is successful with 60% of her first serves and 95% of her second serves.

a) Calculate the probability that Gabriella serves a double fault.

If Gabriella is successful with her first serve she has a probability of 0.75 of winning the point.

If she is successful with her second serve she has a probability of 0.5 of winning the point.

b) Calculate the probability that Gabriella wins the point.

MEG

10 Peter and Asif are both taking their driving test for a motor cycle for the first time.

The table below gives the probabilities that they will pass the test at the first attempt or, if they fail the first time, the probability that they will pass at the next attempt.

	Probability of passing at first attempt	Probability of passing at next attempt if they fail the first attempt
Peter	0.6	0.8
Asif	0.7	0.7

On a particular day 1000 people will take the test for the first time.

For each person the probability that they will pass the test at the first attempt is the same as the probability that Asif will pass the test at the first attempt.

a) Work out an estimate for how many of these 1000 people are likely to pass the test at the first attempt.

b) Calculate the probability that both Peter and Asif will pass the test at the first attempt.

c) Calculate the probability that Peter will pass the test at the first attempt and Asif will fail the test at the first attempt.

d) Calculate the probability that Asif will pass the test within the first two attempts.

London

Mixed exercise 18.4 *continued*

11 Mr McTaggart lives on the island of Fluva. He walks to work but is quite often late, particularly when the weather is wet. During the last year there were 240 working days. The state of the weather, and Mr McTaggart's punctuality at work, are summarised in the table below.

		Weather	
		Dry	Wet
Mr McTaggart	On time	72	120
	Late	8	40

A day is selected at random for next year. Estimate the probability

a) that it will be wet

b) that Mr McTaggart will be late for work.

One day Mr McTaggart is late for work.

c) Estimate the probability that it is wet (assuming that you do not know whether or not it really is wet).

12 A test for a disease gives a positive result 95% of the time when used on someone who has the disease. When tried on someone who does not have the disease, it gives a positive result 8% of the time. In a particular group of patients 30% of them have the disease.

a) Copy and complete the following tree diagram:

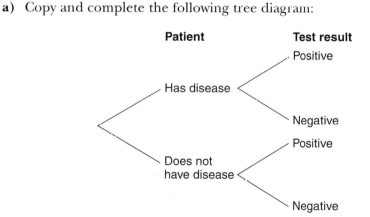

b) Use the tree diagram to find the probability that:

    (i)   a patient chosen at random has the disease and tests positive

    (ii) a patient chosen at random does not have the disease and tests negative

    (iii) the test result is correct

    (iv) the test result is wrong.

Trigonometry

Reminder

Pythagoras' theorem is:

$$a^2 + b^2 = c^2$$

Remember that c is the hypotenuse

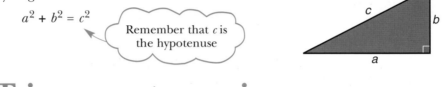

Trigonometry review

This section revises the work on trigonometry.

The three trigonometrical ratios are:

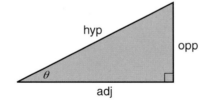

$$\sin \theta = \frac{\text{opp}}{\text{hyp}} \qquad \cos \theta = \frac{\text{adj}}{\text{hyp}} \qquad \tan \theta = \frac{\text{opp}}{\text{adj}}$$

You can use these ratios to find sides and angles in right-angled triangles.

Finding a side

Example 1

Find the value of x in this triangle.

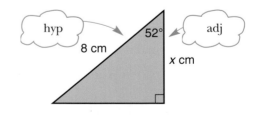

Solution

The first step is to decide whether to use sin, cos or tan.

The side that is 8 cm is the hypotenuse, and the side that is x is the adjacent side, so you use cos.

$$\cos 52° = \frac{x}{8}$$
$$x = 8 \cos 52°$$
$$x = 4.93 \text{ (in cm)}$$

In the next example an extra step is needed, because the unknown side is the denominator of the fraction.

Example 2

Rachel is standing on top of a cliff 150 m high. She can see a boat out at sea. The angle of depression of the boat is 28°.

How far is the boat from the foot of the cliff?

Solution

$$\tan 28° = \frac{150}{d}$$

$$d \tan 28° = 150$$

$$d = \frac{150}{\tan 28°}$$

$$d = 282 \ (3 \text{ s.f.})$$

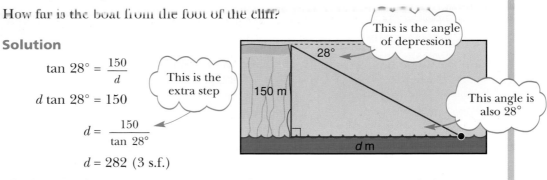

This is the angle of depression

This is the extra step

This angle is also 28°

The boat is 282 m from the foot of the cliff.

? *Check that you know how to use the sin, cos and tan functions on your calculator by working out the answers to the examples above.*

Finding an angle

To find an angle in a right-angled triangle, you need to use the inverse of sin, cos or tan. On your calculator these may be labelled arcsin, arccos and arctan, or $\sin^{-1}$, $\cos^{-1}$ and $\tan^{-1}$.

Example

Find the angle marked θ in this triangle.

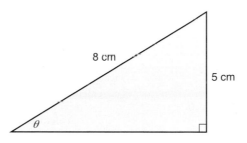

Solution

The 5 cm side is the opposite side, and the 8 cm side is the hypotenuse, so you need to use sin.

$$\sin \theta = \frac{5}{8} \qquad \theta = 38.7°$$

Three-dimensional problems

When solving a problem in three dimensions, always draw a true shape diagram (so that right angles look like 90°) of the right-angled triangle you are using.

The angle between a line and a plane is the angle between the line and a line immediately below it on the plane. You may find it helpful to think of it as the shadow of the line if a light were shining from directly above.

Example

Find the angle between the edge AE and the base ABCD of this pyramid.

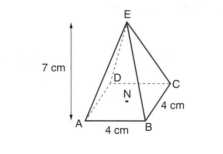

Solution

This is the triangle you need to use, and θ is the angle you need to find. The point N is directly below E (at the centre of the face ABCD).

First you need to find the distance AN. This is half the distance AC, which you can find using Pythagoras' theorem in this triangle.

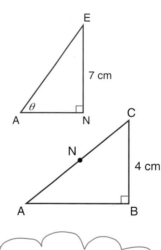

$$AC^2 = 4^2 + 4^2 = 32$$

$$AC = \sqrt{32}$$

$$AN = \frac{1}{2}\sqrt{32}$$

Store this value in the calculator to use in the next part of the calculation

Now you can find the angle θ.

$$\tan \theta = \frac{7}{AN} \qquad \theta = 68.0°$$

Explain why the angle EAN, *found in the example above, is the smallest possible angle between the line* EA *and the plane* ABCD. *(Consider some other possible angles, such as* EAB.)

Review exercise 19.1

1 Find the value of x in these triangles.

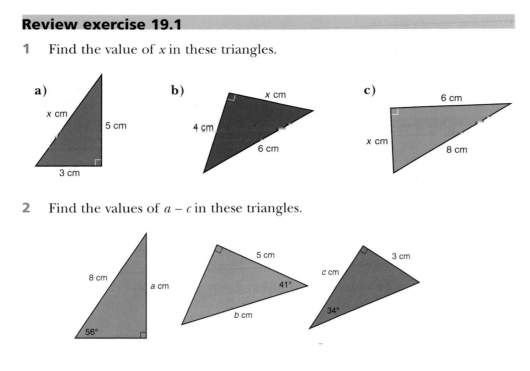

a)

x cm, 5 cm, 3 cm

b)

x cm, 4 cm, 6 cm

c)

6 cm, x cm, 8 cm

2 Find the values of $a - c$ in these triangles.

8 cm, a cm, 56°

5 cm, 41°, b cm, c cm

3 cm, 34°

3 Find the angles marked with letters in these triangles.

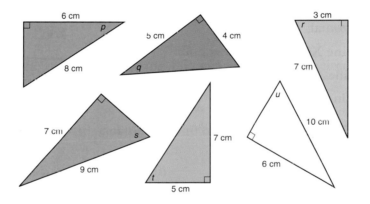

6 cm, p, 8 cm

5 cm, 4 cm, q

3 cm, r, 7 cm

7 cm, s, 9 cm

t, 7 cm, 5 cm

u, 10 cm, 6 cm

4 A rectangular field is 120 m long and 70 m wide.

What is the diagonal distance across the field?

5 In this cuboid, X is the mid-point of AD, Y is the mid-point of CG and Z is the mid-point of GH.

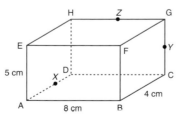

Find the lengths of

a) AG   b) AY   c) AZ

d) GX   e) XY   f) XZ

Finding an angle using the sine rule

You have used the sine rule to find the length of a side. You can also use the sine rule to find an angle.

To find an angle, it is easier to write the sine rule like this.

$$\frac{\sin A}{a} = \frac{\sin B}{b}$$

 Why is this the same as the other version of the sine rule?

Example

Find the angle x in this triangle.

Solution

$$\frac{\sin x}{7} = \frac{\sin 58}{8}$$

$$\sin x = \frac{\sin 58}{8} \times 7$$

$$x = 47.9° \quad \text{or} \quad x = 132.1°$$

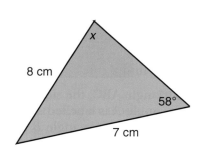

 Why are there two possible values for x?

In fact, $x = 47.9°$ is the only possible correct answer.

 Why is it impossible for x to be $132.1°$?

Sometimes both answers are possible, as in the next example.

Example

Find angle y in this triangle.

Solution

$$\frac{\sin y}{8} = \frac{\sin 42}{5.5}$$

$$\sin y = \frac{\sin 42}{5.5} \times 8$$

$$y = 76.7° \quad \text{or} \quad y = 103.3°$$

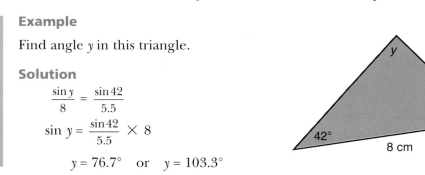

Why are both of these solutions possible?

Note: Do not be influenced by what the diagram looks like. You can't assume that an angle is acute or obtuse just because it has been drawn that way.

19: Trigonometry

Exercise 19.4

1 Use the sine rule to find x in each of these triangles.

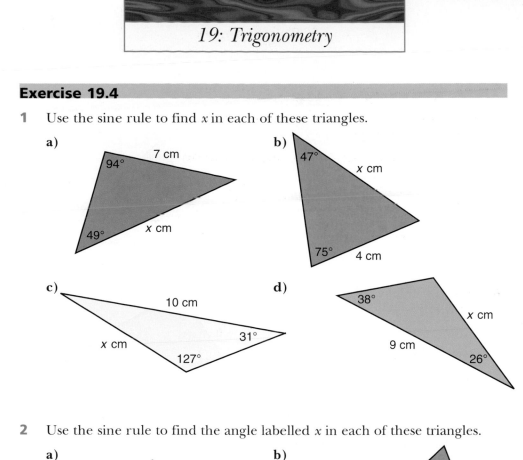

a)

94° 7 cm

49° x cm

b)

47° x cm

75° 4 cm

c)

10 cm

x cm 31°

127°

d)

38° x cm

9 cm 26°

2 Use the sine rule to find the angle labelled x in each of these triangles.

a)

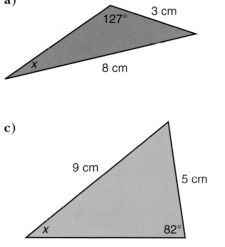

127° 3 cm

x

8 cm

b)

10 cm 6 cm

43° x

c)

9 cm 5 cm

x 82°

d)

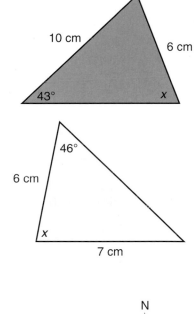

46°

6 cm

x

7 cm

3 Neil is on a countryside walk. He notices a windmill in the distance and finds that the bearing of the windmill is 142°. He then walks 3 km on a bearing of 053° and finds that the bearing of the windmill is now 206°.

a) Copy the diagram and fill in the known angles.

b) Find the distance of the windmill from each of the points where Neil took a bearing.

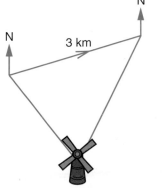

N

N 3 km

The cosine rule

 Why can't you use the sine rule to find x in this triangle?

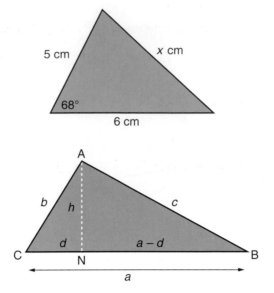

5 cm

x cm

68°

6 cm

 How could you find x by dividing the triangle into two right-angled triangles?

Again, you can find a rule by generalising the method.

Pythagoras' theorem for triangle ANB: $\quad h^2 + (a-d)^2 = c^2$

Pythagoras' theorem for triangle ANC: $\quad h^2 + d^2 = b^2$

Subtract to eliminate h: $\quad (a-d)^2 - d^2 = c^2 - b^2$

Expand the brackets: $\quad a^2 - 2ad + d^2 - d^2 = c^2 - b^2$

Tidy up: $\quad a^2 - 2ad = c^2 - b^2$

Using triangle ACN: $\quad \cos C = \dfrac{d}{b}$

$\quad d = b \cos C$

Substitute in ①: $\quad a^2 - 2ab \cos C = c^2 - b^2$

$\quad a^2 + b^2 - 2ab \cos C = c^2$

This is the **cosine rule**. It is usually written like this.

$$c^2 = a^2 + b^2 - 2ab \cos C$$

The cosine rule can be used to find the third side of a triangle when you know the other two sides and the angle between them.

 What happens to the cosine rule if C is 90°? Why?

Example

Use the cosine rule to find x in the triangle at the top of the page.

Solution

$\quad x^2 = 5^2 + 6^2 - 2 \times 5 \times 6 \cos 68°$

$\quad x = 6.21$ (in cm)

Work this out on your calculator all in one go. Then take the square root of the answer

 Work this out on your calculator and check that you get the same answer.

Using the cosine rule to find an angle

If you know all three sides of a triangle, you can use the cosine rule to find any of the angles.

It is easiest if you use a rearranged form of the cosine rule.

$$\cos C = \frac{a^2 + b^2 - c^2}{2ab}$$

c is the side opposite the angle that you want to find

? *Check that you can rearrange the other form of the cosine rule to get this one.*

Example

Find the angle C in this triangle.

Solution

$$\cos C = \frac{a^2 + b^2 - c^2}{2ab}$$

Work this out on your calculator and then use $\cos^{-1}$

$$\cos C = \frac{6^2 + 7^2 - 8^2}{2 \times 6 \times 7}$$

$$\cos C = \frac{21}{84}$$

$$C = 75.5°$$

? *Check that you get the same answer on your calculator.*

? *Why is there only one possible answer, unlike when you use the sine rule to find an angle?*

For some situations, you need to use both the sine and cosine rules.

? *Explain how you would find x and y in these triangles.*

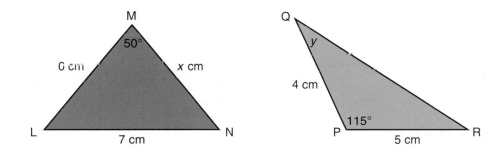

Exercise 19.5

1 Use the cosine rule to find *x* in each of these triangles.

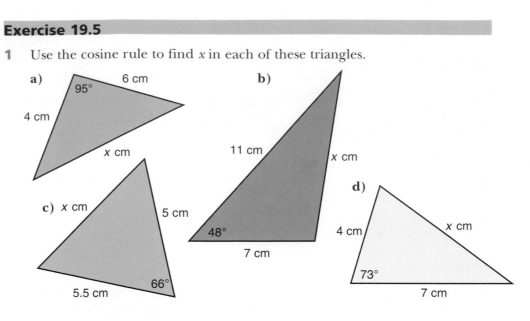

a) 95° 6 cm
4 cm
x cm

b) 11 cm
x cm
48°
7 cm

c) *x* cm
5 cm
66°
5.5 cm

d) 4 cm
x cm
73°
7 cm

2 Use the cosine rule to find the angle marked *x* in each of these triangles.

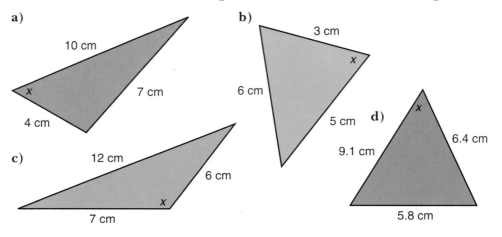

a) 10 cm
x
7 cm
4 cm

b) 3 cm
x
6 cm
5 cm

c) 12 cm
6 cm
x
7 cm

d) *x*
9.1 cm
6.4 cm
5.8 cm

3 Find all the unknown sides and angles in these triangles.

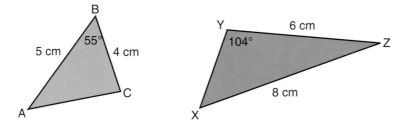

B
55°
5 cm   4 cm
A   C

Y   6 cm
104°   Z
X   8 cm

4 Prove the cosine rule for this triangle.

☆
☆
☆
☆
☆
☆
☆

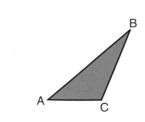

B
A   C

Solving problems using the sine and cosine rules

When solving a problem involving triangles, you have to decide whether you need to use the sine rule, the cosine rule or a combination of both. Sometimes there is more than one possible approach.

Remember:

- To use the sine rule you need to know an angle, the side opposite it, and one other side or angle.

- To use the cosine rule you need to know two sides and the angle between them, or all three sides.

Example

A ship starts from point A and sails 40 km on a bearing of 318° to point B. It then changes course and sails a further 35 km on a bearing of 236°, to reach point C.

Find the distance and bearing to get back from C to A.

Solution

First draw a clear diagram showing the known sides and angles.

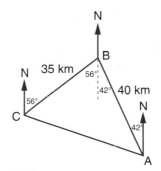

You can find the side AC by using the cosine rule.

$$AC^2 = 40^2 + 35^2 - 2 \times 40 \times 35 \cos 98°$$
$$AC = 56.698$$

Store this value in your calculator

You can now use the sine rule to find the angle BCA.

$$\frac{\sin 98}{AC} = \frac{\sin C}{40}$$
$$\sin C = \frac{\sin 98}{AC} \times 40$$
$$C = 44.3° \quad \text{or} \quad 135.7° \qquad \text{(to 1 decimal place)}$$

The angle BCA cannot be obtuse, as angle ABC is obtuse,

so   ∠BCA = 44.3°.

Bearing of A from C = 56° + 44.3° = 100.3°.

The ship must sail 56.7 km (to 1 decimal place) on a bearing of 100.3°.

Working in three dimensions

You have already solved three-dimensional problems involving right-angled triangles. You can use the same sort of approach when using the sine and cosine rules in three dimensions. The important thing is to draw a clear true shape diagram of any triangles you use.

Exercise 19.6

1 Nicole walks 5 km on a bearing of 128°. She then walks a further 3 km on a bearing of 245°.

How far and on what bearing does she need to walk to get back to her starting point?

2 For the cuboid ABCDEFGH

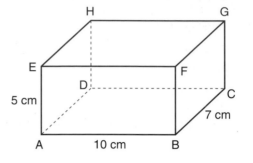

   a) Find the lengths of these lines. Leave the square roots in your answers.

      (i)   AC

      (ii) CH

      (iii) AH.

   b) Find the angle ACH.

3 Three points P, Q and R in three-dimensional space have co-ordinates (3, 1, –2), (5, –2, 1) and (–1, 0, 4) respectively.

Find the angle PQR.

4 A statue stands on a column.

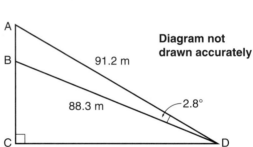

Diagram not drawn accurately

In the diagram AB represents the statue and BC represents the column.

Angle ACD = 90°.

Angle BDA = 2.8°.

AD = 91.2 m and BD = 88.3 m.

ABC is a vertical straight line.

   a) Calculate the height, AB, of the statue. Give your answer, in metres, correct to 3 significant figures.

   b) Calculate the height, BC, of the column. Give your answer, in metres, correct to 3 significant figures.

Edexcel

5 Find the angles A, B and C in this quadrilateral.

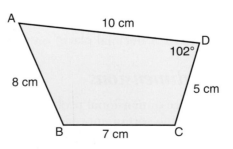

The area of a triangle

You have seen that the area of a triangle is given by the rule:

Remember:
a and *b* are two sides of the triangle and *C* is the angle between those two sides

$$\text{Area} = \frac{1}{2}ab\sin C$$

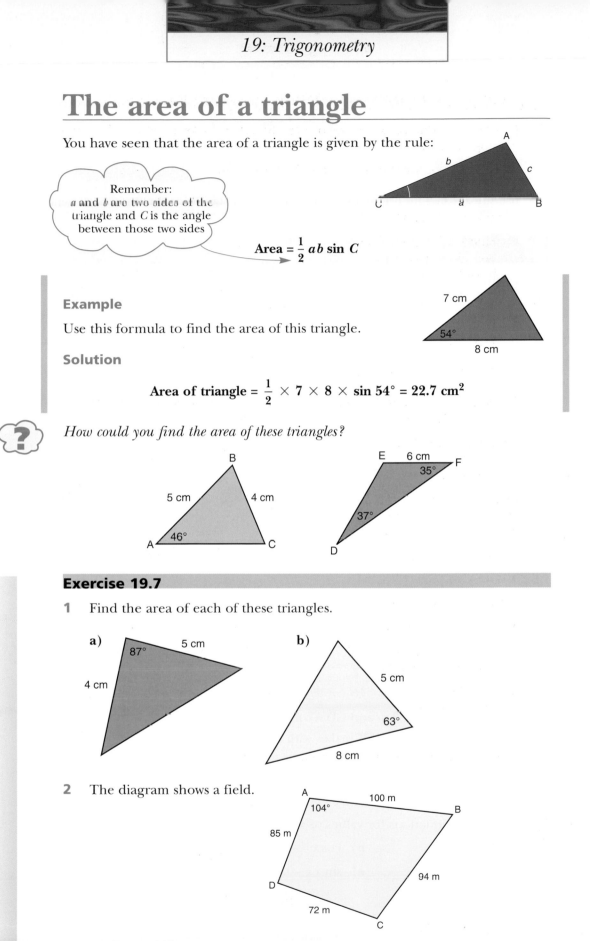

Example

Use this formula to find the area of this triangle.

Solution

$$\text{Area of triangle} = \frac{1}{2} \times 7 \times 8 \times \sin 54° = 22.7 \text{ cm}^2$$

? *How could you find the area of these triangles?*

Exercise 19.7

1 Find the area of each of these triangles.

a)

b)

2 The diagram shows a field.

a) Find the length of the diagonal BD.
b) Find the angle DCB.
c) Find the area of the field.

Finishing off

Now that you have finished this chapter you should be able to:

★ use sine, cosine and tangent to find sides and angles of right-angled triangles in two or three dimensions

★ recognise and sketch the graphs of sine, cosine and tangent functions

★ use the relationships between angles which have the same sine, cosine or tangent

★ use the sine and cosine rules to find sides and angles in triangles

★ use the sine and cosine rules to solve problems in two or three dimensions

★ find the area of a triangle.

Use the questions in the next exercise to check that you understand everything.

Mixed exercise 19.8

1   In this question give both answers to a sensible degree of accuracy.

The diagram shows the end ABCD of a building.

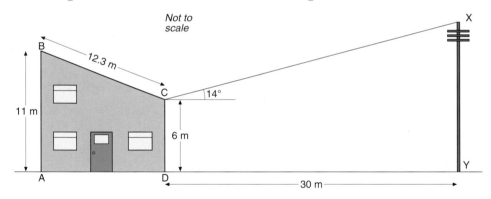

AB = 11 m, BC = 12.3 m and CD = 6 m.

a) Find the angle that CB makes with the horizontal.

b) A telegraph pole XY is 30 metres from the house.
    The angle of elevation of X from C is 14°.
    Find the length of the wire CX.   *MEI*

2   Solve these equations for values of x between 0° and 360°.

a) $\sin x = 0.81$ **b)** $\cos x = -0.64$ **c)** $\tan x = 1.6$

d) $\cos x = 0.93$ **e)** $\sin x = -0.35$ **f)** $\tan x = -0.78$

Mixed exercise 19.8 *continued*

3 The diagram shows a marquee.

A, B, C and D are four corners of a rectangle on horizontal ground.

E, F, G and H are all in the same horizontal plane and are vertically above A, B, C and D respectively.

PQ and SR are equal vertical poles such that P and S are on the ground and QE = QH = RF = RG.

AB = 18 m, BC = 10 m, AE = 2 m, QR = 12 m and PQ = 5.5 m.

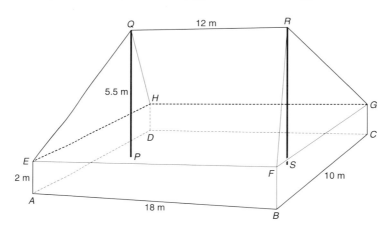

a) Calculate the length RG.

b) Calculate the angle between RG and the horizontal.

MEI

4 From a point P, on level ground, a surveyor measures the angle of elevation of R, the top of a building, as 32°.

He walks 12 metres towards the building to point Q and measures the angle of elevation of R as 57°.

X is the point on PR such that angle PXQ = 90°.

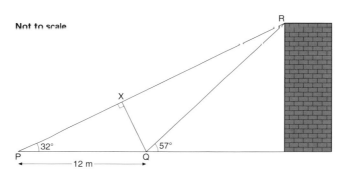

a) Show that QX = 6.36 m

b) (i) Explain why angle PRQ is 25°;

(ii) hence find the length of QR.

c) Calculate the height of the building.

MEI

Trigonometrical functions

Situations where events recur regularly are called **cyclic**. These can often be modelled using a sine or cosine curve, as in the next example.

Ben works for Avonford Council and is preparing a cash flow forecast for next year. In order to calculate the amount needed to spend on street lighting, he needs to know the hours, h, when street lighting is needed for each day of the year, d.

He finds that the formula connecting h and d is given by

$$h = 12 + 5\sin\left(\frac{360d}{365}\right)^\circ$$

The graph shows how the number of hours of non-daylight, h, in Avonford changes during the year, where d is the number of days after 21st September.

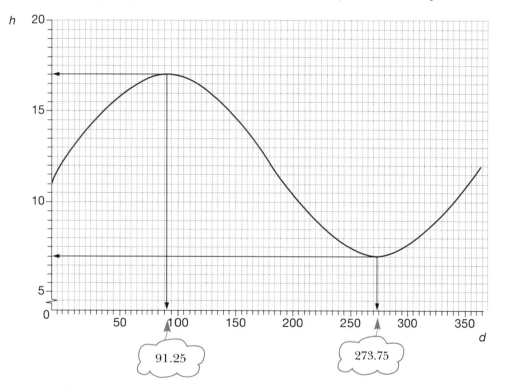

Mid-summer's day is the day with the greatest hours of daylight, and least hours of lighting up time. From the graph there are 7 hours of non-daylight on mid-summer's day, which occurs 273.75 days after 21st September.

? *Mid-winter's day is the day with least hours of daylight and longest lighting up period. How many hours of lighting up time are there on mid-winter's day?*

How many days after 21st September will mid-winter's day occur?

Why does d start from 21st September?

When is the springtime equivalent to 21st September?

? *What other situations are cyclic?*

Exercise 20.5

In this exercise use a graphic calculator or sketch the graphs and use your knowledge of trigonometry.

1   Solve the equations for $0 \leqslant x \leqslant 360°$ using the following graphs.

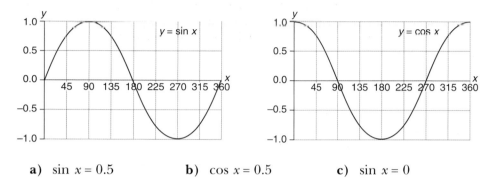

  a) $\sin x = 0.5$ **b)** $\cos x = 0.5$ **c)** $\sin x = 0$

2   The depth of water in metres in a harbour entrance over a 24-hour period starting at midnight is $d = 7 - 2 \sin (30t)°$ metres where t is the number of hours after midnight on Wednesday.

The graph shows the depth of water in the harbour entrance for the first 12 hours of the 24-hour period.

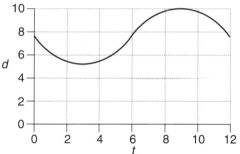

  a) Copy and complete the graph for the rest of the 24-hour period.

  b) What is the greatest and least depth of water in the harbour?

  c) At what time is low tide on Thursday morning?

  d) A fishing boat needs a depth of 6 metres to enter the harbour. Using the graph or otherwise, state the times over the 24-hour period during which it is impossible for the boat to do this.

3   The graph of $y = 5 + 3 \sin (30t)°$ shows the level of water in a tidal river passing under a bridge The height of the bridge is 10 metres. Draw the graph for $0 \leqslant t \leqslant 12$.

  a) At what time is   (i) high tide   (ii) low tide?

  b) How deep is the water at   (i) high tide   (ii) low tide?

  c) A vessel needs 3.5 metres of water to keep it afloat. Find the times between which it cannot pass under the bridge.

  d) The mast of a yacht requires a clearance of 3.5 metres. Find the times between which it can pass under the bridge.

4   A water board knows that the amount of water stored in a reservoir, W million gallons, is given by $W = 2 + \cos (30t)°$, where t is the number of the month in the year (i.e. $t = 1$ for January, etc.)

  a) Find the volume of water in the reservoir in
       (i) February   (ii) August.

  b) The local council would need to consider water rationing in any month in which the volume of water stored is likely to be less than 1.13 million gallons. When is this likely to be?

Investigation

The diagram shows the graph of $y = 3 + 5\sin x$.

Notice that the curve has the following properties:

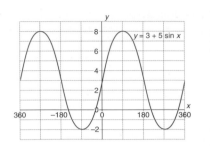

- it oscillates between −2 and 8
- it oscillates about $y = 3$ (the mean position) and has amplitude 5
- the period of the oscillation is 360°
- when $x = 0$, $y = 3$, and as x increases above 0 the value of y initially also increases.

a) Use a computer graph-drawing package or a graphic calculator to draw the graphs of

    (i) $y = 6 - 2\sin x$ (ii) $y = 4 + 3\sin x$ (iii) $y = 3 - 5\sin 2x$
    (iv) $y = 5 + 2\sin 3x$ (v) $y = 1 + 5\sin 4x$ (vi) $y = 7 - 2\sin 4x$

b) Assume that the numbers p, q and k are all positive.

Use the results that you have obtained to describe the main features of the graph of $y = p + q\sin kx$.

Use the results that you have obtained to describe the main features of the graph of $y = p - q\sin kx$.

c) Determine the equations of the curves shown in the following diagrams, giving brief reasons for your answers.

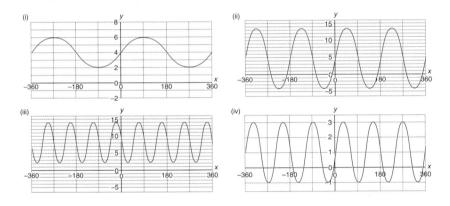

d) Investigate curves whose equations are of the form

    $y = p + q\cos kx$ or $y = p - q\cos kx$

and summarise your findings clearly.

e) Determine the equation of each of the following curves.

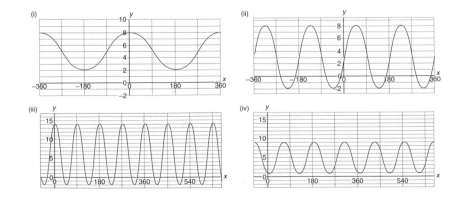

Linear sequences

Anna is investigating matchstick patterns. Here is part of her work, showing her first two matchstick patterns. She has drawn five patterns altogether.

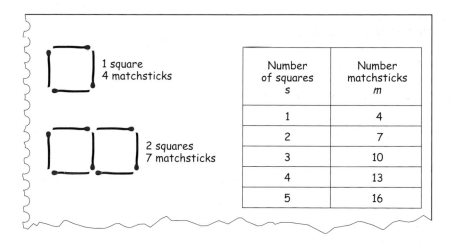

| 1 square
4 matchsticks |
| 2 squares
7 matchsticks |

Number of squares s	Number matchsticks m
1	4
2	7
3	10
4	13
5	16

What do you notice? Predict the next two entries in the table.

Anna's teacher asks her how many matchsticks she would need to make a pattern with 100 squares. To answer this, Anna wants to find a formula connecting the number of squares with the number of matchsticks.

Here is her formula. Check that it fits the results.

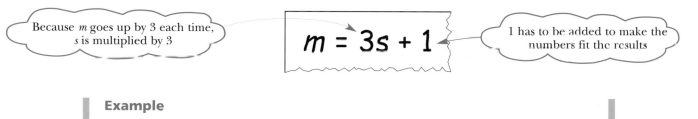

Because *m* goes up by 3 each time, *s* is multiplied by 3

$$m = 3s + 1$$

1 has to be added to make the numbers fit the results

Example

Find the *n*th term in the sequence 1, 5, 9, 13, ...

Solution

The terms in the sequence go up in fours. So the *n*th term must be something to do with $n \times 4$, or $4n$.

The sequence with *n*th term $4n$ has terms 4, 8, 12, 16, ...

You can see that you need to subtract 3 from this sequence to get the sequence 1, 5, 9, 13, ...

So the formula for the *n*th term is

   *n*th term = $4n - 3$

When you are doing an investigation, it is important to remember that you can sometimes work out a formula by thinking about the problem itself, rather than just looking for a pattern in the results.

How could you work out the formula for the matchstick investigation by looking at the problem itself, without using the table of results?

Quadratic sequences

James is investigating the sequence whose rule is

nth term $= 2n^2 - 5n + 7$

He calculates

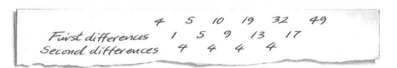

and then considers the differences between consecutive terms.

He notices that all the second differences of this sequence are 4.

 Investigate the sequences whose rules are

a) nth term $= n^2 + 3n + 2$
b) nth term $= 4n^2 - 2n - 3$
c) nth term $= 5n^2 + 3n + 7$

What do you think can be said about the second differences of these quadratic sequences?

a) nth term $= 7n^2$
c) nth term $= 10n^2 + 13n - 11$
b) nth term $= 5n^2 - 3n - 73$
d) nth term $= an^2 + bn + c$

As part of an investigation, James has obtained the sequence

2, 15, 34, 59, 90, 127

and he wishes to obtain a rule for the sequence.

He starts by investigating the differences between consecutive terms.

Noticing that all the second differences are 6, he decides that the rule must be of the form

nth term $= 3n^2 + bn + c$

Why does James think the rule takes this form?

James continues like this.

1st term = 2
The rule says
1st term = 3 × 1² + b × 1 + c = 3 + b + c

so 2 = 3 + b + c
or −1 = b + c
Similarly 2nd term = 15
and the rule says
2nd term = 3 × 2² + b × 2 + c = 12 + 2b + c
so 15 = 12 + 2b + c
or 3 = 2b + c

　　3 = 2b + c
　　−1 = b + c
　　4 = b　　　so −1 = 4 + c
　　　　　　　　or −5 = c
so b = 4 and c = −5
and the rule is
nth term = 3n² + 4n − 5

> Now I've got a pair of simultaneous equations for b and c which I can solve in the normal way

Having done all this work, James decides it is worth *checking* that his rule works.

His rule *predicts* that the sixth term of the sequence is given by

$$6\text{th term} = 3 \times 6^2 + 4 \times 6 - 5 = 108 + 24 - 5 = 127$$

and this does agree with the sequence.

Exercise 20.6

1　Write down the first 8 terms and the nth term of these sequences. Write the term number above each term.

　　a)　2,　4,　6,　8, ...　　　　**b)**　10,　12,　14, ...

　　c)　1,　3,　5,　7, ...　　　　**d)**　0,　3,　6,　9, ...

　　e)　1,　4,　9,　16, ...　　　　**f)**　1 × 2,　2 × 3,　3 × 4,　4 × 5, ...

2　For each of these sequences

　　　　(i)　write down the next three terms of the sequence

　　　　(ii)　find a formula for the nth term of the sequence.

　　a)　2, 6, 10, 14, ...　　　　**b)**　1, 3, 5, 7, ...
　　c)　10, 7, 4, 1, ...　　　　**d)**　2, 2½, 3, 3½, ...

3　Look at this sequence.

　　1, 1 + 3, 1 + 3 + 5, 1 + 3 + 5 + 7, ...

　　You can see that when you work them out, the first four terms are 1, 4, 9 and 16.

　　a)　Write down the next two terms in the sequence and work out their values.

　　b)　Without working out any more terms, complete these sentences.

　　　　When the first 10 odd numbers are added together, their sum is ...

　　　　When the first n odd numbers are added together, their sum is ...

Transformations and graphs

Transforming graphs

Drawing an accurate graph of $y = f(x)$ by plotting points and joining them (usually with a smooth curve) can take a long time. Sometimes there is no need for such detailed work – often just sketching the general shape and position of a curve is enough. This chapter shows how transformations can help you do this.

Translations

The blue curve is the graph of $y = x^2$. Note that it is symmetrical about $x = 0$ (the y axis), and has a minimum point at $(0, 0)$.

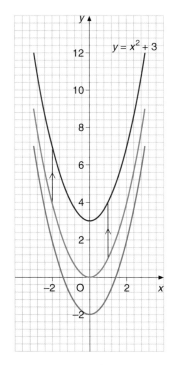

If the equation is changed to $y = x^2 + 3$ then, for every value of x, the value of y is 3 more than before. So the graph of $y = x^2 + 3$ is the same shape as $y = x^2$ but shifted up 3 units: the red curve is the image of the original blue curve when translated by $\begin{pmatrix} 0 \\ 3 \end{pmatrix}$.

The axis of symmetry is still $x = 0$, but the minimum point is now $(0, 3)$.

 If the green curve is the image of the original blue curve when translated by $\begin{pmatrix} 0 \\ -2 \end{pmatrix}$, what is the equation of the green curve?

Find the vector of the translation which maps the graph of $y = x^2$ to the graph of $y = x^2 + b$. Where is the minimum point of $y = x^2 + b$, and what is the equation of its axis of symmetry?

Working out $x^2 + 3$ is a combination of two processes: square, then add 3. If you do these in the reverse order (add 3, then square) you get $(x + 3)^2$. The way in which the graphs of $y = x^2$ and $y = (x + 3)^2$ are related is clear from this table.

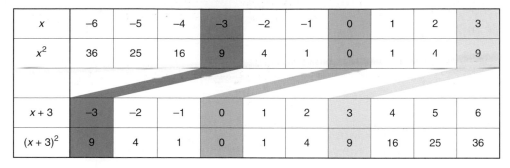

x	−6	−5	−4	−3	−2	−1	0	1	2	3
x^2	36	25	16	9	4	1	0	1	4	9
$x + 3$	−3	−2	−1	0	1	2	3	4	5	6
$(x + 3)^2$	9	4	1	0	1	4	9	16	25	36

The coloured shading shows that the graph of $y = (x + 3)^2$ is the same shape as $y = x^2$, but shifted 3 units to the left, i.e. translated by $\begin{pmatrix} -3 \\ 0 \end{pmatrix}$. It may seem strange that *adding* 3 moves the curve to the *left*. To remember this, note that the minimum point is where $x + 3 = 0$, i.e. $x = -3$.

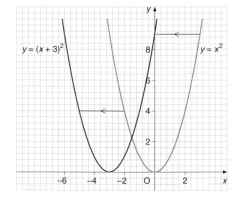

Sketch $y = x^2$ and its image under $\begin{pmatrix} 5 \\ 0 \end{pmatrix}$.
What is the equation of the image curve?

Find the vector of the translation which maps the graph of $y = x^2$ to the graph of $y = (x + a)^2$. Where is the minimum point of $y = (x + a)^2$, and what is the equation of its axis of symmetry?

These horizontal and vertical shifts can be combined. For example, to sketch the graph of $y = (x - 2)^2 + 4$ you start with $y = x^2$ (blue curve), translate this by $\begin{pmatrix} 2 \\ 0 \end{pmatrix}$ (green curve), and then translate this by $\begin{pmatrix} 0 \\ 4 \end{pmatrix}$ to reach the final red curve.

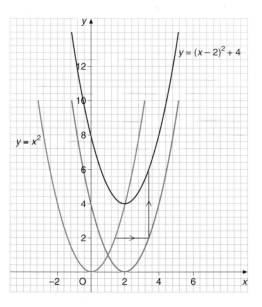

The minimum point is $(2, 4)$, and the axis of symmetry is $x = 2$.

Does the order of the translations make any difference to the end result?

With practice you can go straight from $y = x^2$ to $y = (x - 2)^2 + 4$ by the single translation $\begin{pmatrix} 2 \\ 4 \end{pmatrix}$. The general result is that $y = x^2$ is mapped to $y = (x + a)^2 + b$ by the translation $\begin{pmatrix} -a \\ b \end{pmatrix}$.

Where is the minimum point of $y = (x + a)^2 + b$, and what is the equation of its axis of symmetry?

Exercise 21.1

1 Sketch on the same axes the graphs of

a) $y = x^2$

b) $y = x^2 + 4$

c) $y = x^2 - 3$

d) $y = (x + 4)^2$

e) $y = (x - 3)^2$

2 Sketch the graphs with these equations.
For each one give the co-ordinates of the minimum point and the equation of the axis of symmetry.

a) $y = (x - 3)^2 + 4$

b) $y = (x + 1)^2 - 1$

c) $y = (x + 0.5)^2 + 2.3$

d) $y = \left(x - \dfrac{5}{2}\right)^2 - 7$

3 Each of these graphs is a translation of $y = x^2$.
Find the equation of each graph in the form

a) $y = (x + a)^2 + b$

b) $y = x^2 + px + q$

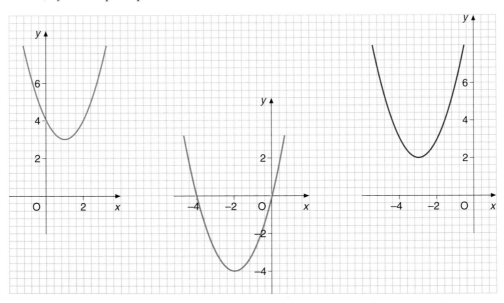

Reflections

If the equation $y = x^2$ is changed to $y = -x^2$ then the sign of each value of y is reversed: the graph of $y = x^2$ (blue curve) is mapped to the graph of $y = -x^2$ (red curve) by reflection in the x axis.

Write down the equations of the reflections of $y = x^2 - 2$ and $y = (x - 4)^2$ in the x axis. Sketch these curves.

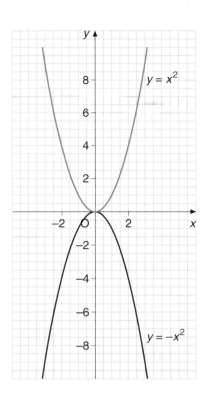

One-way stretches

If the equation $y = x^2$ is changed to $y = 2x^2$ then each value of y is multiplied by 2, so that the distance of each point of the original curve from the x axis is doubled.
The transformation which maps the blue curve to the red curve is called a **one-way stretch** with **scale factor 2** and **invariant line** the x axis.

Describe the transformation which maps the red curve to the blue curve.

The general result is that $y = x^2$ is mapped to $y = kx^2$ by the transformation in which each y co-ordinate is multiplied by k; this is called a one-way stretch with scale factor k and invariant line the x axis.

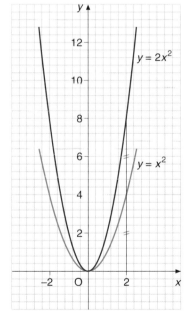

Note that if k is negative then the sign of y changes too. In particular, if $k = -1$ the one-way stretch is simply a reflection in the x axis.

How many transformations would you need to map $y = x^2$ to $y = 3x^2 + 2$? Describe them.
Do the same mapping for $y = x^2$ to $y = 3(x^2 + 2)$.
Does the order of the transformations make any difference?

Writing vectors

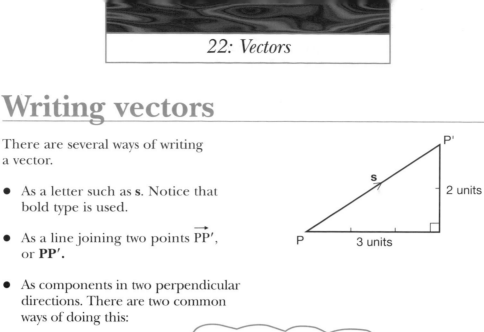

There are several ways of writing a vector.

- As a letter such as **s**. Notice that bold type is used.

- As a line joining two points $\overrightarrow{PP'}$, or **PP'**.

- As components in two perpendicular directions. There are two common ways of doing this:

  (i) $\begin{pmatrix} 3 \\ 2 \end{pmatrix}$ ← Top number relates to x direction; bottom number to y direction

  (ii) $3\mathbf{i} + 2\mathbf{j}$, where **i** and **j** are vectors of length 1, (unit vectors).

  They are often in the x and y directions, so $3\mathbf{i}$ means '3 units along' and $2\mathbf{j}$ means '2 units up'.

- As a magnitude (size) and a direction. In this case

  magnitude: $\sqrt{3^2 + 2^2} = \sqrt{13}$
  (Pythagoras' theorem)

  direction: $\tan \alpha = \dfrac{2}{3}$ so $\alpha \approx 33.7°$

  The vector is $\sqrt{13}$ at $33.7°$.

Notice that in mathematics angles are usually measured from the x direction, anticlockwise. This is not the same convention as that for compass bearings; bearings are measured clockwise from North.

- The vector joining the origin to a point is called the **position vector** of the point.

  The position vector of a point A is $\overrightarrow{OA}$ where O is the origin.

The next two examples show you how to convert between different ways of writing the same vectors.

Example

The vector **v** is 2**i** − 5**j**. Write **v** in magnitude–direction form.

Solution

Magnitude: $\sqrt{2^2 + 5^2} = \sqrt{29} = 5.39$

(to 3 significant figures).

Direction: The angle θ in the diagram is given by

$\tan\theta = \dfrac{5}{2}$ and so $\theta = 68.2°$

(to 3 significant figures)

The direction is given by α and in this case

$\quad \alpha = 360° − \theta$

$\quad\quad = 291.8°$

The vector has magnitude 5.31, direction 291.8°.

Example

The vector **w** has magnitude 30 units and direction 20°. Write it in component form.

Solution

The vector $\mathbf{w} = \begin{pmatrix} a \\ b \end{pmatrix}$ where a and b are shown in the triangle.

Using trigonometry

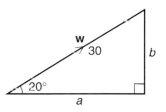

$\dfrac{a}{30} = \cos 20° \qquad \dfrac{b}{30} = \sin 20°$

$a = 30 \cos 20° \qquad b = 30 \sin 20°$

$a = 28.2 \qquad\qquad b = 10.3$

(3 sig. figs.) $\qquad$ (3 sig. figs.)

The vector **w** is $\begin{pmatrix} 28.2 \\ 10.3 \end{pmatrix}$. It can also be written 28.2**i** + 10.3**j**.

What about the vector (−**s**)?

By drawing:

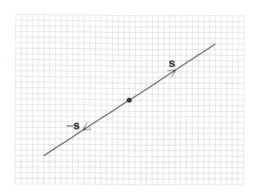

By calculation:

$$\mathbf{s} = \begin{pmatrix} 3 \\ 2 \end{pmatrix}.$$

$$-\mathbf{s} = \begin{pmatrix} -3 \\ -2 \end{pmatrix}.$$

You can see that the vector (−**s**) has the same length (or magnitude) as **s**, but is in the opposite direction.

Which of these vectors are parallel?

$$\begin{pmatrix} 4 \\ 1 \end{pmatrix}, \begin{pmatrix} 5 \\ 2 \end{pmatrix}, \begin{pmatrix} -10 \\ -4 \end{pmatrix}, \begin{pmatrix} 20 \\ 4 \end{pmatrix} ?$$

How can you tell?

Subtracting vectors

Subtracting a vector is just the same as adding its negative, and this is shown in the next example.

Example

Given that $\mathbf{s} = \begin{pmatrix} 3 \\ 2 \end{pmatrix}$ and $\mathbf{t} = \begin{pmatrix} 1 \\ -4 \end{pmatrix}$, find $\mathbf{s} - \mathbf{t}$,

a) by drawing **b)** by calculation.

Solution

Since $\mathbf{t} = \begin{pmatrix} 1 \\ -4 \end{pmatrix}$, $(-\mathbf{t}) = \begin{pmatrix} -1 \\ +4 \end{pmatrix}$.

> Notice that
> − −4 = +4

a)

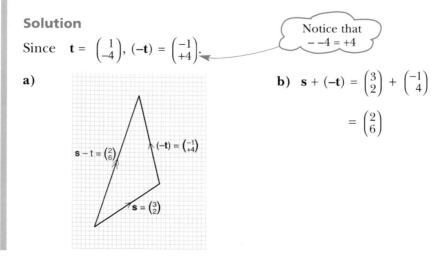

b) $\mathbf{s} + (-\mathbf{t}) = \begin{pmatrix} 3 \\ 2 \end{pmatrix} + \begin{pmatrix} -1 \\ 4 \end{pmatrix}$

$$= \begin{pmatrix} 2 \\ 6 \end{pmatrix}$$

The vector joining two points

P is the point (3, 4). Q is the point (5, 8).

What is the vector $\vec{PQ}$?

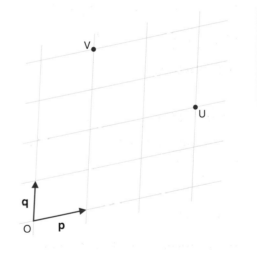

In this case, $\vec{OA}$ and $\vec{OB}$ are given as letters, not numbers

Look at the triangle OAB in the diagram.

What is the vector $\vec{AB}$?

You can see from the diagram that

$$\vec{OA} + \vec{AB} = \vec{OB}$$
$$\vec{AB} = \vec{OB} - \vec{OA}$$

This can be written as $\vec{AB} = \mathbf{b} - \mathbf{a}$, where $\mathbf{a}$ and $\mathbf{b}$ are the position vectors of A and B.

What is the position vector of the mid-point of AB?

What about the point one quarter of the way from A to B?

You can use vectors even when the axes are not at right angles as in the next example.

Example

Find, in terms of $\mathbf{p}$ and $\mathbf{q}$, the vectors

a) $\vec{OU}$ **b)** $\vec{OV}$ **c)** UV

shown in the diagram.

Solution

a) $\vec{OU} = 3\mathbf{p} + 2\mathbf{q}$

b) $\vec{OV} = \mathbf{p} + 4\mathbf{q}$

c) $\vec{UV} = \vec{OV} - \vec{OU}$

$$= (\mathbf{p} + 4\mathbf{q}) - (3\mathbf{p} + 2\mathbf{q})$$

$$= -2\mathbf{p} + 2\mathbf{q}$$

Example

$$\mathbf{p} = \begin{pmatrix} 1 \\ 1 \end{pmatrix}, \quad \mathbf{q} = \begin{pmatrix} 2 \\ 0 \end{pmatrix}, \quad \mathbf{r} = \begin{pmatrix} 0 \\ 1 \end{pmatrix}$$

Find the magnitude and direction of $3\mathbf{p} + \mathbf{q} - 2\mathbf{r}$.

Solution

$$3\mathbf{p} + \mathbf{q} - 2\mathbf{r} = 3\begin{pmatrix} 1 \\ 1 \end{pmatrix} + \begin{pmatrix} 2 \\ 0 \end{pmatrix} - 2\begin{pmatrix} 0 \\ 1 \end{pmatrix}$$

$$= \begin{pmatrix} 3 \\ 3 \end{pmatrix} + \begin{pmatrix} 2 \\ 0 \end{pmatrix} + \begin{pmatrix} 0 \\ -2 \end{pmatrix}$$

$$= \begin{pmatrix} 5 \\ 1 \end{pmatrix}$$

Magnitude: $\sqrt{5^2 + 1^2} = \sqrt{26} = 5.1$ (2 significant figures)

Direction: $\tan \alpha = \dfrac{1}{5}$ $\alpha = 11°$ (nearest degree)

Exercise 22.2

1 Add these vectors:

a) $\begin{pmatrix} 2 \\ 3 \end{pmatrix}$, $\begin{pmatrix} 4 \\ -1 \end{pmatrix}$ and $\begin{pmatrix} 0 \\ 6 \end{pmatrix}$

b) $\begin{pmatrix} 1 \\ 1 \end{pmatrix}$, $\begin{pmatrix} 2 \\ 2 \end{pmatrix}$ and $\begin{pmatrix} -3 \\ -3 \end{pmatrix}$

c) $\begin{pmatrix} 4 \\ 1 \end{pmatrix}$, $\begin{pmatrix} 1 \\ 4 \end{pmatrix}$ and $\begin{pmatrix} 2 \\ 2 \end{pmatrix}$

d) $\begin{pmatrix} -1 \\ -3 \end{pmatrix}$, $\begin{pmatrix} -3 \\ -4 \end{pmatrix}$, $\begin{pmatrix} 2 \\ 1 \end{pmatrix}$ and $\begin{pmatrix} 0 \\ -6 \end{pmatrix}$

e) $6\mathbf{i} + 3\mathbf{j}$, $3\mathbf{i} - \mathbf{j}$ and $-8\mathbf{i} - \mathbf{j}$

2 Given that $\mathbf{p} = \begin{pmatrix} 3 \\ 2 \end{pmatrix}$, $\mathbf{q} = \begin{pmatrix} -1 \\ 4 \end{pmatrix}$, and $\mathbf{r} = \begin{pmatrix} -6 \\ -2 \end{pmatrix}$, simplify:

a) $\mathbf{p} + \mathbf{q} + \mathbf{r}$

b) $2\mathbf{p} + 3\mathbf{q} + \mathbf{r}$

c) $2\mathbf{p} + \mathbf{q} - \mathbf{r}$

d) $-\mathbf{p} - \mathbf{q} - \mathbf{r}$

e) $3\mathbf{p} - 4\mathbf{q} - 2\mathbf{r}$

3 Three vectors are defined as follows

$$\mathbf{u} = \begin{pmatrix} 4 \\ 1 \end{pmatrix}, \quad \mathbf{v} = \begin{pmatrix} -2 \\ -3 \end{pmatrix}, \quad \mathbf{w} = \begin{pmatrix} 3 \\ 0 \end{pmatrix}$$

For each of the following

(i) draw a diagram to illustrate it

(ii) give the answer in component form.

a) $\mathbf{u} + \mathbf{v}$

b) $\mathbf{u} + \mathbf{v} + \mathbf{w}$

c) $2\mathbf{v}$

d) $\mathbf{u} - \mathbf{v}$

4 The diagram shows three vectors, **p**, **q** and **r**.

a) Write the following vectors in component form:

(i) $\mathbf{p} + \mathbf{q}$

(ii) $\mathbf{p} + \mathbf{r}$

(iii) $\mathbf{p} - \mathbf{r}$

(iv) $\mathbf{p} + \mathbf{q} - \mathbf{r}$

b) State the magnitude and direction of the vectors.

(i) $2\mathbf{p} + \mathbf{q} + 2\mathbf{r}$

(ii) $2\mathbf{p} + \mathbf{q} + 3\mathbf{r}$

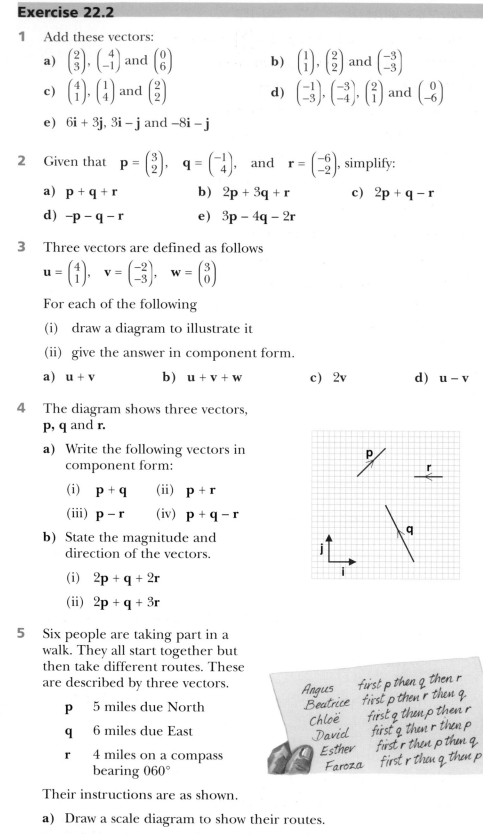

5 Six people are taking part in a walk. They all start together but then take different routes. These are described by three vectors.

p   5 miles due North

q   6 miles due East

r   4 miles on a compass bearing 060°

Their instructions are as shown.

a) Draw a scale diagram to show their routes.

b) What do you notice?

Exercise 22.2 *continued*

6 Vectors **l** and **m** are defined by $\mathbf{l} = \begin{pmatrix} 3 \\ 4 \end{pmatrix}$ and $\mathbf{m} = \begin{pmatrix} 4 \\ -3 \end{pmatrix}$.

   a) State the magnitudes and directions of **l** and **m**.

   b) Find the angle between **l** and **m**.

   c) Write, in component form, the vectors

      (i) $3\mathbf{l} + 4\mathbf{m}$ (ii) $4\mathbf{l} - 3\mathbf{m}$

   d) Use your answers to part **c)** to write the vectors

      (i) $\begin{pmatrix} 1 \\ 0 \end{pmatrix}$ (ii) $\begin{pmatrix} 0 \\ 1 \end{pmatrix}$

   in terms of **l** and **m**.

7 Vectors **p**, **q**, **r** and **s** are defined as follows

      $\mathbf{p} = 4\mathbf{i} + \mathbf{j}, \qquad \mathbf{q} = \mathbf{i} + 5\mathbf{j}, \qquad \mathbf{r} = -6\mathbf{i} - 2\mathbf{j}, \qquad \mathbf{s} = \mathbf{i} - 4\mathbf{j}$

   a) Draw a diagram showing $\mathbf{p} + \mathbf{q} + \mathbf{r} + \mathbf{s}$.

   b) What is the magnitude of $\mathbf{p} + \mathbf{q} + \mathbf{r} + \mathbf{s}$?

   c) Three vectors, **l**, **m** and **n** are such that $\mathbf{l} + \mathbf{m} + \mathbf{n} = \mathbf{0}$. What can you say about them?

8 Look at the diagram.

   a) Write, in terms of **p** and **q**, the vectors

      (i) $\overrightarrow{AB}$

      (ii) $\overrightarrow{DC}$

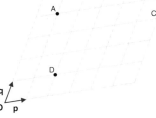

   b) What does this tell you about the quadrilateral ABCD?

   c) Write, also in terms of **p** and **q**, the vector $\overrightarrow{OM}$ where M is the mid-point of CD.

   d) Describe the quadrilaterals ABMD and ABCM.

Investigation

The point A is $(-4, 4)$ and the point B is $(8, 4)$. The position vectors, $\overrightarrow{OA}$ and $\overrightarrow{OB}$, are denoted by **a** and **b**.

a) Using graph paper, draw a diagram showing the origin and the points A and B.

b) Mark on your diagram the point M, with position vector **m** given by
$\mathbf{m} = \frac{1}{2}\mathbf{a} + \frac{1}{2}\mathbf{b}$. What can you say about M?

c) Now mark the points L and N with position vectors
$\mathbf{l} = \frac{3}{4}\mathbf{a} + \frac{1}{4}\mathbf{b}$ and $\mathbf{n} = \frac{1}{4}\mathbf{a} + \frac{3}{4}\mathbf{b}$.
What can you say about the points L and N?

d) T is the point $(4, 4)$. Show that its position vector **t** can be written in the form $(1 - \alpha)\mathbf{a} + \alpha\mathbf{b}$ for a certain value of α which you are to find.

e) State a general rule for points on the line AB.

Exercise 22.4 *continued*

8 The diagram shows a triangle

OAB, in which $\overrightarrow{OA}$ = **a** and $\overrightarrow{OB}$ = **b**.

The points L and M are the mid-points of OA and OB.

a) Write down the vector $\overrightarrow{AB}$ in terms of **a** and **b**.

b) Find the vector $\overrightarrow{LM}$.

c) Describe the relationship between LM and AB.

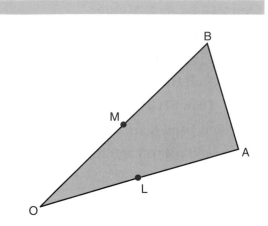

9 In the diagram O is the origin, **a** is the position vector of A and **b** is the position vector of B.

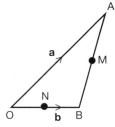

M is the mid-point of AB and N is the mid-point of OB.

a) Find the position vector of M in terms of **a** and **b**.

b) G is the point where $\overrightarrow{OG} = \frac{2}{3}\overrightarrow{OM}$.

Find the position vector of G in terms of **a** and **b**.
Write your answer in its simplest terms.

c) H is the point where $\overrightarrow{AH} = \frac{2}{3}\overrightarrow{ON}$.

Show clearly that G and H are the same point.

d) What can you say about the point where BG meets OA?

MEI

10 a)

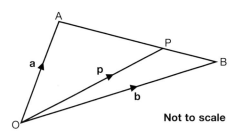

Not to scale

In the diagram **a**, **b**, **p** are the position vectors of A, B and P respectively.

$\overrightarrow{AP} = \frac{3}{4}\overrightarrow{AB}$.

(i) Write AB in terms of **a** and **b**.

(ii) Use this to write **p** in terms of **a** and **b**. Simplify your answer.

Exercise 22.4 *continued*

b) $\overrightarrow{QA} = \frac{1}{2}\overrightarrow{AB}$.

Find **q**, the position vector of Q, in terms of **a** and **b**. Simplify your answer.

c) R is another point on the line AB where

$$\mathbf{r} = m\mathbf{a} + n\mathbf{b}$$

What can you say about *m* and *n*?

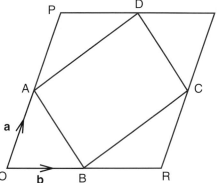

Not to scale

MEI

11 In the diagram, OPQR is a parallelogram.

A, B, C, D are the mid-points of the sides.

$\overrightarrow{OA} = \mathbf{a}$ $\overrightarrow{OB} = \mathbf{b}$

a) Find, in terms of **a** and **b**,

   (i) $\overrightarrow{OP}$ (ii) $\overrightarrow{PQ}$

   (iii) $\overrightarrow{AB}$ (iv) $\overrightarrow{AD}$

   (v) $\overrightarrow{DC}$ (vi) $\overrightarrow{BC}$

b) What can you say about the shape ABCD?

12 The diagram shows a triangle UVW.

The points L, M and N are the mid-points of its sides.

a) State the vector $\overrightarrow{UL}$, in component form.

b) The point P is on $\overrightarrow{UL}$,

and $\overrightarrow{UP} = \frac{2}{3}\overrightarrow{UL}$.

Find the co-ordinates of P.

c) The point Q is on $\overrightarrow{VM}$ and $\overrightarrow{VQ} = \frac{2}{3}\overrightarrow{VM}$.

Find the co-ordinates of Q.

d) The point R is on $\overrightarrow{WN}$ and $\overrightarrow{WR} = \frac{2}{3}\overrightarrow{WN}$.

Find the co-ordinates of R.

What do you notice?

e) The position vectors $\overrightarrow{OU}$, $\overrightarrow{OV}$, $\overrightarrow{OW}$ and $\overrightarrow{OP}$ are denoted by **u, v, w** and **p**.

Show that $\mathbf{p} = \frac{1}{3}(\mathbf{u} + \mathbf{v} + \mathbf{w})$.

f) Show that the result in part **e)** is true in general, not just for the particular points U, V and W in this question.

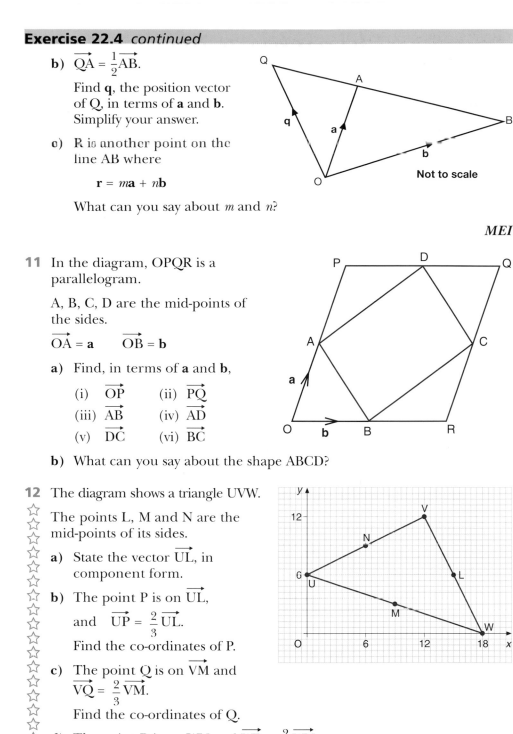

Mixed exercise 22.5 *continued*

11 **p** is the vector $\begin{pmatrix} 3 \\ 1 \end{pmatrix}$ and **q** is $\begin{pmatrix} 0 \\ 2 \end{pmatrix}$.

    a) Write down the vector $\mathbf{p} - \dfrac{1}{2}\mathbf{q}$

    b) Write these vectors in the form $a\mathbf{p} + b\mathbf{q}$ where a and b are numbers that you must find in each case.

        (i) $\begin{pmatrix} 3 \\ 3 \end{pmatrix}$ (ii) $\begin{pmatrix} 3 \\ 5 \end{pmatrix}$ (iii) $\begin{pmatrix} 0 \\ 1 \end{pmatrix}$

        (iv) $\begin{pmatrix} 1 \\ 0 \end{pmatrix}$ (v) $\begin{pmatrix} 63 \\ -47 \end{pmatrix}$

    c) Can you express *any* vector in the form $a\mathbf{p} + b\mathbf{q}$?

    d) Can you express *any* vector in terms of *any* two others?

Chapter 23

Circles

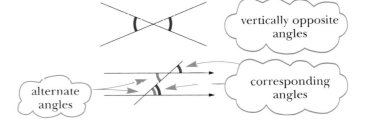

Before you start this chapter you should:

★ know that angles on a straight line add up to 180° and those around a point to 360°

★ know that the angle sum of a triangle is 180° and that of a quadrilateral is 360°

★ know the meaning of vertically opposite, alternate and corresponding angles, and that they are equal

★ be able to recognise congruent and similar triangles

★ know that the base angles of an isosceles triangle are equal

★ recognise that the perpendicular from the centre of a circle to a chord is a line of symmetry and so bisects the chord.

Reminder

Angles

Vertically opposite angles are equal.
Corresponding angles are equal.
Alternate angles are equal.

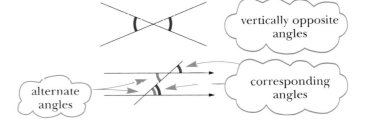

Circles

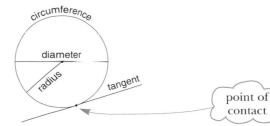

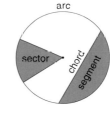

 Which of the arcs below comes from the largest circle?

 Why do so many containers have circular cross-sections?

 A circle is the locus of points in two dimensions that are a fixed distance from a given point. What is the locus of such points in three dimensions?

Finishing off

Now that you have finished this chapter you should be able to use these results:

★ the angle at the centre is twice the angle at the circumference standing on the same arc

★ angles in the same segment are equal

★ the angle in a semi-circle is a right angle

★ opposite angles of a cyclic quadrilateral add up to 180°

★ the tangent is perpendicular to the radius at the point of contact

★ tangents from a point to a circle are equal in length

★ the alternate segment theorem.

Use the questions in the next exercise to check that you understand everything.

Mixed exercise 23.5

1   Find the angles marked with letters, giving reasons for your answers.

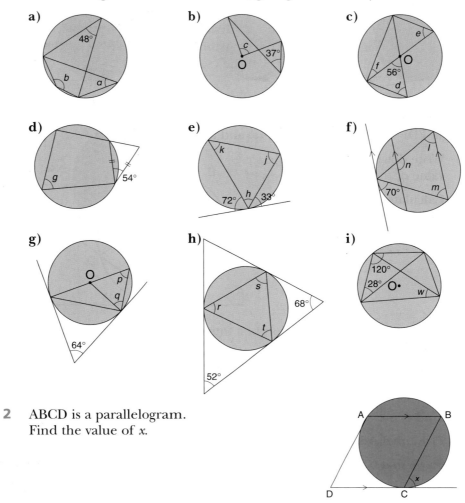

2   ABCD is a parallelogram.
    Find the value of *x*.

Mixed exercise 23.5 *continued*

3 In the diagram the chord AC is parallel to the tangent BT. Prove that triangle ABC is isosceles.

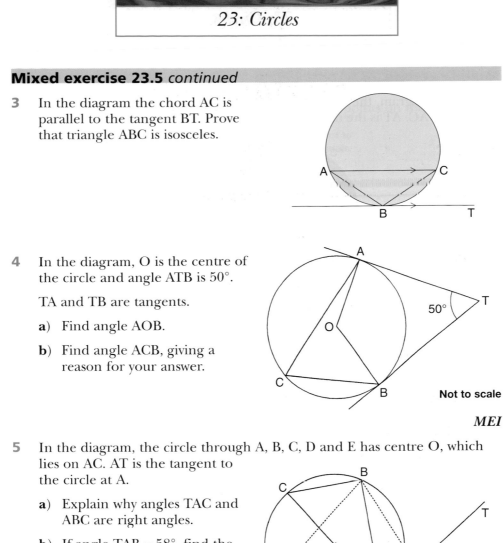

4 In the diagram, O is the centre of the circle and angle ATB is 50°.

TA and TB are tangents.

a) Find angle AOB.

b) Find angle ACB, giving a reason for your answer.

Not to scale

MEI

5 In the diagram, the circle through A, B, C, D and E has centre O, which lies on AC. AT is the tangent to the circle at A.

a) Explain why angles TAC and ABC are right angles.

b) If angle TAB = 58°, find the following angles, in each case giving a reason for your answer.

(i) BAC   (ii) ACB

(iii) ADB   (iv) AEB

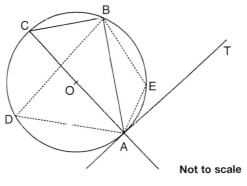

Not to scale

MEI

6 A, B, C, D and E are points on the circumference of a circle centre O. BD̂C is 32°.

Write down the values of

a) CÂB

b) CÔB

c) DĈB

d) DÊC

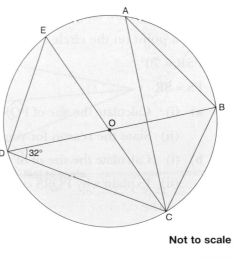

Not to scale

NEAB

Answers

Chapter 1: Basic arithmetic

Review exercise 1.1

1 a) 25   b) 275

2 about 5.5

3 a) 25   b) 121   c) 225   d) 64
   e) 125   f) 8   g) 12   h) 14

4 a) 5   b) -3 c) -3 d) 5
   e) -11 f) 2   g) -3 h) -5

5 a) -24 b) 21   c) -40 d) -5
   e) -4 f) 5   g) -8 h) 0

6 a) 20   b) 14   c) 14   d) 2
   e) 7   f) 7   g) 12   h) 15

7 a) $\frac{5}{8}$ b) $\frac{7}{16}$ c) $\frac{1}{10}$ d) $1\frac{5}{12}$
   e) $\frac{5}{8}$ f) $\frac{2}{15}$ g) $\frac{1}{8}$ h) $1\frac{1}{5}$

8 a) $\frac{5}{4}$ b) $\frac{11}{3}$ c) $\frac{23}{5}$ d) $\frac{55}{16}$

9 a) $1\frac{1}{2}$ b) $2\frac{3}{4}$ c) $3\frac{5}{6}$ d) $6\frac{5}{8}$

10 a) Anna £5000; Harry £6000; Kashmir £6000; Paul £3000
   b) $\frac{3}{20}$

11 a) 7.33   b) 6.6   c) 1.897   d) 1.17

12 a) $\frac{2}{3}$, 0.67, $\frac{7}{10}$, 0.72, $\frac{3}{4}$ b) 0.04, 0.3, 0.33, $\frac{1}{3}$, $\frac{7}{20}$

13 a) Union   b) Management   c) £320

14 a) £1350   b) £177.60

Exercise 1.2

1 a) 2×7 b) 3×5
   c) $2 \times 2 \times 7$ d) $2 \times 2 \times 3 \times 3$
   e) $2 \times 3 \times 5$ f) $3 \times 3 \times 3$
   g) $2 \times 3 \times 3 \times 5$ h) $2 \times 3 \times 3 \times 7$
   i) $2 \times 3 \times 5 \times 5$ j) $2 \times 3 \times 5 \times 7$
   k) $7 \times 7 \times 11$ l) $2 \times 2 \times 5 \times 7 \times 11$

2 a) 5   b) 1   c) 9   d) 2
   e) 7   f) 11   g) 9   h) 14
   i) 6   j) 8

3 a) 30   b) 21   c) 54   d) 16
   e) 70   f) 40   g) 72   h) 30

4 a) 35   b) $\frac{14}{35}$ c) $\frac{15}{35}$ d) $\frac{3}{7}$

5 a) 8   b) 5   c) 7

Exercise 1.3

1 a) $5\frac{1}{2}$ b) $2\frac{3}{8}$ c) $4\frac{1}{6}$ d) $3\frac{7}{12}$
   e) $2\frac{13}{20}$ f) $17\frac{1}{2}$ g) $14\frac{23}{60}$ h) $74\frac{17}{24}$

2 a) $2\frac{1}{2}$ b) $1\frac{1}{2}$ c) $8\frac{3}{4}$ d) $7\frac{4}{5}$
   e) $28\frac{1}{8}$ f) 9   g) $8\frac{5}{9}$ h) $4\frac{1}{3}$

3 a) $1\frac{1}{2}$ b) 6   c) $\frac{7}{10}$ d) 16
   e) $1\frac{1}{6}$ f) $1\frac{1}{9}$ g) $\frac{7}{16}$ h) $4\frac{1}{2}$

4 c) (i) $\frac{4}{3}$ (ii) $\frac{16}{5}$ (iii) $\frac{11}{6}$

5 a) $\frac{4}{11}$ b) $\frac{2}{7}$ c) $\frac{5}{38}$

6 $4\frac{1}{8}$

7 a) $3\frac{7}{8}$ miles   b) $4\frac{5}{8}$ miles
   c) $\frac{7}{8}$ mile   d) $5\frac{1}{2}$ miles

8 a) £282   b) 42 hours

9 648

10 a) (i) $1\frac{1}{2}$ (ii) 2   (iii) $2\frac{1}{2}$
   b) (i) $5\frac{1}{2}$ (ii) $50\frac{1}{2}$ (iii) $\frac{n+1}{2}$
   c) odd   d) 2

Exercise 1.4

1 a) 0.72   b) 0.162   c) 22.4   d) 0.765
   e) 0.08   f) 1.545   g) 1.521   h) 0.0009

2 a) 18   b) 25   c) 200   d) 45.6
   e) 0.35   f) 4   g) 7.5625   h) 180

3 a) 420   b) 0.39   c) 0.002   d) 14700
   e) 1710   f) 4.8   g) 0.1175
   h) 30 000 000

4 a) 106 lb   b) 55 kg   c) 53 kg

5 a) 9.45 g   b) 21.4 g   c) 1.41 cm^3
   d) 1.34 cm^3

6 a) 76.2 mm   b) 182.88 mm
   c) 24 inches   d) 4 feet 11 inches

Exercise 1.5

1 a) 22.2%   b) 42.9%   c) 81.3%   d) 46.7%

2 Patel's (£426.55)

3 a) £200   b) £135.32

4 a) £1650   b) £2700
   c) subscriptions 79°; social events 130°; fundraising 151°

5 a) £18 760   b) 4.22%   c) £25 392.16
   d) £20 000

6 a) (i) £9000   (ii) £5062.50
   b) £12 000 3 $(0.75)^n$ c) after 5 years

7 a) Church Road £10 000; Agora £10 000;
       High Street £30 000
    b) You cannot combine percentage changes by adding them
    c) −4%
    d) No – it distorts the truth
8 a) 5, 6 (5 in 6)   b) Kingshill
    c) Abbey, Queensfield   d) Queensfield
    e) Woodgate
9 £656.88
10 2.41 inches
11 £9567
12 a) 10.8%   b) 11.8%
13 a) 0.85   b) £12 484   c) £8560
14 10.24%

Exercise 1.6

1 a) (i) £72   (ii) £44.80   b) 12.5%   c) £40
2 a) (i) 65%   (ii) 56%
    b) (i) £3651   (ii) £1351; 58.7%
3 a) £1377.28   b) £337.28   c) 32%
4 a) £29 830   b) 21.5%
5 a) £4718   b) £21 782
    c) It will be reduced by £67
6 a) £80   b) £816.75
    c) £168   d) Karen £16.80; Tiffany £13.50
7 a) 1.037   b) £4796.82
8 a) £315.25   b) £151.79   c) £1623.57
9 a) £10 000 × $(1.06)^n$ b) after 80 years

Mixed exercise 1.7

1 a) $2\frac{11}{16}$ b) $8\frac{7}{12}$ c) $5\frac{1}{5}$ d) $3\frac{3}{4}$
    e) $2\frac{1}{2}$ f) 6   g) $10\frac{3}{4}$ h) $\frac{4}{7}$
    i) $4\frac{1}{2}$ j) $7\frac{3}{4}$
2 4000 litres
3 a) 2.28 litres   b) 2.6 pints
4 a) Southwood 61.0%   b) Riverside 86.2%
    c) 20.9%
5 a) £11   b) £5.70   c) £121.80   d) 34.1%
6 a) £20 666   b) 15.0%   c) £120
7 a) 4.5%   b) £2282.33
8 £122 500
9 £61.50
10 £1829.74

Chapter 2: Shapes and angles

Review exercise 2.1

1 a) $a = 60°$, $b = 70°$, $c = 120°$
    b) $d = 90°$, $e = 100°$,
    c) $f = 110°$
2 a) $a = 111°$, $b = 69°$, $c = 111°$, $d = 111°$, $e = 69°$
    b) $t = 50°$, $u = 130°$, $v = 50°$, $w = 130°$, $x = 130°$

3 a) $a = 58°$
    b) $b = 67°$, $c = 113°$, $d = 74°$, $e = 106°$, $f = 74°$
    c) $g = 89°$, $h = 89°$, $i = 47°$
4 a) $a = 40°$
    b) $b = c = d = 25°$
    c) $l = 20°$
    d) $m = 85°$, $n = 95°$, $o = 70°$
5 a) 20 cm^2 b) 112.5 cm^2 c) 126 cm^2
6 a) 42 cm^2 b) 92 cm^2 c) 63 cm^2 d) 60 cm^2
7 10 000 cm^2 (or 1 m^2)
8 Parallelogram 0, 2; rhombus 2, 2;
   rectangle 2, 2; square 4, 4

Exercise 2.2

1 a) A — regular pentagon
       B — irregular octagon
       C — irregular hexagon
       D — irregular quadrilateral
       E — irregular pentagon
       F — regular octagon
    b) 540°, 1080°, 720°, 360°, 540°, 1080°
2 a) 120°   b) 90°   c) 72°
    d) 60°   e) 45°   f) 36°
3 144°
4 a) 125°   b) 120°   c) 126°
5 Hexagon

Mixed exercise 2.3

1 a) 48 cm^2 b) 15 cm^2 c) 48 cm^2
2 a) 133°   b) $b = 118°$, $c = 84°$
    c) $d = 22°$, $e = 58°$
3 Equilateral triangle 3, 3; square 4, 4; regular pentagon 5, 5;
   regular hexagon 6, 6; regular octagon 8, 8
4 102°
5 a) $a = b - 120$
    b) a would be negative

Chapter 3: Equations and inequalities

Review exercise 3.1

1 a) $2x - 1$ b) $2a - 4b + 3$ c) $9p + 2pq$
2 a) $x > 3$ b) $x \leq -2$ c) $-1 \leq x < 5$
3 a) $6ab$ b) $15x^2$ c) $12p^2q$ d) $6a^3$
    e) $-12cd$ f) $6xy^2$ g) $4s^2$ h) $18z^3$
4 a) $3a + 6$ b) $4x - 4y$
    c) $6p - 9q$ d) $2a - 8b + 4c$
    e) $10x - 15$ f) $m^2 + 2mn$
    g) $9d^2 - 6de$ h) $x^2y + xy^2$
    i) $4a^2b - 4abc$ j) $6p^2q - 8pqr$
5 a) $11x - 13$ b) $-a - 7b$
    c) $16p + 23q + 3$ d) $3mn + 3m - 4n$
    e) $14a^2 + a - 5$ f) $2x^2 - 12xy - 3y^2$

6 a) $a = 3$ b) $b = 6$ c) $x = 6$ d) $y = 5$
  e) $p = -3$ f) $t = 3.5$ g) $d = 9$ h) $x = 11$
  i) $y = -1$ j) $x = -9$ k) 24 l) 12
  m) 84 n) 10 o) 11

7 a) $a = 2$ b) $x = 3$ c) $y = 1$ d) $z = -1$

8 $50 + 0.4m = 82.4$; 81 miles

9 a) $50 - n$ b) $4n + 6(50 - n) = 256$
  c) 22 children, 28 adults

Exercise 3.2

1 a) $x = 0.5$ b) $x = -1.75$ c) $x = 0.6$ d) $x = -3$
  e) $x = -6$ f) $x = 6$ g) $x = -11$ h) $x = -4.4$

2 a) $x = 1.75$ b) $x = 0.75$ c) $x = -3$ d) $x = 1.5$
  e) $x = -0.1$ f) $x = 3$ g) $x = 6$ h) $x = -1$

3 a) $x = 0.75$ b) $x = 0.7$ c) $x = -1.5$ d) $x = 2$
  e) $x = -6$ f) $x = -1$ g) $x = 1.5$ h) $x = 0.55$

4 a) $5n + 2 = 3(n + 3) + 5$; 6 children
  b) 32 sweets

5 a) Andrew is 12 and his grandmother is 60
  b) (i) When Andrew is 24 and his grandmother is 72
    (ii) When Andrew is 48 and his grandmother is 96

6 a) $x = 4.6$ b) $x = -2.2$ c) $x = -0.4$

Exercise 3.3

1 a) $a = 2, b = 5$ b) $p = 1, q = -1$
  c) $s = 2, t = -1$ d) $x = 4, y = -3$

2 a) $x = 2, y = -1$ b) $m = 3, n = 3$
  c) $a = 2, b = 6$ d) $y = -2, z = 3$

3 a) $x = 3, y = 5$ b) $a = 3, b = 11$
  c) $c = 2, d = 7$ d) $p = 2, q = -2$

4 a) $x = 1, y = 2$ b) $a = 2, b = 2$
  c) $x = 1.25, y = 1.75$ d) $m = -2, n = -3$
  e) $c = 5, d = 1$ f) $s = 3, t = -1$
  g) $w = 3, z = 4$ h) $g = 1, h = -2$
  i) $p = 2, q = -1$ j) $r = 8, s = 3$

5 A cone costs 85p and a choc-ice costs 60p

6 $a = 3, b = -1$

7 a) $x = -2, y = 1.5$ b) $x = 3, y = 2$
  c) $x = 1, y = 2.5$ d) $x = -2, y = 4$
  e) $x = 1, y = 3$ f) $x = -1, y = 2$

8 $x = 1, y = -3, z = -2$

Exercise 3.4

1 a) $x \geqslant -3$ b) $x < 1$ c) $-4 < x \leqslant 3$

2 a) $x < 4$ b) $x \leqslant -2$ c) $x \leqslant 3$
  d) $x > -1$

3 a) $x > 5.5$ b) $x > -1.6$ c) $x \leqslant -1.5$
  d) $x < 3.75$ e) $x \geqslant -2.25$ f) $x > 0.5$
  g) $x > -5.5$ h) $x \geqslant -1$

4 a) 1000 miles b) $m < 250n$

5 $x > 3$

6 $x > 2\frac{1}{2}$

7 2, 3, 4

8 $x > 2$ or $-3 < x < 0$

9 $0 < x < 2$ or $x < -2$

Mixed exercise 3.5

1 a) $x = -0.5$ b) $x = -3$
  c) $x = 6$ d) $x = -5$
  e) $x = 4$ f) $x = -1$
  g) $x = -2.5$ h) $x = 2.6$
  i) $x = -6.2$ j) $x = 9$
  k) $x = -2.2$ l) $x = 1.2$
  m) $x = 0.5$ n) $x = 14.5$

2 a) $x = 3, y = 1$ b) $a = 2, b = -1$
  c) $p = -2, q = 2$ d) $s = 5, t = 2$
  e) $c = -1, d = -4$ f) $x = -3, y = -10$
  g) $p = 5, q = -3$ h) $f = 2.5, g = -2$
  i) $c = -1, d = 1$

3 a) $x > 2.25$ b) $x \leqslant -3$ c) $x < 1$
  d) $x \geqslant -3$ e) $x > -\frac{4}{3}$ f) $x \geqslant 10.5$
  g) $x \leqslant 1.5$ h) $x < 0.5$

4 $A = 56°, B = 28°, C = 96°$

5 77 adults, 153 children

6 2.57 km

7 (0.9, 0.8)

8 Dog food costs 56p, cat food costs 45p

9 8 doughnuts

10 5

11 B (8, 1), c (3, 6)

12 $x = 1.1, y = 2.2$

Chapter 4: Statistics review

Review exercise 4.1

1 a) 65 b) 30 c) 23
  d) Conservative e) 17 million

2 b)

Word length	1	2	3	4	5	6	7	8	9	10	11
Frequency	1	7	6	7	3	10	8	3	0	2	3

  d) Chrystal uses short words mainly. Kevin's spread is more uniform except that four-letter words predominate! Nigel uses short and medium length words mainly and a few longer words.
  e) With 12 categories the pie charts would get too cluttered.

3 a) 110 b) Car
  d) With just 4 categories a pie chart would show the comparisons well.

4 a) The bar chart is the best – easier to see the frequencies as age increases – the pie chart is the least good as it just highlights the larger categories.
  b) (i) $\frac{3}{60} = \frac{1}{20} = 5\%$
    (ii) New car owners might well wish to park in better class areas fearing that their cars are more likely to be stolen or 'knocked' or scratched, etc.

6 a) 120

b) (i) 7   (ii) 7   (iii) 7.01 (2 d.p.)

7 Sheila is not correct (e.g. 1, 1, 5, 6, 7 has mode 1, mean 4 and median 5)

Exercise 4.2

1

	Part time	Full time
Female	12	15
Male	10	13

2 The very young could not tick a box.

No box for people over 70.

Not clear where 20, 40 or 60 year olds tick.

3 Ask your teacher to check your answers

4 a) Numerical, continuous

b) Categorical

c) Numerical, continuous

d) Numerical, discrete

5 a) Is more likely to get the owner's opinion as to whether he/she is in favour or not.

b) People not in favour would exaggerate their closeness

c) Invites the comment 'derisory' amount

d) Invites the answer Yes – less pleasant

e) The local tradesmen might tick (i) otherwise for everyone else the reasons are frivolous and irrelevant.

6 Ask your teacher to check your answers

7 a) Lower 49, middle 36, and upper 15

b) Ask your teacher to check your answer

8 a) Statified sample by year and possibly by sex.

b) Use the electoral register and take a single random sample

9 a) No. They might be regulars

b) Seems OK.

c) Should be randomly selected, or the manufacturer will take advantage.

d) Leading question. Children should be randomly selected.

10 a) SV 91, LC 70, JV 39

11 a) e.g. The 3rd DP is even (heads) or odd (tails)

b) Number the students from 000 to 999

c) Treat as integers from 000 to 995 (ignoring 996 – 999) and take the remainder on division by 6 (with zero counted as 6).

12 Ask your teacher to check your answers

13 Ask your teacher to check your answers

14 a) Ask your teacher to check your answers

b) 15

15 Ask your teacher to check your answers

16 Ask your teacher to check your answers

Exercise 4.3

1 a) Negative correlation if these were the only two available activities but in practice no correlation e.g. little television does not imply lots of reading – sporting activity is another alternative.

b) There will usually be a positive correlation.

c) There will usually be a positive correlation.

d) No correlation.

2 b) Positive correlation. Yes.

3 b) 297, 48   d) about 55 seconds

4 b) about 36.1 seconds (36 to 36.2 seconds)

5 a) 18

b) We cannot be sure of the effect of such overfertilisation – likely to cause a larger fall in numbers produced.

6 b) 50.7, 44.9

d) The % of arable land falls as the % of land over 500 m increases.

e) 48 to 49%

f) No. Flooding will have adverse effects, sandy ground, …

7 44

Exercise 4.4

1 a) Alun: 11.56, 12, 12, 23

David: 16.09, 4, 0, 55

Martin: 24.38, 24.5, None, 8

b) (i) Mean

(ii) Martin for consistency or David for his 'blue patches'.

c) No. Not over a small number of innings.

2 a) Mean £4.55   Median £3.50   Mode £5

b) Mean £4.60   Median $\geqslant$ £3.50   Mode £5

3 a) Mode 0   Median 3.5   Mean 6

b) The 40 is an extreme outlier so the median is best.

c) John has at least 5 × 2 = 10 bus journeys and so must be the one with 40.

New Mean = 2.91   New Median = 3

4 a) Mean £385   Mode £0   Median £200

c) (i) Mode

(ii) Median (or perhaps Mean if outlier is a big spender)

5 a) Mode 1   Median 2   Mean 2.28

b) (i) Mode   (ii) Mean

Exercise 4.5

1 29

2 a) 81

3 b) 652.75, 624, 626.75, 623, 624.75, 594, 624, 621.5, 640.75, 690.75, 696.5, 701.75, 666.75

No clear pattern

4

Year	Food and drink index	Restaurants and hotels index
2001	100	100
2002	102	107.3
2003	105.8	113.0
2004	109.3	119.4

5 b) 409, 406, 413.25, 410.25, 409.25, 406.25, 407.5, 404.5, 396, 393, 382.25, 379.25, 370, 367, 363.25, 360.25, 351.25

Decrease in number of births

6 b) 176.6, 173.4, 176.1, 173.7, 174.0, 175.7, 168.3, 166.3, 166.4, 163.7, 164.7, 169.0, 169.7, 171.9, 173.6, 174.3, 173.0, 172.6, 169.4, 163.7, 162.1, 160.9, 160.6, 164.6, 163.6

Some evidence of decline but relatively short period considered

7 b) Numbers: 38, 36.8, 37, 37.8, 36, 36.8, 36.8, 35.4, 35.4, 35.8, 38.4, 40.2, 41, 43, 42

Slight increase in recent years in numbers

%AB: 41.66, 43.86, 41.56, 45.2, 46.2, 48.12, 53.54, 58.34, 59.28, 57.44, 59.62, 62.62, 64.56, 63.9, 70.34

Clear increase in % obtaining A or B

Mixed exercise 4.6

1 a)

	Women	Men
Under 21	6	4
21 and over	6	9

3 a) ✔   b) ✗   c) ✗

d) ✗   e) ✔

4 a) (Strong) positive correlation

b)

Shoe size	$5\frac{1}{2}$	6	7	$7\frac{1}{2}$	8	$8\frac{1}{2}$	9	10	$10\frac{1}{2}$	12
Height	145	155	155	165	170	165	185	180	185	190

c) Mean point (8.4, 169.5)

e) (ii) 138 – 140 cm   (ii) 202 – 204 cm.

These two extremes are unlikely to follow the same pattern. The original data is not randomly selected – it is unlikely all 10 would have different shoe sizes. Male and female differences in shoe sizes mean the two sexes should be taken separately.

5 a) Swimming: 10 s, Run: 5 s

b) Swimming: 64.7 s, Run: 23 s

e) 66.6 s

6 a) The theatre is open for 6 days each week.

b) $\dfrac{600 + 582 + 241 + 316 + 372 + 521}{6}$

c) The attendances are decreasing.

7 a) 39, 40

b) The sales are increasing.

8 a) Alex: Mode 5, Mean 2.9, Median 3; Sam: Mode 4, Mean 2.9, Median 3.5

b) (i) Mode   (ii) Median

9 b) Mean = 1.43, Range = 5

c) Mean = 1.28, Range = 7

City pupils have fewer pets on average.

Greater spread in number of pets owned by city pupils.

10 Mean = 4.17, Median = 4, Mode = 5, Range = 9

The charges have slightly increased average loadings of buses and increased the range.

11 a) 100, 494, 67, 49, 4, 72

b) $\dfrac{100 - 20 - 5 - 18 - 12.5 - 4}{6} = 6.75$

This is not a fair assesment, as all the crime figures except for gun-related crime have decreased.

Chapter 5: Formulae and expressions

Review exercise 5.1

1 a) $b = a + 3$ b) $b = 3a$ c) $b = a - 2$ d) $b = \dfrac{3a}{2}$

2 a) $P = 12a + 6b$, $A = 10ab$

b) (i) $P = 42$, $A = 60$ (ii) $P = 90$, $A = 280$

3 a) $6n - 5$ b) 13   c) −17

d) add 5, then divide by 6

4 a) 1   b) −2   c) −7   d) −5

e) −11   f) 4   g) −10   h) 21

i) 16   j) −4   k) −5   l) 9

5 a) −17   b) −7   c) −2   d) 8.5

e) 7   f) −1.2   g) −16   h) −4

i) 25   j) 2

6 a) 13   b) 6   c) −29

7 a) 11   b) −0.6   c) 9.5

8 a) 1   b) −2   c) −12.5

Exercise 5.2

1 a) $xy + x + 3y + 3$ b) $a^2 + 7a + 12$

c) $2pq + 4p + q + 2$ d) $6z^2 + 7z + 2$

e) $m^2 + m - 2$ f) $2cd + 6c - d - 3$

g) $3x^2 - 14x - 5$ h) $8p^2 - 10p - 7$

i) $4y^2 - 4y - 3$ j) $6a^2 - 13a + 6$

2 a) $2(a + 3b)$ b) $x(x - 2y)$

c) $3p(3q - 2r)$ d) $4mn(m + 2n + 1)$

e) $2a(a^2 + 2b^2 - 3ab)$ f) $cd(e - 2c - 3d)$

g) $5s^2t^2(2t + 3s + 1)$ h) $3pqr(4pqr - 5q - 3r)$

i) $2xy^2(2z^2 - 3xz - 5y)$ j) $pq^2(7p^2q + 2p - 5)$

3 a) (i) $x^2 - 4$ (ii) $4y^2 - 9$

(iii) $9p^2 - 1$

4 a) (i) $a^2 + 6a + 9$ (ii) $z^2 - 8z + 16$

(iii) $4n^2 + 4n + 1$

c) (i) $b^2 + 4b + 4$ (ii) $9q^2 - 6q + 1$

(iii) $1 - 2x + x^2$

5 a) $3x^2 + x - 13$ b) $6x + 3$

c) $3x^2 - 9x - 1$

6 a) $x = -1$ b) $x = 0.2$ c) $x = -1.2$

d) $x = 3$ e) $x = -8$ f) $x = 3$

7 a) $\dfrac{2x}{y}$ b) $\dfrac{x}{5}$ c) $\dfrac{3y}{2}$ d) x

e) $\dfrac{x-1}{2}$ f) $\dfrac{x+4}{3}$ g) $\dfrac{x+1}{4}$

8 top row: $2x - 1$;

middle: $x^2 - 1$;

bottom: $x^2 + 4x + 4$

9 a) $2a^2 - 3b^2 - 5ab - 3a - 5b - 2$

b) $2x^3 + 9x^2 + 7x - 6$

c) $x^4 + 4x^3 - 2x^2 - 12x + 9$

d) $s^3 + 6s^2 + 12s + 8$

Exercise 5.3

1 a) $x = b - a$ b) $x = \dfrac{z}{y}$

   c) $x = \dfrac{r + q}{p}$ d) $x = mn$

   e) $x = bc - a$ f) $x = \dfrac{s(v + t)}{r}$

   g) $x = g - h$ h) $x = \dfrac{c - e}{d}$

   i) $x = y - wz$ j) $x = q(p - r)$

   k) $x = \dfrac{bc}{ad}$ l) $x = \dfrac{mn - n}{m}$

   m) $x = \dfrac{q + s}{p - r}$ n) $x = \dfrac{5 + s}{p - 2}$

   o) $x = \dfrac{-b - d}{a - c} = \dfrac{b + d}{c - a}$ p) $x = \dfrac{b + d}{a + c}$

2 a) $p = \pm\sqrt{r + q}$ b) $p = \pm\sqrt{b} - a$

   c) $p = (n - m)^2$ d) $p = s^2 - r$

   e) $p = \pm\sqrt{yz - x}$ f) $p = \dfrac{d^2 - c}{b}$

   g) $p = w(x + y)^2$ h) $p = \pm\sqrt{r - s}$

   i) $p = a(\pm\sqrt{c} - b)$ j) $p = q - rs^2$

   k) $p = \pm\sqrt{f - gh}$ l) $p = (q - qr)^2$

3 a) $a = \dfrac{p}{q}$ b) $a = \dfrac{b}{c + d}$

   c) $a = \dfrac{x}{z} - y$ d) $a = \dfrac{s}{r - t}$

   e) $a = g - \dfrac{f}{h}$ f) $a = \pm\sqrt{\dfrac{p}{r} + q}$

   g) $a = \dfrac{b}{(d - c)^2}$ h) $a = \left(n - \dfrac{m}{p}\right)^2$

   i) $a = x \pm \sqrt{\dfrac{w}{y}}$

4 a) $r = \dfrac{C}{2\pi}$ b) $r = \sqrt{\dfrac{A}{\pi}}$

   c) $r = \sqrt{\dfrac{3V}{\pi h}}$ d) $r = \sqrt[3]{\dfrac{3V}{4\pi}}$

5 a) $h = \dfrac{2A}{a + b}$ b) $a = \dfrac{2A}{h} - b$

6 a) $l = \dfrac{T^2 g}{4\pi^2}$ b) $g = \dfrac{4\pi^2 l}{T^2}$

7 a) $f = \dfrac{uv}{u + v}$ b) $u = \dfrac{fv}{v - f}$

Mixed exercise 5.4

1 a) $4n - 1$ b) $2n - 7$ c) $n^2 + 2$

   d) $10 - 3n$ e) $(n + 1)(n + 2)$

2 a) $ab + 3a + 2b + 6$ b) $x^2 + 3x - 10$

   c) $2p^2 + 7p + 3$ d) $2st - 8s - t + 4$

   e) $6z^2 + 11z - 10$ f) $-2d^2 + d + 1$

   g) $x^2 + 8x + 16$ h) $8q^2 - 26q + 15$

   i) $4y^2 - 9$ j) $9a^2 - 12a + 4$

   k) $4pq - 7p + 9q + 7$ l) $5x^2 + 2x - 2$

3 a) $p(q + 2r)$ b) $2(a - 3b)$

   c) $4(3x - 2y + 4z)$ d) $mn(m - 1)$

   e) $3x(x + 3y)$ f) $5f(g - 2f - 3h)$

   g) $2cd(3c - 4d)$ h) $4st(1 + 2s - t)$

   i) $p^2 q^2(q + p)$ j) $2xyz(xz - 5y)$

   k) $3ab(2ab - 1)$ l) $6s(3r^2 - 4rs + 2)$

4 a) $2p(p + 2q + 3pq)$ b) $d(9c - 2)$

   c) $2(2n + 7)$ d) $y(3y + 13)$

   e) $2b(4a + 7b)$ f) $8s(s + 2)$

5 a) $x = \dfrac{r + q}{p}$ b) $x = \dfrac{z^2}{y^2}$

   c) $x = \dfrac{g(g - h)}{f}$ d) $x = t(s - r)$

   e) $x = a - bc$ f) $x = \pm\sqrt{p(r - q)}$

   g) $x = (wz + y)^2$ h) $x = f \pm \sqrt{gh}$

   i) $x = \dfrac{r^2}{s}$ j) $x = \dfrac{a}{c} + b$

   k) $x = \pm\sqrt{\dfrac{q}{p - r}}$ l) $x = d - \dfrac{a}{c}$

6 a) $l = \dfrac{S - \pi r^2}{\pi r}$ b) $S = \pi r(l + r)$

   c) $l = \dfrac{S}{\pi r} - r$

7 a) $1 - x^2$ b) $1 - x^3$ c) $1 - x^4$

8 a) $\dfrac{x}{3} + 3$ b) $8x^{12}$

9 a) $\dfrac{2}{q^3}$ b) Always > 2

10 a) $b = \dfrac{2A}{h} - a$ b) $t = \sqrt{\dfrac{2s}{a}}$ c) $u + \sqrt{v^2 - 2as}$

11 a) $1 - x^2$ b) $1 - x^3$ c) $1 - x^4$

Chapter 6: Ratio, proportion and variation

Review exercise 6.1

1 a) 6 litres   b) $\dfrac{2}{5}$ c) 60%

   d) 30 litres

2 a) $3 : 4$ b) $4 : 5$ c) $5 : 2$ d) $1 : 3$

   e) $3 : 5$ f) $5 : 2$ g) $2 : 3$ h) $5 : 7$

   i) $1 : 2 : 4$ j) $4 : 5 : 10$ k) $6 : 8 : 13$ l) $2 : 3 : 6$

3 a) $5 : 1$ b) $5 : 2$ c) $8 : 3$ d) $1 : 6$

   e) $5 : 2$ f) $10 : 3$ g) $1 : 50\,000$ h) $3 : 1$

   i) $3 : 4$ j) $400 : 1$ k) $5 : 3$ l) $5 : 4$

4 a) 15   b) 4

5 a) £480, £320   b) £240, £320

   c) £350, £525, £875   d) £590, £1770, £1180

6 a) 8 m   b) 2 m   c) 4.2 m^2

   d) 14 mm, 12.5 mm

7 a) 252 g   b) 45 g   c) 14 g

8 £567

9 £55 000

14 a) $a = 52\,000$, $b = 6$

   b) They must sell at least $13\,000$

15 a) $(5, 0)$ and $(-4, 3)$

16 11 m

17 a) $y = -\dfrac{1}{2}x + 1$
           b) $\left.\begin{array}{l} y = -\dfrac{1}{2}x + 1 \\[4pt] x^2 + y^2 = 25 \end{array}\right\}$

   c) A $(-4, 3)$, B $(4.8, -1.4)$
   d) 59.03 minutes

Chapter 17: Similarity and congruence

Exercise 17.1

1 a) $\dfrac{OA}{OC} = \dfrac{AB}{CD} = \dfrac{OB}{OD}$
    b) $\dfrac{PQ}{ST} = \dfrac{PR}{RT} = \dfrac{QR}{RS}$

   c) $\angle A = \angle X$
        d) $\angle V = \angle Y$

2 a) $p = 4\dfrac{1}{5}$
         b) $q = 1$, $r = 1\dfrac{1}{3}$

   c) $s = 2\dfrac{1}{3}$

3 $x = 6$ cm; 39 cm²

4 7.5 m

5 CA = 6.125 m

6 Ask your teacher to check your answer

7 20 km

Exercise 17.2

1 a) Use triangles AXY and AX'Y. They are congruent (SSS).

   b) Use triangles QYZ and QY'Z. They are congruent (SSS). So $\angle YQZ = \angle Y'QZ$. Since they are on a straight line $\angle YQZ = \angle Y'QZ = 90°$.

   c) Start with triangles PAB and PA'B. They are congruent (SSS) and so $\angle APB = \angle A'PB$.
Now take triangles PAX and PA'X. They are congruent (SAS) and so $\angle AXP = \angle AX'P$.
Since they are on a straight line $\angle AXP = \angle AX'P = 90°$.

Exercise 17.3

1 a) yes, SSS   **b)** no   **c)** yes, AAS
   d) yes, SAS   **e)** no   **f)** yes, SSS
   g) no

2 Ask your teacher to check your answer

3 Ask your teacher to check your answer

4 It is a rhombus

5 Ask your teacher to check your answer

6 b) CD is the line through C which is perpendicular to AB
   d) ACBD is a kite

7 Ask your teacher to check your answer

8 Ask your teacher to check your answer

9 Ask your teacher to check your answer

10 Ask your teacher to check your answer

11 Ask your teacher to check your answer

12 Ask your teacher to check your answer

13 Ask your teacher to check your answer

14 CF is the line through C which is parallel to AB

Exercise 17.4

1 6.3 cm, 4.3 cm
   4.5 cm, 7.9 cm

2 a) AC = 5.3 cm, BC = 6.5 cm
   b) PR = 9.2 cm, QR = 6.4 cm

3 a) 94°, 56°, 30°   **b)** 87°, 30°, 63°
   c) 94°, 36°, 50°   **d)** 102°, 56°, 22°

5 a) Can   **b)** Cannot   **c)** Cannot
   d) Can   **e)** Cannot

6 a) DF = 6.8 cm
   b) YX = 8.9 cm

7 a) GH = 7.4 cm, GFH = 84°
   b) LM = 3.9 cm, LNH = 43°

9 b) $p = 85°$ $q = 128°$ $r = 23°$ $s = 70°$
   c) $a = 3.8$ m $b = 6.0$ m
      $c = 6.4$ m $d = 10.9$ m

10 a) Left hand triangle 45°, 45°, 90°
      Right hand triangle 34°, 56°, 90°
   b) Parallelogram 53°, 127°
      Triangle 53°, 37°, 90°
   c) Left hand triangle 60°, 60°, 60°
      Right hand triangle 45°, 45°, 90°

Exercise 17.5

1 a) Ask your teacher to check your answer
   b) Ask your teacher to check your answer.
      PQ = 12.1 cm

2 Ask your teacher to check your answer

3 Ask your teacher to check your answer

4 a) Ask your teacher to check your answer
   b) Slower
   c) 0.72 : 1

Mixed exercise 17.6

1 e) is the only true statement

2 Ask your teacher to check your answer

3 a) Ask your teacher to check your answer
   b) AB = 8.5 m

4 Ask your teacher to check your answer

5 a) 70°   **b)** 10 cm

6 Ask your teacher to check your answer

7 The triangle formed is similar to triangle ABC

8 Ask your teacher to check your answer

9 a) Ask your teacher to check your answer
   b) Ask your teacher to check your answer
   c) (i) 6.5 km (ii) 7.5 km

10 a) Ask your teacher to check your answer
   b) 36.1 cm

Chapter 18: Probability

Review exercise 18.1

1 a) imp.   b) likely
   c) certain   d) unlikely

2 a) 6

b) (i) $\dfrac{1}{6}$ (ii) $\dfrac{1}{2}$ (iii) $\dfrac{5}{6}$

3 a) $\dfrac{15}{22}$ b) $\dfrac{1}{22}$ c) $\dfrac{3}{22}$ d) $\dfrac{21}{22}$

4 a)

	1	2	3	4	5	6
Head	H, 1	H, 2	H, 3	H, 4	H, 5	H, 6
Tail	T, 1	T, 2	T, 3	T, 4	T, 5	T, 6

b) (i) $\dfrac{1}{2}$ (ii) $\dfrac{1}{4}$ (iii) $\dfrac{1}{6}$

5 a) Yes

b) (i) $\dfrac{1}{3}$ (ii) $\dfrac{1}{6}$ (iii) $\dfrac{1}{3}$

6 a) $\dfrac{14}{31}$ b) $\dfrac{15}{31}$ c) $\dfrac{22}{31}$

7 a) $\dfrac{3}{25}$ b) $\dfrac{22}{25}$ d) 180

8 a) Ask your teacher to check your answer

b) (i) $\dfrac{1}{8}$ (ii) $\dfrac{1}{2}$

c) A child is equally likely to be a boy or a girl

9 a) Ask your teacher to check your answer

b) (i) $\dfrac{1}{36}$ (ii) $\dfrac{35}{36}$ (iii) $\dfrac{6}{36} = \dfrac{1}{6}$

(iv) $\dfrac{8}{36} = \dfrac{2}{9}$

c) The probability that each number comes up is the same

Exercise 18.2

1 a) $\dfrac{1}{11}$ b) $\dfrac{19}{66}$

2 a) 0.0459   b) 0.3941

3 b) (i) $\dfrac{1}{8}$ (ii) $\dfrac{3}{8}$ (iii) $\dfrac{1}{4}$

4 a) 0.01   b) 0.09   c) 0.09   d) 0.18

5 a) 0.09   b) 0.42   c) 0.343

6 a) (i) $\dfrac{13}{50}$ (ii) $\dfrac{22}{50}$ (iii) $\dfrac{15}{50}$

c) (i) $\dfrac{78}{1225}$ (ii) $\dfrac{88}{175}$ (iii) $\dfrac{18}{35}$

7 a) 0.52   b) 0.07

8 a) (ii) 0.99   b) (i) 20

9 a) 0.51   b) 0.34

10 a) 0.42   b) 0.46

11 a) 0.732   b) 0.268   c) 0.237

12 b) $\dfrac{1}{12}$ c) $\dfrac{1}{4}$

13 a) $\dfrac{1}{6}$ b) $\dfrac{1}{9}$ c) $\dfrac{1}{3}$

14 a) (i) 31   (ii) $\dfrac{1}{64}$

b) (i) $\left(\dfrac{7}{8}\right)^n$ (ii) $1 - \left(\dfrac{7}{8}\right)^n$

15 a) $\dfrac{1}{1}$

b) (i) $\dfrac{1}{8}$ (ii) $\dfrac{1}{2}$

16 0.1205

Exercise 18.3

1 a) $\dfrac{3}{4}$ b) 15

2 a) Ask your teacher to check your answer

b) $\dfrac{1}{3}$ c)   About 10

3 a) (i) $\dfrac{1}{10}$ (ii) $\dfrac{9}{10}$

b) Ask your teacher to check your answer

c) (i) $\dfrac{1}{110}$ (ii) $\dfrac{1}{11}$ (iii) $\dfrac{1}{11}$ (iv) $\dfrac{89}{110}$

4 $\dfrac{470}{870} = \dfrac{47}{87}$

5 $\dfrac{5}{12}$

6 a) Ask your teacher to check your answer

b) 0.15

7 a) (i) $\dfrac{9}{30} = \dfrac{3}{10} = 0.3$ (ii) $\dfrac{28}{123} \approx 0.23$

(iii) $\dfrac{142}{365} \approx 0.39$

b) Either May to Sept (inclusive) or June to October (inclusive)

c) No. The weather on any day is random

8 a) $\dfrac{66}{84} = \dfrac{11}{14}$ b) $\dfrac{66}{70} = \dfrac{33}{35}$

c) $\dfrac{22}{150} = \dfrac{11}{75}$

Mixed exercise 18.4

1 a) 0.35   b) 0.4225   c) 0.455

2 a) 0.027   b) 0.370   c) 0.441

3 a) 0.7   b) 0.15

4

Prob. of flowering	Sunny	Shady
Dry	$\dfrac{15}{24} = 0.625$	$\dfrac{24}{30} = 0.8$
Damp	$\dfrac{27}{45} = 0.6$	$\dfrac{12}{18} = 0.667$

so Dry and Shady conditions are best.

5 a) $\dfrac{113}{340} = 0.332$ b) $\dfrac{285}{340} = 0.838$

6 a) the test renders them useless

b) (i) 0.97

(ii) For 200, P (fail) = 0.02;

For 300, P (fail) = 0.023

7 a) 0.343　　　b) 2

8 a) (i) $\dfrac{1}{25}$　　(ii) $\dfrac{1}{5}$　　b) (i) 0.28　　(ii) 0.228

9 a) 0.02　　b) 0.64

10 a) 700　　b) 0.42　　c) 0.18　　d) 0.91

11 a) $\dfrac{2}{3}$　　b) $\dfrac{1}{5}$　　c) $\dfrac{40}{48} = \dfrac{5}{6}$

12 a) Ask your teacher to check your answer

b) (i) 0.285　(ii) 0.644

(iii) 0.929　(iv) 0.071

Chapter 19: Trigonometry

Review exercise 19.1

1 a) 5.83 cm　　b) 4.47 cm　　c) 5.29 cm

2 $a = 6.63$ cm　$b = 6.63$ cm　$c = 4.45$ cm

3 $p = 41.4°$　$q = 38.7°$　$r = 64.6°$　$s = 51.1°$

$t = 54.5°$

4 139 m

5 a) 10.2 cm　　b) 9.29 cm　　c) 7.55 cm

d) 9.64 cm　　e) 8.62 cm　　f) 6.71 cm

6 a) 39.1 m　　b) 6.37°

7 a) 24.6 km north, 17.2 km west

b) 222.8°

8 a) 23.0°　　b) 40.3°　　c) 56.1°　　d) 80.6°

9 a) (i) 5.83　　(ii) 5.83

b) (i) 3　　(ii) 4.90

10 61.1°

Exercise 19.2

1 Ask your teacher to check your answer

2 a) (i) 37°, 143°　　　　(ii) 17°, 153°

(iii) 192°, 348°

b) They add up to a multiple of 180°

c) Ask your teacher to check your answer

4 a) (i) 46°, 314°　　　　(ii) 114°, 246°

(iii) 143°, 217°

b) They add up to 360°

c) Ask your teacher to check your answer

5 a) Ask your teacher to check your answer

b) (i) 24°, 66°　　　　(ii) 44°, 46°

c) They add up to 90°

d) Ask your teacher to check your answer

8 a) (i) 11°, 191°　　　　(ii) 27°, 207°

(iii) 149°, 329°

b) They have a difference of 180°

Exercise 19.3

1 a) 48.6°, 131.4°　　　　b) 111.8°, 291.8°

c) 35.9°, 324.1°　　　　d) 199.9°, 340.1°

d) 126.2°, 233.8°　　　　f) 44.1°, 224.1°

2 a) $\sqrt{2}$

b) $\sin 45° = \dfrac{1}{\sqrt{2}}$, $\cos 45° = \dfrac{1}{\sqrt{2}}$

c) (i) −1　　(ii) $\dfrac{1}{\sqrt{2}}$

(iii) $-\dfrac{1}{\sqrt{2}}$　(iv) $-\dfrac{1}{\sqrt{2}}$

(v) 1　　(vi) $\dfrac{1}{\sqrt{2}}$

3 a) $\sqrt{3}$

b) $\cos 30° = \dfrac{\sqrt{3}}{2}$, $\tan 30° = \dfrac{1}{\sqrt{3}}$

c) $\sin 60° = \dfrac{\sqrt{3}}{2}$, $\cos 60° = \dfrac{1}{2}$, $\tan 60° = \sqrt{3}$

d) (i) $\dfrac{1}{2}$　　(ii) $-\dfrac{1}{2}$　　(iii) $-\sqrt{3}$

(iv) $-\dfrac{\sqrt{3}}{2}$　(v) $\dfrac{1}{\sqrt{3}}$　(vi) $\dfrac{\sqrt{3}}{2}$

(vii) $-\dfrac{1}{\sqrt{3}}$　(viii) $-\dfrac{\sqrt{3}}{2}$　(ix) $-\dfrac{\sqrt{3}}{2}$

4 Ask your teacher to check your answer

Exercise 19.4

1 a) 7.93 cm　　b) 5.28 cm

c) 6.45 cm　　d) 6.16 cm

2 a) 17.4°　　b) 77.0° or 103.0°

c) 33.4°　　d) 95.9°

3 a) Ask your teacher to check your answer

b) 1.52 km and 3.34 km

Exercise 19.5

1 a) 7.50 cm　　　　　　b) 8.18 cm

c) 5.73 cm　　　　　　d) 6.97 cm

2 a) 33.1°　　　　　　b) 93.8°

c) 134.6°　　　　　　d) 39.3°

3 AC = 4.25 cm, ∠BAC = 50.5°, ∠BCA = 74.5°

∠YXZ = 46.7°, ∠YZX = 29.3°, XY = 4.04 cm

4 Ask your teacher to check your answer

Exercise 19.6

1 4.51 km, bearing 344.3°

2 a) (i) $\sqrt{149}$　(ii) $\sqrt{125}$　　(iii) $\sqrt{74}$

b) 42.9°

3 74.1°

4 a) 5.26 m　　b) 46.9 m

5 A = 57.6°, B = 107.0°, C = 93.4°

Exercise 19.7

1 a) 9.99 cm²　　b) 17.82 cm²

2 a) 146.1 m　　b) 122.7°　　c) 6971 m²

Mixed exercise 19.8

1 a) 24.0°   b) 30.9m
2 a) 54.1°, 125.9°   b) 129.8°, 230.2°
   c) 58.0°, 238.0°   d) 21.6°, 338.4°
   e) 200.5°, 339.5°   f) 142.0°, 332.0°
3 a) 6.80 m   b) 31.0°
4 a) Ask your teacher to check your answer
   b) (i) Ask your teacher to check your answer
       (ii) 15.0 m
   c) 12.6 m
5 a) 8.89 cm   b) 8.16 cm
   c) 10.73 cm   d) 7.31 cm
6 a) 81.8°   b) 87.7° or 92.3°
   c) 44.3°   d) 55.8°
7 a) 23.8 cm^2 b) 24.6 cm^2
8 a) 33.3 cm   b) 44.3 cm
9 58.1° or 121.9°
10 a) Ask your teacher to check your answer
   b) 2.17 or –3.84   c) 4.46 cm
11 a) 696 m   b) 1525 m
12 a) 62.9 m   b) 51.6°
13 a) 81.6 m   b) 52.5 m
14 45.7 km

Chapter 20: Working with graphs and sequences

Exercise 20.1

1 a) 1011   b) 1005 to 1009
   c) between 1000 and 1005
2 a) 1260 ft per minute   b) 960 ft per minute
3 a) 0.15 ms^{-2} b) 20 seconds
   c) 3375 m   d) 0.3 ms^{-2}
4 b) (i) 306 m   (ii) 1.8 ms^{-2}
5 b) 13 ms^{-1} c) 3.5 ms^{-2}
   d) 620.48 m
6 b) 5.66 seconds   c) 84 cm
   d) (i) 6 cms^{-2} (ii) –2 cms^{-2} decelaration
7 2 a) (i) Nothing   (ii) rate of increase of mass
      b) (i) Volume   (ii) nothing useful
      c) (i) Total earnings   (ii) nothing
8 $V = 5$, $T = 4$
9 b) (ii) 2 cm per minute
10 b) 12 ms^{-1} c) $12t – 72$ m   d) $16t – 160$ m
   e) after 22 seconds   f) 192 m

Exercise 20.2

1 Ask your teacher to check your answers
2 a), c), d), e) Ask your teacher to check your answers
   b) Moderate positive linear correlation
   e) $y = 24.1x + 55.3$
3 a), b), d) Ask your teacher to check your answer
   c) Brenda

Exercise 20.3

1 a) $y = 7x$ b) $y = 3x + 10$
2 $L = 0.449x + 24.2$
3 a) $y = 3x + 7$ b) $y = -2x + 9$ c) $y = 4x + 6$
   d) $y = 5x – 18$ e) $y = -3x + 19$
4 a) $y = 3x – 7$ b) $y = \frac{1}{2}x – 3$ c) $y = 7x$
   d) $y = bx + 9$
5 a) A $(0, 12)$ B $(8, 0)$ b) $-\dfrac{3}{2}$
   c) Ask your teacher to check your answers
   d) $y = \dfrac{2}{3}x + 12$
   e) $y = -\dfrac{3}{2}x + \dfrac{63}{2}$
   f) $(9, 18)$
   g) Rectangle

Exercise 20.4

1 b) (i) 19 300   (ii) 26 000
   c) (i) 2.3 years   (ii) 4.6 years
   e) 2 021 000
2 b) (i) 39 units   (ii) 21.9 units
   c) (i) 2.4 hours   (ii) 5.6 hours
   d) $a = 60$, $b = 0.75$
3 b) (i) £5584   (ii) £6142
   c) (i) 2.35 years   (ii) 6.6 years
   d) A $= 4000(1.1)^t$
   e) £26 910
4 a) 0.9
   b) (i) 98   (ii) 89
   d) (i) 1.73   (ii) 3.85
5 b) 1.2   c) 7.45 years
6 b) $y = 50 \times 1.15^t$ c) $1430
7 b) $\theta = 95 \times 0.9^t$ c) 4°
8 b) After 6 hours
   c) Dose at 12 hours should be the last (98.85 milligrams)

Exercise 20.5

1 a) 30° 150°   b) 60° 300°   c) 0° 180° 360°
2 b) 9 m, 5 m   c) 3 am
   d) Between 1 am and 5 am and between 1 pm and 5 pm
3 a) (i) $t = 3$ (ii) $t = 9$
   b) (i) 8 m   (ii) 2 m
   c) Between $t = 7$ and $t = 11$
   d) Before $t = 1$ and after $t = 5$
4 a) (i) 2.5 million gallons
       (ii) 1.5 million gallons
   b) Between $t = 5$ (May) and $t = 7$ (July)